Praise for *The Once an[d Future Sex]*

"Hugely entertaining and informative. . . . [R]eminds us that we can only tackle present injustices if we remember that there is nothing universal about the ways in which people treat one another." —Hannah Skoda, *BBC History* magazine

"Robust and well-sourced. . . . There are colourful anecdotes on almost every page." —Rachel Cunliffe, *New Statesman*

"Both the subject matter and the author's engaging conversational style make this a book of many delights. . . . [V]ery entertaining." —Gillian Kenny, *Spectator*

"Entertaining and revealing . . . Janega skilfully weaves a modern cultural commentary through her research into the medieval world, highlighting similarities and differences to today's world for women and focussing our attention on the importance of analysing history as a way to understand the present." —Emily Staniforth, *All About History*

"[A] lively exploration of medieval women's social roles." —Laura Kalas, *Conversation*

"A startling rethinking of why the medieval past still matters. Eleanor Janega tells how women's roles are fundamentally constructed and the ways they have both changed over time and unfortunately stayed the same. With erudition and humor, this book offers the reader a perfect case study of how a fuller accounting of the past opens up new, better possible worlds." —Matthew Gabriele, coauthor of *The Bright Ages: A New History of Medieval Europe*

"Humorous, slightly irreverent. . . . This book offers fresh, insightful takes on the medieval period from a feminine standpoint."

—*Booklist*

THE
ONCE
AND
FUTURE
SEX

GOING MEDIEVAL ON WOMEN'S
ROLES IN SOCIETY

ELEANOR JANEGA

W. W. NORTON & COMPANY
Independent Publishers Since 1923

For my mother

Copyright © 2023 by Eleanor Janega

Printed in the United States of America
First published as a Norton paperback 2024

For information about permission to reproduce selections from this book, write to
Permissions, W. W. Norton & Company, Inc., 500 Fifth Avenue, New York, NY 10110

For information about special discounts for bulk purchases, please contact
W. W. Norton Special Sales at specialsales@wwnorton.com or 800-233-4830

Manufacturing by Lakeside Book Company
Book design by Chris Welch
Production manager: Louise Mattarelliano

ISBN: 978-1-324-07446-5 pbk.

W. W. Norton & Company, Inc.
500 Fifth Avenue, New York, N.Y. 10110
www.wwnorton.com

W. W. Norton & Company Ltd.
15 Carlisle Street, London W1D 3BS

1 2 3 4 5 6 7 8 9 0

CONTENTS

———

INTRODUCTION

In late fourteenth-century Prague, Archdeacon Pavel of Janovice embarked on a tour of the grand imperial city's parish churches to see if locals had any religious issues that they wanted addressed. In the parish of St. Andre the Greater, in the Old Town, the archdeacon was alerted to the presence of "a certain woman called Domka." According to her fellow parishioners, Domka was living with, and even heading, a group of "suspect women" in the house of a man called Henry, even though she was married to one of the king's chamberlains. To make a living, the women were selling blessed herbs to customers who complained of head ailments.[1] This arrangement was a "suspect" religious emergency for several reasons: first, Domka was living outside her husband's control, while the others didn't seem to be attached to any man at all other than their landlord; second, while their herb business was technically licit, the fact that a bunch of women were participating in it made it seem to be pushing the bounds from standard herbal medicine into magical remedies; and third, a group of women living together like this meant that they must be running and working in an unlicensed brothel.

The community concern about Domka and her roommates shows us that women in medieval Europe had it bad, but not in the way most of us think they did. We know they had a difficult time, because our society was built by theirs, and women are still at a disadvantage with men. Today women face, among other things, lower wages in return for the same work; a disproportionate workload at home; disbelief from medical professionals about our pain levels; an expectation that we will always look sexually attractive but engage in sex *only* with our correct and designated partners and in *exactly the right amount*; and sexual harassment and huge risks of sexual and physical assault while we go about our daily business. If we are still going through all this now, in the era of feminism, it stands to reason that medieval women had it worse, lacking the benefits of the Pill, the Equal Rights Act, and Dolly Parton's *Nine to Five*. Yet we seldom take the time to learn how medieval women were considered and treated in their own time and why, instead assuming that they just faced a more draconian version of our same issues. This is somewhat true, as Domka and her pals were reported to the archdeacon, who had the power to excommunicate them from the Church and have them driven from their homes. In this case, however, nothing seems to have happened at all. Were these women "suspect" and the subjects of communal monitoring and gossip? Yes! Was the Church going to do anything about it? No. After all, these women seemed just to be doing what women naturally did—suspicious stuff. There was no real way to stop that.

When we ignore history like this and assume that women have always been treated in one particular way that we are only now beginning to overcome, we accept that our society has always been this way and indeed *should* be this way. Our world, as a collective, is simply responding to the natural deficiencies of women and is organizing itself to adjust for them. We tend to agree that our society is beginning to address such shortcomings now. Yet we assume that women in the past were treated as we are treated, for the same reasons, just without the benefits of the modern world to help them make up for their own innate and natural deficiencies.

The fatalism of the such assumptions is rage-inducing. The idea that this is how things always were, and that our societal expectations of women have developed as a result of some immutable truth about over half of the world's population is just too convenient. More to the point, it is also wrong and has no historical basis. Whatever problems we may have with women now, we don't generally agree that they are so sex-crazed and heretical that when left to their own devices they will start a brothel with a nice little side racket in magical herbs. Clearly some things have changed.

If we want to understand how Western society got its current attitudes about women, we have to retrace its steps back to medieval Europe. Sadly, we often treat medieval European history as the ultimate in obscure or unnecessary knowledge. We use the term *medieval* as shorthand for "backward" or "barbaric," as something that we have learned from, moved past, and bettered ourselves as a result of. We are so sure of what we would find if we took a look at medieval history that we often don't bother. But this attitude is not only incorrect, it is also one reason our society is not moving toward an equitable future.

Medieval literally means "middle time." It describes a span of about eleven hundred years, from the fall of Western Rome in 476 to sometime in the sixteenth century, the interval between the ancient period and our modern period. In other words, it acts as a kind of bridge, explaining how modern society moved from the ancient world to its current state, or rather it would if we paid attention to it.

Because of the period's placement between two eras, studying its gender norms allows us to see where some of our ongoing assumptions about gender come from. Our consideration of women as "naturally" weak and inferior, and therefore requiring protection and guidance, is an ancient and medieval holdover. Understanding that allows us to interrogate why we still believe it. If we think medieval people are so backward, why do we agree with them about this?

Moreover, studying medieval gender norms allows us to see that many assumptions about women have, in actuality, changed drastically since the medieval era. When we realize that gender expectations have massively shifted in a number of ways, but our worst and most parochial behaviors have not, we can reject them. The only unbroken tradition in terms of gender norms is treating women as inferior. And we can stop doing that at any time.

Over the course of this book, we will examine the historical problem with our societal insistence that women are X and we therefore respond to that with Y. In this book, we will focus first on the intellectual underpinnings of the medieval approach to women. The ancient writings of Plato, Aristotle, Galen, and Hippocrates shaped medieval society's philosophical approach to women and gender. Further, to understand the religious bedrock of medieval Europe, we will consider the Church fathers like Augustine and Jerome, whose works provided the framework for Christian theology. Armed with a good understanding of ancient thinkers, we can encounter their medieval counterparts. They will include theologians like Albertus Magnus, Aquinas, and Hildegard of Bingen, but also secular writers like Chaucer and Christine de Pizan, whose literary works reflect the views that their academic counterparts argued over.

Once we have a solid grasp of whose ideas these were and how they were transmitted, we will move on to a consideration of beauty, that most important of feminine features. We will see that just as medieval people looked to the past to guide their understandings of knowledge, so too did they look back to learn how to identify which women were hot. Understanding the medieval checklist for attractive attributes helps to explain medieval women's beauty and fashion regimes and allows us to consider the work that they put into living up to the specific beauty standard. Even though they were told that there was exactly one way to be attractive, women were also instructed that they should under no circumstances attempt to live up to that expectation. Women were simply meant to *be* beautiful effortlessly. To attempt to meet the beauty standard was to face ridicule and even to gamble with their own soul. Medieval women were forced to walk a tightrope between living up to stringent criteria for public adoration and successful marriages and what was deemed an unseemly interest in the beauty regimens that allowed for these things.

Frustratingly, the beauty that women had to embody was often also condemned because it distracted men's minds from lofty civic and religious considerations to the most base and feminine of subjects, sex. To better understand medieval attitudes toward sex, we have to understand the theological expectations that medieval people navigated. Yet most medieval Christians were happy to gamble with their souls, here and there, for a good time and put it upon women to trespass against the Holy Church's prohibitions on sex. Unlike in our day, women were conceptualized both as sex-addled and as insatiable in their demands, to the point that there was constant worry that women would be adulterous. They were even thought to turn to magic if their sexual demands were stymied. Overall, the medieval concept of women's sexuality looks almost nothing like ours, except that it was considered wrong.

After we establish how women were meant to look and love, we will turn more broadly to the expectations of medieval women outside the bedroom. First and foremost, women were seen as wives and mothers. The Church at times attempted to intervene and set them on a path to religious contemplation and celibacy. By and large, however, to be a woman meant to be viewed as breeding stock.

While most women did marry and have children, they were also expected to be heavily involved in any number of occupations. The majority of medieval women were peasants, performing agricultural labor that ground on month after month and year after year. Outside farmwork, peasant women, like their city counterparts, might be involved in cottage industries like weaving, baking, or brewing beer. Some women worked in rarefied occupations as artists and artisans, as shopkeepers and traders, medical professionals, and when the Church got its wish, as nuns. Still, wealthy women did not have lives of leisure. Being a noble or royal woman was in and of itself a form of specific and taxing work. So while women were first and foremost wives and mothers, they were never considered *just* that. To be a medieval woman was to be a worker, even if that work was not necessarily valued in the same way that men's labor was.

Finally, we will move on to our own expectations in these same areas. We will see how the philosophical and academic justifications we've developed about women's nature are used to insist that our attitudes toward women have always been in place, but that we are also now living in a golden age for women. Knowing both the presumptions about medieval women and the reality of their lives, the current expectations we place on women will appear as anything but "traditional." Our notions of the ideal woman have changed a great deal over time, as has our concept of what exactly is wrong with women. What has remained static, unfortunately, is our desire to subjugate women—to judge them by the harshest possible standards and find them wanting. The outcome is the same—it's just that the justification for reaching it has changed.

This work is not, however, fatalistic. If our ideas about women are continuously remade to justify our poor treatment of women, they can be remade to respect women's abilities and desires. Once we understand that our biases about women are culturally constructed, we can deconstruct them and start again. So in Chapter 1, let us begin the demolition at its base: the philosophical framework of the medieval understanding of women.

THE
ONCE
AND
FUTURE
SEX

1

BACK TO BASICS

IN 1371 GEOFFROY IV DE LA TOUR LANDRY BEGAN TO WRITE a book for his daughters. In its preface, he recorded his overwhelming love and devotion for their mother, who was "practiced to all honor and to every excellence; and hers was courtly carriage and demeanor; of the good she was the best." Her death sent him into a decades-long depression over the loss of his "perfect love," and at the same time it made him aware of what he needed to do to bring up his daughters to follow in her footsteps. His "soul's desire was, that all honor and advantage might be theirs; for they were yet young and small . . . so that they would require to be early taken in hand, and to be gently broken." So he decided he "would make a book, wherein [he] would have collected the memorable instances of admirable women . . . so as to show, by their pattern, what was true feminacy and good conduct; and also how, by their virtues, they were held in honor and estimation, and will ever continue to be so."[1]

When he committed these words to parchment, Geoffrey not only gave his daughters a social and moral guide; he also provided a perfect example of his society's attitudes toward women. Every woman had the possibility of attaining the apogee of femininity—being a cherished wife and mother, with a devoted husband who would compose poetry for her and write of her fondly years after her death. However, women like this were not born but made, through the timely intervention of their male family members and with examples from the past. It was men who knew what women should be, and men who were best able to understand and tame the nature of women to be exactly that. For a beloved daughter to become a cherished wife, men must break her worst feminine attributes, to tame her into a helpmeet, the ultimate status for any medieval woman. At least, that was the case if you asked medieval men (and sometimes even when you didn't).

If ideal women could be made, it was also true that without targeted intervention, women were emphatically not that. The ideal default humans were men, while women were an afterthought or mirror of them that was meant to work for and complement the dominant sex. They were also seen to lack the beneficial characteristics that men had. Where men were strong, constant, rational, and pious, women left to their own devices would end up weak, flighty, conceited, lustful, and—worst of all—unmarried as a result. The arrival of a girl into the world was therefore not necessarily unwelcome but meant that parents like Geoffroy had their work cut out for them if they wanted their daughters to be functioning parts of the family and society.

These ideas about women and their nature did not spring fully formed from the head of Zeus: they were derived from ancient scholars. The intellectuals of the time believed they were "standing on the shoulders of giants," a phrase that was coined by the scholar and philosopher Bernard of Chartres (ca. twelfth century). What Bernard meant was that knowledge was cumulative, begun by the great philosophers and thinkers of the ancient world and steadily built upon by later scholars.

In fact, the entire medieval educational system was constructed around and upon the work of writers from ancient Greece and Rome. When it came to sex differences, the ideas of a core group had an outsize influence on medieval thought.

Medieval intellectuals revered their forefathers as having had a philosophical system that was not only superior but almost divine in nature, based on the very fact of their being ancient. That meant they were born closer in time to the existence of the Garden of Eden, where God had been present. Since then, as humanity retreated further and further from that time and place of divinity, it had steadily been losing knowledge. The creation myth, meanwhile, provided a fertile theological starting point for medieval philosophers and theologians. It was just one part of a sophisticated Christian theological framework, added to in the Patristic Era (which lasted from roughly A.D. 100 to 450) by the Church fathers, on which medieval European scholars sought to expand.

To understand how medieval people thought about women, first we have to understand where they got their ideas. This means looking back to the ancient past to see the giants whose shoulders the medieval people were standing on.

Theorizing Women's Bodies: Hippocrates

The most ancient of the writers whom medieval thinkers revered was the Greek physician Hippocrates of Cos (ca. 460–370 B.C.E.). Even today Hippocrates, as close to a household name as you can be when you're 2,500 years old, is hailed as "the father of medicine."[2] His name is forever attached to the Hippocratic Oath, which all doctors take as their main tenet and which commands them to, among other things "abstain from all intentional wrong-doing and harm," "apply, for the benefit of the sick, all measures [that] are required,"

and "remember that [they] remain a member of society, with special obligations to all [their] fellow human beings." Hippocrates
founded a school for physicians and thus gave rise to an entire class
of well-trained medical practitioners, all of whom stressed professionalism and careful observation of systems and techniques. Con-
fusingly, because of this school and the number of people it trained,
a lot of "Hippocratic" texts weren't necessarily written by this one
man. Instead, it is a corpus of texts written by his acolytes and those
trained using Hippocratic methods.

You may wonder how people in medieval Europe could have been
reading and writing about Hippocrates, since as an ancient Greek,
he was, well, reading and writing in ancient Greek. The answer is
that they were reading him in translation, as generations of students
had been doing for centuries. Hippocratic texts had long formed the
backbone of medical training in the classical world. They were still
taught in Alexandria when it became the center of learning for the
Roman world. Romans, as you may well know, spoke Latin and were
intent on translating important works into Latin in order to save
themselves the trouble of learning ancient Greek. The Hippocratic
texts thus entered Roman libraries in their common tongue.

When the Western Roman Empire fell, Hippocrates's popularity
did not fall with it.[3] The Ostrogoths (the so-called barbarians who
toppled the dying Western Roman Empire) copied the Alexandrian-
Hippocratic model for training their physicians in their new capital at Ravenna. In fact, the Ostrogoths liked Hippocrates so much
that they went out of their way to translate texts that hadn't made
the jump to Latin yet. These included works like *Diseases of Women*,
which pretty much does what the title says, as well as his *Aphorisms*,
which had short pithy statements to guide physicians, starting with
"Life is short, and Art long; the crisis fleeting; experience perilous,
and decision difficult. The physician must not only be prepared to
do what is right for himself, but also to make the patient, the attendants, and externals cooperate."[4]

The Hippocratic school and its texts are absolutely critical to understanding classical and medieval medical thought, but although its system was based on observation, we would not call what they practiced "medicine" or "science" today. As a case in point, one of the absolute cornerstones of Hippocratic thought was something called humoral theory, or humorism.[5] The idea behind humorism was that "humors" existed as four liquids in every human body: blood, phlegm, yellow bile, and black bile. These humors were associated with the four elements: air, water, fire, and earth, respectively. There were also four temperaments associated with the humors: sanguine, phlegmatic, choleric, and melancholic.

While all human bodies contained all four humors, humorism taught that they existed in varying quantities within the bodies of men and women. Men were seen as hot and dry, or naturally sanguine and socially useful. Women, in contrast, were cold and wet and therefore more likely to be phlegmatic, or placid. Having said that, the fact that all humans had all four humors meant that people's humoral balance allowed some wiggle room for how they behaved. The historian Sherry Sayed Gadelrab has characterized these differences as a "sliding scale" between the sexes, meaning that Hippocrates and his acolytes accepted "the possibility that a person could be more masculine or feminine than others in his or her own sex."[6]

A person's humoral balance also changed over their life span, a process depicted much like the passage of seasons through the year. Young people were considered dryer and warmer, and older people colder and wetter. These were not merely descriptions or observations; they served as a system for how the humors should interact with each other. Women *should* be cold and wet and behave in a particular way, but you might meet some who were hotter and drier than the average. There could be feminine men and masculine women. The temperament of various sexes could change because of certain activities. By certain activities, of course, I mean sex.

In his treatise *On Generation,* for example, Hippocrates announced that women should "have intercourse with men [because] their health is better than if they do not. . . . Intercourse by heating the blood and rendering it more fluid gives an easier passage to the menses; whereas if the menses do not flow, women's bodies are prone to sickness."[7] This is instructive in several ways. It tells us that the Hippocratic concept of women's bodies was that they were (a) strange and (b) prone to failure, specifically because they have uteruses. This makes sense from the standpoint of a physician who is attempting to explain to other physicians how bodies work. The thing about women, as opposed to men, was that they had all this stuff that men did not, and it was inside them, where it was difficult to observe. As a result, Hippocratic scholars' concern figured primarily on the unruly and unknowable uterus and what it was up to inside the secretive female body.

For them, the uterus was an independent entity inside women. As a result, it could wander around and cause medical problems that men didn't have, including a condition known as hysteria, which caused a sense of suffocation, trembling, anxiety and in extreme cases convulsions and paralysis.

One surefire way to alleviate hysteria was to become pregnant. During pregnancy, the womb couldn't wander, as it was pinned in one place while the fetus was growing.

If a postpubescent woman was not currently pregnant, and ideally was married, she should have sex regularly in order to keep the uterus well moistened and warm. Otherwise, without sex, the uterus might not bleed on time, or it might move toward the other, wetter organs in the body—the brain, or heart, or liver—in order to absorb their moisture. A woman with her womb on her brain could act irrationally, making life difficult for everyone around her. Undersexed women were therefore a matter of public concern.

In the Hippocratic world—and therefore in the medieval world— a liver was a liver, and a brain was a brain, but women had an extra weird thing that made them *incomparable* to men. Women were physically more complicated, and their complication was mysterious and unknowable by virtue of it being inside them. This prevented much medical study because anatomical dissection was essentially unheard of in ancient Greece. This was because corpses were seen as a potential pollutant, especially if the skin was cut, and because legal and religious prohibitions upheld the sanctity of the dead. All in all, then, women's internal anatomy stayed a "secret" over this period.[8]

Spiritually Philosophizing Women: Plato

Physicians weren't the only ancient thinkers to hold forth on sex. The philosopher Plato had a lot to say on the subject as well.[9] What Plato thought about women was particularly influential because, much like Hippocrates before him, he didn't philosophize in a vacuum; he started a school and thereby guaranteed his own legacy. Plato's was outside Athens, and it was called the Academy. At the Academy, Plato inaugurated whole branches of thought and began the European tradition of dialectic and dialogue. He also thought about sex.

In the ancient world, it is fair to say, Plato's writing was as big a deal for philosophers as Hippocrates's was for physicians. And his dialogue *Timaeus* was an equally big influence on medieval thinkers.[10] The *Timaeus* was particularly popular in the medieval period, crucially, because it was circulating in Latin translations. (There were two versions circulating during the period, both from the fourth century, but the translation attributed to the fourth-century Roman philosopher Calcidius was generally favored.)

The medieval interest in the *Timaeus* is of note for us because within it Plato approaches women as a spiritual quandary. Here he presented his creation myth, which established the physical world as a moral proving ground wherein men—who were considered to be the only humans—strove to achieve a higher state of being. Those who failed to do so were returned to earth to live again. (Yes, it is more or less an ancient Greek version of the Buddhist concept of reincarnation.) But guess what—the men who were returned? They were punished for their inability to live a moral life by being sent back as women.

Once women existed alongside men, the gods created sexual desire. Plato argued that sexual desire existed in a gendered manner. In men, the gods opened a special passage, from the brain going along the spine, that allowed semen to travel from the brain into the testicles. The semen itself had a soul and wanted to be released into uteruses in order to create new life. This desire was *eros*. The thing about *eros* was that it made men's penises act in an involuntary manner. Plato saw the penis as essentially out of control, a type of living willful animal. This, in turn, mirrored his concept of the uterus. Much like the Hippocratic thinkers before him, Plato felt that this corresponding generative organ for women was an erratic creature, climbing around inside the body and animated by a corresponding female sexual desire. Like Hippocrates, he argued that the uterus had to be pacified and pinned in place by pregnancy. Therefore, the unruly aspects of both penises and uteruses could be calmed through generative sexual activity.[11]

The fact that Plato accorded wild-card status to both penises and uteruses might seem like a kind of evolution or marker of progress over Hippocratic thought. It was not. While the unruly penis makes a brief appearance in his characterizations, the wandering uterus is a major figure, as well as the necessity of keeping it held in place by making babies. At the same time, there is a hierarchy to the way that Plato describes the generative desires of these organs. Semen *wants* to be released because it has a soul. Uteruses, meanwhile, desire to be given this material and its soul to make babies.

Plato understood women as fallen men and naturally inferior to men as a result. Correspondingly, he contended that society should organize itself in such a way that that men would be able to control women. After all, women had already proven themselves incapable of making correct moral decisions. Otherwise, they wouldn't even *be* women.

Philosophizing Women's Bodies: Aristotle

While Plato's *Timaeus* was immensely important in the Middle Ages, medieval thinkers lionized one philosopher above all others, and that was Aristotle (384–322 B.C.E.).[12] Aristotle continues to be famous enough that he barely needs introduction even now. He is the *other* philosopher everyone knows. And once again, this was partly guaranteed by his presiding over his own school, where his ideas would find disciples and heirs. His was called the Lyceum, and it was also a temple dedicated to the god Apollo. Here philosophers were trained in the Peripatetic school, named for the Lyceum's *peripatoi* or walkways. The Peripatetics largely focused on preserving and commenting on Aristotle's works after his death, and they managed to keep the school running into the third century A.D. After that, Aristotle's works were picked up by the Romans, who were keen on demonstrating that they were the logical heirs to the Hellenistic world.

To say that medieval intellectuals revered Aristotle would be an understatement. They were so enamored of Aristotle that they often referred to him simply as "the Philosopher." As a result, much of medieval philosophy can be treated as Peripatetic, and medieval philosophers classed themselves as such. Not to put too fine a point on it, but anyone who was literate in the medieval period (which meant specifically that they could read in Latin) was basically raised on Aristotle, and they saw themselves as charged with continuing his tradition.

Much like Hippocrates and Plato, Aristotle wrote in Greek, and medieval scholars read his work in Latin translation. Boethius (ca. 477–524), a philosopher and consul in early medieval Rome, did many of the translations. No man could possibly translate all of Aristotle's work, however, so early medieval people without any Greek were mostly reading what Boethius had deemed worth translating. The most widely studied of his translations were *The Categories* and *On Interpretation*. Beyond the translations from Aristotle, in the high to late medieval era, people worked with a lot of explanations and interpretations of Aristotle made by the Arabic polymath Ibn Sinna (ca. 980–1037), or Avicenna as he was known by Latinists.

Like Plato, Aristotle was convinced that men were essentially the default humans. As far as he was concerned, men were the basis by which all humans should be judged, and women were a pale imitation of men. According to his *Politics*, men were "superior, and the female inferior, the male ruler, and the female subject."[13] As frustrating as this is to read, it is important to notice that Aristotle insisted that societal roles should be based on human nature: men ruled, women were ruled.

Aristotle, like any good Hellenic thinker who was aware of Hippocratic texts, thought humans were ruled by their humors. Because women were cold and wet, he thought, they were also "more mischievous, less simple, more impulsive . . . more compassionate . . . more easily moved to tears . . . more jealous, more querulous, more apt to scold and strike . . . more prone to despondency and less hopeful . . . more void of shame or self-respect, more false of speech, more deceptive, or of more retentive memory . . . more wakeful; more shrinking, more difficult to rouse to action" than were men.[14] You'll note that in this laundry list of complaints about what is "naturally" wrong with women, but Aristotle threw in a few small compliments. Sure, women were shrill harpies who could stop crying only long enough to lie to you, but they sure did have sharp memories and were *complex*! Still, men needed to keep them under their rule because women couldn't be trusted.

Aristotle's proof lay in women's physiognomy. Women, he claimed (incorrectly), have fewer teeth than men. Women don't have external genitals. (This is meant to be an obvious negative, for reasons

that are not fully explained.) As a result, Aristotle posited that
women were *inside-out men*, who had lost some of their power in the
process of becoming inverted.

Medicalizing Women: Galen

Before the medieval period, Aristotle's musings on women and sex
were codified by Galen (129–ca. 216). Galen, also known as Aelius or
Claudius Galen, aka Galen of Pergamon, was an extremely influential physician. Like the three men we've already encountered, Galen
was Greek, but his world was much different from theirs, as he was
born several centuries later, in a thoroughly Roman era. Coming
from a wealthy family in Pergamon (present-day Bergama, Turkey),
Galen was lavishly educated and well traveled. And like any social
climber during the height of Roman power and influence, he eventually settled in the eternal city itself. Galen nevertheless wrote in
Greek. Medieval people came to most of his work after it was translated first into Arabic, then from Arabic into Latin in the twelfth
century, followed by a second wave in the late fifteenth and early
sixteenth centuries.[15]

In Rome, Galen set about expanding on extant medical knowledge to the best of his ability. He augmented Hippocratic and Aristotelian concepts of humoral theory by performing dissections.
Unfortunately for him, the Roman Empire banned dissection of
humans, so he spent his time dissecting monkeys and pigs to further develop humoral theory. At the time, humans were considered
to resemble bears or apes *externally* and pigs *internally*.

Performing real experiments on real bodies was a big step forward. However, Galen didn't see physiological work as contradicting
to philosophical beliefs, let alone something that would overhaul
them. Instead, he saw it as corresponding to and embellishing the
philosophical practice of his predecessors. He was so convinced of
it that he wrote a treatise called *The Best Physician Is Also a Philoso-*

pher.[16] Given that this was Galen's starting point, you will likely be unsurprised to learn that all that dissection did absolutely nothing to overhaul the Aristotelian concept of women as inside-out men.

Instead, Galen kept the Peripatetic tradition alive and encouraged his readers, when considering women, to "think first . . . of the man's [genitals] turned in and extending inward between the rectum and the bladder. If this should happen, the scrotum would necessarily take the place of the uterus with the testes lying outside, next to it on either side." Note that while everyone had genitals, and they were more or less the same but in different places, the genitals that you should think of *first* were the male ones. No number of dissections was going to change the way that Galen approached women, because the treatment of women as secondary had nothing to do with medical facts. Women weren't quite people, what with their cold, wet humors, inside-out genitals, and irrational brains.

Educated Ancient Women

Women weren't considered stable enough to vote in Rome, and they certainly weren't considered able to join in scholarly debate about their humanity.[17]

However—and this is very important—they still tried. In both Greek and Roman society, women who were a part of the wealthy elite were often educated and often worked as teachers, wrote poetry, and created art. They were also brilliant philosophers. Famously, the mathematician Pythagoras (you may have heard of his theorem?) was educated by the philosopher Themistoclea (sixth century B.C.E., aka Aristoclea, aka Theoclea), though unfortunately none of her works survive.[18] Hipparchia the Cynic (ca. 350–280 B.C.E.), a philosopher, shocked Greek society and gained fame by wearing male clothing and living in equality with her husband, the cynic Crates. Her philosophical work was famous enough that she was the only woman to be referred to in Diogenes Laertius's *Lives and Opin-*

ions of Eminent Philosophers, which was an encyclopedia of famous Greek thinkers.[19] Though sadly very little of her actual work survives, her life itself was considered a philosophical argument for the equality of women. Under Rome, the philosopher Hypatia (ca. 350–415) lived and worked in Alexandria and was a polymath who taught astronomy and neo-Platonic philosophy. Again, her extraordinary intelligence was seen as an argument for her equality with men, and the Church historian Socrates of Constantinople (ca. 380–439) wrote glowingly that she did not "feel abashed in going to an assembly of men. For all men on account of her extraordinary dignity and virtue admired her the more."[20] This was high praise indeed coming from a Christian toward a pagan woman, and indicative of the esteem that she enjoyed.

As intelligent and independently powerful as these women were, and as compelling a case as some of them were able to make for their humanity, they were still treated as a sideshow. The fact that Hipparchia had to dress like a man to make a case for her equality gives some hint as to whether people took the work of women seriously. We may know the name of Themistoclea, but we don't even know when she lived. While she was undoubtedly a famous intellectual in her day, her major accomplishment is historically recorded as having taught a man. Neither of these women's philosophical work survives for us in a great enough quantity to scrutinize it. Instead, we have to content ourselves with their society's understanding of them as oddballs. Or worse: Hypatia was murdered in 415 by an angry mob who accused her of practicing dark magic.

Medieval Education

During the medieval period, theologians communicated this foundation through a pedagogical network of philosophers and clergymen in cultivated schools centered first in monasteries and later in universities. These more rarefied educational apparatuses, meanwhile, were augmented by culture more broadly. People who were unable to access formal education were nevertheless taught at home; they learned about theology and cosmology in their parish churches, through popular literature, and at times even in the theater. Medieval people were much attached to the idea of themselves as the successors of the glorious ancient empires, which provided a mythic element to their reverence of the ancients. If they claimed Aristotle hard enough, they could also claim to be the second coming of the Lyceum.

This need to be connected to the ancients occasionally tipped over into absurdity. Sometimes, for example, chroniclers (who were like medieval historians but also acted as propagandists for their patrons) would portray various rulers as descendants of mythical ancients. The twelfth-century French poet Benoît de Sainte-Maure (d. 1173), for example, wrote that the emperor Charlemagne (748–814) was descended from the mythical Trojan Francus.[21] Similarly, Geoffrey of Monmouth (ca. 1095–1155), a Benedictine monk and avid chronicler, wrote in his *Historia regnum Britanniae*, or *History of the Kings of Britain,* that Britain itself was named for its first king, Brutus, a grandson of Aeneas, who set sail to the island of Britain to slay the race of giants living there.[22] The fact that both of these myths involve Trojans specifically is no mistake, as Trojans were a mythological two-for-one. By claiming descent from a Trojan, you could in one fell swoop connect yourself with the glory of the Hellenistic world *and* to Rome. This was important, because everyone agreed that Rome and the ancient Greek city-states were the height of human endeavor. If you could add Christianity to the equation, it would be almost optimal—at least as far as terrestrial civilization was concerned.

For Charlemagne, part of *proving* his theoretical "Roman-ness" (and that he was the rightful ruler of the largest contiguous land mass in Europe) was spreading ancient knowledge and texts. Hence he began what historians refer to as the Carolingian Renaissance,[23] a flourishing of the arts and culture in monasteries throughout the Carolingian Empire with specific backing from the emperor. Along with his court scholar Alcuin of York (ca. 735–804), Charlemagne called for major educational reforms for the betterment of his Christian subjects. All cathedrals and monasteries were to establish schools where boys would learn how to read and write so that they could understand the Bible, copy important texts, and contribute to a Christian society. The best way to do this, it was agreed, was to focus on the seven liberal arts, which were broken into two sections. The first and most important was the Trivium, which was composed of Grammar, Logic, and Rhetoric. Once students mastered it, they could proceed to the Quadrivium: arithmetic, astronomy, geometry, and music.

As a result of Charlemagne's dictates, every monastery and cathedral was soon teaching whichever boys showed up that day how to read and write in Latin. In order to do so, they sought out available classical texts. They studied Plato and read the *Odyssey*. They read Ovid and argued about Virgil. Under Charlemagne's rule, learning was identical with studying the classics, and students had to fully grasp them in order to move on to understand biblical thought.

These same clergy members contributed to the spread of knowledge not only by teaching but also by copying and distributing texts. Monastic life in general was dedicated to the concept that work took place alongside and as a type of prayer, which was referred to as *ora et labora* or "prayer and work." Given that most monks were well educated and had access to libraries, one form of work to which they were uniquely suited was copying texts. As a result, they were able to ensure that there was plenty of Plato, Aristotle, and Galen to go around, as monastic and cathedral schools proliferated throughout the European continent.

Even after Charlemagne's dynasty and empire fell apart, his contributions to learning and knowledge stayed firmly in the medieval imagination. Three hundred years later the twelfth century hosted its own renaissance, which historians creatively call the Twelfth-Century Renaissance.[24] It was centered on universities, which had come into being at the end of the eleventh century and were gaining traction as the preferred mechanism for in-depth education. Universities were established in Bologna (in 1088, by a group of super-keen students), Paris (in 1150, by the clergy associated with the cathedral school at Notre Dame), and Oxford (by clergy who were either uninterested in the trip to Paris or prevented from making it after Henry II [1133–89] forbade the English from studying there in 1167). Students attended these schools in the hopes of attaining lucrative positions in the Church or in various royal courts. What they studied was largely the same as what Charlemagne's monks had, but with an added emphasis on Rhetoric, meaning there was more disputation and argument in general.

As a result of these emphases, students were educated on a steady diet of the classics. That was a perfect way to unthinkingly proliferate ancient thoughts about women and sex, no matter how absurd. For medieval scholars, philosophy was not unlike the golden rule of improv comedy: if someone gives you a line of thought, you accept the premise, say "Yes, and," and expand on it. If you were raised and educated expressly to revere particular works, to think that ancient knowledge was more complete, and to see upholding it as proof of your place in the world, you likely would not attempt to overhaul it. This is especially true if your own theological beliefs happened to align with the classical concepts of women that had been drilled into you during your education.

The Doctrine of Original Sin

Throughout medieval Europe, an overall concept of women was being constantly refined and argued over, but all Christians could agree on one immutable truth: women were responsible for the existence of sin, for the mortality of humans, and for their own pain during childbirth. This cheery social conceit was brought to us all courtesy of—once again—the creation myth, in which all those ills arose from Eve's decision to eat the fruit of knowledge.

This concept was, and indeed still is, known as the doctrine of Original Sin. Augustine (354–430), a theologian and philosopher whose works became so important to the canon of Christianity that he is known as a Church father and a saint, conceptualized the sin as a sort of infection that was passed down through all generations of humans as its corporeal embodiment. Before the fall, Adam and Eve had been more akin to spiritual incarnations than to physical bodies. After they sinned and were expelled from the Garden of Eden, however, they were made of flesh and were doomed to die.[25] For many of the devout, this was a cause for some actual anger. Dying has never been popular, so it was easy to be mad at some possibly real, probably allegorical, forebears who were responsible for everyone living as what Augustine called a *massa peccati* or mess of sin and were repugnant as a result.

Before you jump to conclusions, it wasn't just women who were culpable. According to the doctrine of Original Sin men were too. After all, Adam chose to eat the fruit of the tree of knowledge and became mortal just as Eve had.

In this instance, however, there were levels of culpability.

Eve had decided to eat the fruit of the tree because when the snake tempted her, she was easily swayed and lacked sufficient mental and moral strength to push back. Adam, according to Augustine, was tempted and ate the fruit not simply because he was weak but because he wanted to participate in an experience with Eve. Yes, he was forced to leave the garden, just as she was, but his reasons for being forced out were certainly purer than hers, or stronger at the very least. Augustine's message was that even when a man disobeyed God, it was probably because a woman had convinced him to do so.

Leaving aside the doctrine of Original Sin, Adam and Eve, as the first people, were meant to be seen as archetypes for the rest of the

The Fall of Man from *Les Très Riches Heures du duc de Berry,* by the Limbourg brothers (active 1385–1416), Bibliothèque du Château, Chantilly. HERITAGE IMAGE PARTNERSHIP LTD / ALAMY STOCK PHOTO.

species. Adam, having been made first, was the default human. He was created in God's image and was exactly as man was meant to be: pious, obedient, hardworking, and oblivious to the call of temptation. Women, on the other hand, were like Eve—an afterthought. Eve had been brought into the world from Adam's rib to entertain him and to procreate with him. As Augustine put it, a woman was "merely man's helpmate . . . She is not the image of God but as far as man is concerned, he is by himself the image of God."[26] Women were appendages to men, and if men left them to their own devices, they would be off talking to the devil and cursing men with mortality.

Lest you think that Augustine was alone in his repugnance for women as a result of Eve's theoretical actions, you need look only as far as Tertullian (155–240) for yet more aspersions. Quintus Septimius Florens Tertullianus was born before Augustine but was also an important Christian Roman thinker of African birth. Also like Augustine, he is considered a father of the Church because of his influence. (Unlike most of the other Church fathers, he was never granted sainthood, because some of his ideas, such as that the Son and the Holy Spirit in the Trinity were subordinate to the Father, were deemed heretical.) Nevertheless, Tertullian was the first Christian to produce a huge theological output in Latin. Medieval Christians, as Latin readers, much enjoyed picking out the bits of his thinking that corresponded with what was considered acceptable Christian dogma. His teachings on women meshed with theirs.

To wit, Tertullian was of the opinion that women were the "devil's gateway . . . the unsealer of that (forbidden) tree . . . the first deserter of the divine law . . . she who persuaded him whom the devil was not valiant enough to attack. [Women] destroyed so easily God's image, man. On account of [their] desert—that is, death— even the Son of God had to die. And do you think about adorning yourself over and above your tunics of skins?"[27] In other words, everything bad that happened was the fault of women, and even worse, instead of thinking about that and reforming their ways, they were obsessed with shopping. If nothing else, this is clear evidence that even eighteen-hundred-year-old theological treatises are not immune from the most hackneyed conceits.

To be fair, just because Eve was the first woman in the Bible doesn't mean she was the only one.[28] There were also faithful women who were upheld as moral lessons for the fairer sex. Brave Esther, for example, stood as a beacon for Jewish and Christian women alike. The same was true for Ruth, the great-grandmother of King David. Christians, though, revered one shining example of femininity to whom all others had to defer: the Virgin Mary. Mary was the ultimate in femininity not solely because she was the mother of God, but because she had managed to be born without original sin, thanks to the Immaculate Conception. Often confused with Jesus's divine conception, it was Mary's conception, without the curse of sin, that was to be considered immaculate. This, in turn, allowed her to be used as God's vessel for the birth of Jesus.

The theological mechanics of the Immaculate Conception were largely put in place by the Greek Church early in the medieval period. According to the archbishop of Constantinople and celebrated rhetorician Gregory of Nazianzus (ca. 329–390), the divine nature of Christ reached back in time to when Mary was conceived. In order to make it possible for Christ to be conceived, he more or less "pre-purified" his mother, to make way for himself.[29] So Mary was an excellent example of everything a woman *could* be—but almost never was. Indeed, even before the doctrine of Immaculate Conception came into play, it was basically accepted fact that Mary was above reproach. Augustine, for example, wrote that "the honor of the Lord does not permit the question of sin to be raised in connection with the Blessed Virgin Mary." His feeling was that Mary, even if she had been tainted with original sin, was able to overcome sin "of every sort" by the merit of her grace.[30]

If women were by their nature more prone to sin, then, they were able to overcome it. After all, this was the very reason God had assumed human form as Christ. He came to absolve the world from the sins of their ancestors. All right-thinking Christians had to do was focus their resolve, and they could overcome their frail nature. Assuredly, women had more to make up for, but they also had an exemplary role model in the Virgin Mary to help them.

All this is not to say that Eve and Mary were the only women considered in early Christian ideas of gender. A range of characters pop up in medieval theological and natural philosophical debates. Mary and Eve, however, can be considered the anchors of medieval Christian femininity. They comprise a Christian shorthand for the best and worst possible outcomes for women and are referenced most often in musings about the nature of women.

Monasteries and Cathedral Schools

You may have noticed that this discussion, while nominally about the women, is also about what a number of men think about women. That largely has to do with whose voices from the past are privileged. Aristotle's ideas are brought to the front, while Hypatia's are sent to the back. Another reason those masculine voices were the ones upheld and passed down to medieval thought, however, was that for the most part, organized education (and all its attendant avenues of learning, writing, and publishing) was explicitly closed to women.

For the wealthy, this was not as much the case. There was a premium on education for everyone at court. The average princess or duchess had someone teaching her to read and write in Latin and to think about the Bible. Anyone who worked in a shop or needed to keep accounts was likely educated to some extent as well. Arithmetic and geometry were prerequisites for much of medieval life: money had to be counted and buildings had to be built. For the most part, women taught their children. Local city groups might also hire women to give children the education they needed to keep society running. We know this from personal accounts as well as from illustrations of women working in classrooms. We also have lots of evidence in the form of books of hours—small works that enumerated the appropriate prayers to say at particular times of day. They were generally seen as a feminine affectation and were used by women to teach children, sometimes including alphabets at the front to help them out. The fact of the matter was that women were the suppliers of education, but they were consumers of it only in a private capacity.

But women weren't the ones writing the curriculum. By and large, the Church, especially the monks, was responsible for education that went beyond literacy and a trade. In the early medieval period, a man's best chance of becoming educated was to become a monk. Discussing early medieval monasticism is a difficult proposition, however, as over the era monasticism changed a great deal.

The earliest monks, who we refer to as the "desert fathers," were mostly solitary individuals of the third century who spent their time alone in the desert in Egypt in religious contemplation. Eventually, they attracted followers, which made Church leaders a bit uncomfortable, since these acolytes could uncharitably be described as cult followers. Many of the desert fathers were charismatic, inspiring their followers to acts of self-sacrifice. While this might seem positive, Church leaders saw it not just as threatening to their own power but also as possibly antithetical to their teachings. In theory, the point of Christianity was to focus on Christ, not on the individuals practicing his word.

These concerns led the Church to regularize religious life and to form monasteries, giving rise to what most of us picture as medieval monks. Benedict of Nursia (480–543) founded the first monastery, at Monte Cassino, outside Rome. Monasteries (and especially early ones) were meant to be self-contained worlds, where the monks did all the work needed to sustain the community, cut off from the venal distractions of the world outside. In exchange, Saint Benedict asked monks to adhere to his rule, a series of seventy-three chapters on how to live a Christian life and effectively administer a monastery. The guiding principle for his and all future monasteries was the aforementioned "prayer and work." If monks weren't sleeping or praying, they were meant to be working. In addition to farming, running the kitchens, brewing the beer, and performing all the general tasks required to feed and clothe a community, the monks' work was their scholarly duties.

In an era before printers, books had to be written out manually, which was a time-consuming and laborious process. The monks meticulously copied works by Aristotle, Galen, and Augustine. All this copying led to several innovations, perhaps most notably the development of spaces between words. This novelty was the work of the monks at Kilmalkedar, in what is now Ireland, who realized that text was easier to read when it was not configured as one massive run-on word. Innovations like these were bound to follow when an educated class of workers engaged on similar tasks many times, which made the monasteries some of the most important schools in early medieval Europe. In addition to Monte Cassino and Kilmalkedar, other celebrated monasteries were Marmutier Abbey (founded in 372 in Tours, France), the Princely Abbey of Stavelot-Malmedy (founded in 651 on the Amblève River in what is now Belgium), the Abbey of St. Gall (founded in 747 at St. Gallen, Switzerland), and the Abbey of Cluny (founded in 910 in eastern France)—and these are just some of the standouts among scores of such institutions.[31]

Of course, the downside (from the perspective of the broader society) to such an educational system was that if you were not part of the aristocracy, to get a good education you had to dedicate yourself to the monastic life and live forever inside a monastery, cloistered and serving God. For those who did not feel themselves called to the monastic life, Charlemagne in his renaissance saw fit to establish and endow so-called cathedral schools alongside monasteries. These schools would take any and all young men who wanted an education. No cloistering was required. Some who enjoyed these educations did go on to join the clergy, but others worked for noble houses or royal courts. Henry I of England (1069–1135) used to send members of the court off to cathedral schools with the express purpose of having well-educated courtiers returned to him. Other cathedral students, meanwhile, would end up in various trades where education was a necessity, like merchant or legal work. The most celebrated cathedral schools included Canterbury in England; Utrecht, Liège, Cologne, Metz, and Speyer in the German-speaking lands; and Chartres, Orleans, Paris, Laon, Reims, and Rouen in what is now France. Laon, incidentally, was Henry I's school of choice.[32]

In the twelfth century, cathedral schools gave way to universities as the premier destination for serious scholars.[33] The university system developed as a result of demand for more rigorous and ongoing education as well as instruction in subjects that were not taught at the cathedrals. While all universities founded in this period taught the seven liberal arts, they also offered specialist courses. Bologna eventually became a center for study of the law, whereas Paris was the place to go for philosophy. Budding physicians, meanwhile, headed to Salerno, which had been functioning as a medical school since the ninth century and saw a boom in interest during the eleventh and twelfth centuries, when Arabic medical texts flowed in. These universities offered students and their families more choice; instead of sending their teenage son to a cathedral, they could send him to argue with his peers about Aristotle and have him return ready to serve whatever institution would have him. The Trivium and Quadrivium that these students took as their curriculum would be barely recognizable to us today. But plenty of evidence suggests that one thing would be very familiar indeed: the student himself.

The medieval student drank, fought, and in general conducted himself with the same swaggering nonsense as undergraduates do today. And just as today, this could lead to tensions between these temporary and rebellious residents of the university towns and the townspeople (and their pesky laws).

In order to ensure that their students never experienced legal consequences for their behavior—a key demand from wealthy medieval parents, as much as it is from well-to-do benefactors now—the universities came up with a unique work-around: all university students would take holy orders. That way, if they got in trouble, say, for running out on the bill at a local inn, as students from the University of Paris were fond of doing, they would be tried in ecclesiastical courts rather than local ones. There they would receive a slap on the wrist and be sent back to their studies, rather than face any meaningful punishment. This meant that every medieval university student was technically a clergy member, with a holy cassock to prove it. In fact, this is where the term *town-gown relations* comes from.

This requirement of holy orders also meant that the two major ways to be educated in the medieval period, joining a monastery school or going to university, were effectively closed to women. So even as Plato and Hippocrates and Galen and the Genesis myth were becoming locked into the standard pedagogic system, and even as pedagogy itself was becoming systematized, women were excluded from weighing in. The nature of our natures was being decided, and we weren't even present for the discussion. Most medieval thought about women was thus written by men, for men, based on readings of work by men.

Most of the medieval writers whom this book considers came from either the monastery or the university system. The luminaries consulted included (but are by no means limited to) Constantine the African (ca. 1020–1087), a Benedictine monk at Monte Cassino; Andreas Capellanus (ca. twelfth century), whose name literally means "Andreas the chaplain," which is a type of religious person who works at a lay institution like a court or a hospital; and Thomas Aquinas (1225–74), a Dominican friar and a saint. A friar is a type of monk found from the thirteenth century on who, rather than escaping the world, tried to be involved in and preach to communities. Indeed, the veritable parade of church councils, popes, and preachers, were all to a man, well, men, because they had to be. Even when we are talking about popular writing such as *The Canterbury Tales,* we are still consulting men. Similarly, courtly love or troubadour literature was largely written by men.

While in and of itself there is no problem per se with men engaging in debates about the nature of women, there is a problem when women are excluded from responding to or carrying on their own debates in any recordable fashion. This is why it is worth seeking out the women writers whose work *did* manage to emerge from the medieval period. Even when medieval women were given the same texts to study, when they were able to engage in debates, they didn't read the texts the same way medieval men did. Since these women thinkers are few, we particularly have to focus on what they left us.

Hildegard and Christine

Obviously, some massive impediments prevented women from participating in scholarly and cultural debates about their sex. Still, some exceptional women managed to do so. Perhaps the most celebrated was Hildegard of Bingen (1098–1179). The reason Hildegard was and is feted is that she was a phenom. She was a polymath, with gifts that allowed her to work as, among other things, a composer, a philosopher, and the founder of the Germanic school of natural philosophy. Eventually, she became a saint. Hildegard involved herself in philosophical discussions about gender by taking a similar route to that taken by early medieval men—she became a nun.

Nuns, in many ways, were like monks. The great majority lived enclosed lives in cloisters, removed from the world so that they could better contemplate and serve God through their works. Much as monks had to be literate and educated in order to do their work, so did nuns. As a result, if a woman came from a family that was wealthy enough to not need her to work at home and if she was religiously or intellectually inclined, the nunnery was her destination of choice. She had to take a vow of celibacy and obedience both to the Church and to her abbess, but in exchange for disavowing familial life, she was granted the chance to think. This was how Hildegard got her start. The youngest child of a lower noble family, at some point between six and ten years old she was sent as an oblate (a child sent to a monastery or nunnery). There she had the opportunity to read all the same ancient Greek and Roman thinkers, Church fathers, and biblical instruction as the men in monasteries.

In her study, she came to different conclusions than her male counterparts did. While she too conceived of Eve as having been fashioned from Adam's rib to provide him with companionship, to her way of thinking it was actually a good thing. Adam, and all men by extension, were made from clay. They were therefore hard and strong. Eve, because she was made from Adam's body, was weaker and softer, but that meant her mind was sharper. She was defined less by what her body could do than by what her mind was free to achieve without the burden of heavy flesh.[34] Women should not therefore be thought of as a more quick-witted and sensitive counterpart to men. They were created by God not as a worse sort of man but as something new and different.

To see women not as inferior but as a different sort of human required a new way of thinking altogether. Instead of accepting that men were necessarily at the top of a hierarchically ordered universe with women below them, Hildegard imagined creation as interconnected and harmonious. Men and women had to understand themselves as complementary, with qualities that should be used to support each other and as equals before God. Sure one sex might excel at some things that the other lacked, but that didn't make one sex worse than the other. Instead, men and women could learn from each other. Men could emulate women as examples of grace and mercy, whereas women could attempt to develop the strength and courage that men held. Hildegard provided a detailed analysis not only of women but of the very concept and use of gender as a whole by reframing the conversation away from expectations about humans based on the masculine.

Obviously then, when medieval women did manage to get their foot in the door, they approached these texts—seminal or no— from a different angle.

Similarly, the lack of classical women to influence medieval concepts of women didn't indicate a lack of interest in the lives of classical women. Again, when women were involved, they approached the classical past in a different way. Christine de Pizan (1364–ca. 1430), a court poet and author for French king Charles VI (1368–1422), had much different views on women in history and philosophy. She received a good education as the daughter of a prominent physician and astronomer. Searching for a way to support her family after the death of her husband, she became a court author, writing works to entertain the French royal family, as well as love ballads. When left to her own devices, she specifically wrote books about great women. Her *The Book of the City of Ladies* (*Le Livre de la Cité des dames*) was the equivalent of a medieval best seller. It was also a polemic against men's negative concepts of women, told through the medium of what we might now describe as fan fiction.

Christine describes herself as initially receptive to the idea that women were naturally inferior to men, and as a result she naturally preferred the company and conversation of men. However, she eventually began to doubt her conviction of women's inferiority because men were constantly announcing to her how difficult and terrible women were. She thought their views were odd because, as she noted, *no matter which way I looked at it and no matter how much I turned the matter over in my mind, I could find no evidence from my own experience to bear out such a negative view of female nature and habits. Even so, given that I could scarcely find a moral work by any author which didn't devote some chapter or paragraph to attacking the female sex, I had to accept their unfavorable opinion of women since it was unlikely that so many learned men, who seemed to be endowed with such great intelligence and insight into all things, could possibly have lied on so many different occasions.[35]*

In her book, the personification of Reason visits her and makes the case that women are, in fact, important, citing historical and mythological women ranging from the medieval countess Marie of Blois (1136–82) to Isis and Dido. That leads Christine to realize that women are virtuous, interesting, and accomplished. Later, with the help of the personification of Rectitude, Christine begins building a city to be filled with "valiant ladies of great renown" throughout history, listing some ninety-two in total. Then with the help of the personification of Justice, she invites all the female saints to the city, whereupon they hold an election to establish their queen, the Virgin Mary.

It is no surprise that *The Book of the City of Ladies* was such a hit with audiences. To challenge the idea of women as naturally inferior, it uses the kinds of rhetorical arguments that medieval men were trained to use. It played on the medieval fascination with the past and reverence for the ancients by forcing audiences to consider mythological and historical women as figures of reverence on par with men. It then smartly includes the Virgin Mary—who all good Christians had to agree was the second-best human to ever live (after her son, naturally)—and her election as head of the city, to show that women can be holy, and that they can come together to honor and elevate that holiness. Readers loved the book so much that she wrote a sequel, *The Treasure of the City of Ladies,* or *The Book of the Three Virtues,* that focused on how to educate women to a standard so that they could live up to the ideals of her fictitious city. Not only did her thinking about women reframe ideals, but people explicitly wanted her to help educate women to be like those she championed.

Hildegard and Christine are two of the most famous medieval women writers. There were, of course, others, but sadly, even an exhaustive list of every medieval woman phenom—from Heloise of Argenteuil (ca. 1090–1164) to Marguerite Porete (d. 1310)—would be much shorter than the list of consequential medieval men. This has nothing to do with the ability of women, then or now. Rather, it is a question of access, in a culture that had a fixed idea of women as lesser than men. Even when the dissenting voices of women do come through, like those of Hildegard and Christine, and of Hypatia and Hipparchia before them, they were outliers. The great majority of women were never given the opportunity to be educated to the point that they could enter into a dialogue with the patriarchy, let alone refute it, which was a loss to us all.

Sermons and Literature

Most medieval people, whether they were male or female, didn't have the opportunity for a lavish education. In theory, anyone could arrive at a cathedral school and be educated, but most medieval people (85 percent) were peasants. They lived and died (like the preponderance of people in recorded history) on farms. They spent their lives growing crops and then bringing the harvest in, so they couldn't spare their children for daily lessons.[36] If a child wanted to become an oblate and then monk, the family had to consider not only the loss of a farm worker but also the financial barrier. Families were expected to give a sum of money or land to the institution they had joined in order to support their children before they were able to contribute significantly to the work life of a monastery. That was a tall order for peasants working the fields, especially before medieval advances in technology and agriculture brought greater yields to farming.

For many, besides monetary considerations, sending a child away wasn't a *legal* option. While 85 percent of Europe's population were peasants, 75 percent were serfs. Being a serf was a way of being unfree. Your body couldn't be forcibly bought or sold, but your labor could be. Serfs also had restrictions on their movement. You couldn't move down the road or into a city without permission from your lord. The wealthy people who could say where you lived and who were expecting your free labor on their land were not predisposed to sending young workers off to read the classics. In other words, an education was out of the question for the vast majority of the population.

Which isn't to say that these peasants were spared the ancient wisdom on inverted penises and hysteria, or Genesis's concepts of womanhood. Some rural parish priests lacked a monastery or university education, but they all had to be literate in order to read the Bible to their flocks and compose sermons for them.

The people who meticulously handwrote their Bibles, on the other hand, most likely did have a lofty education. A Bible could not transmit classical and contemporary gender discourse through osmosis, and medieval Bibles were not just the words of biblical text. They also contained glosses, or in-depth annotations written in the margins, around the biblical text. Glosses were considered an absolute necessity for anyone consulting or using a Bible, so much so that especially in the mid- to late medieval period, to read without one was referred to as "reading blind."

In particular, from the twelfth century on, people read the *Glossa Ordinaria,* along with a section of the Bible, like Paul's Letters to the Corinthians, though other glosses were available.[37] The biblical text was in the middle of the page, and surrounding it in the margins were writings that would explain how readers should interpret the passage in question. The gloss would include reference to Church fathers and theologians, so that for any given passage, readers would have recourse to, for example, Augustine's thoughts on the matter. Thus, while reading a medieval Bible,

All of the gloss information would be contained around the main biblical text. It would start above, continue through the midsection, moving on with the text, and then finally wrap itself along the bottom.

You would then read all of the main biblical text in the middle of the page.

As a result, even the lowliest servant of the Church had access to sophisticated theological interpretations of the biblical texts that he read day in and day out. He could then preach these ideas to his parishioners during his sermons.

And it was in sermons that the real work of medieval epistemology happened on a large scale. Medieval people were wild about sermons. In a world with limited entertainment options, where people did not have the opportunity to go to school and read books, having someone explain the Bible—why it was relevant to their lives, and how they could improve themselves—was an exciting prospect. Medieval Europeans saw themselves and each other as Christians first and foremost. Within the expressly religious context of medieval society, learning religious stories and theological doctrine felt personal and immediate in a way that it doesn't—or can't—for many of us today.

Hundreds of people would attend the sermons of popular preachers, and sermon collections were some of the period's most influential works. These written records would circulate, allowing people who lived too far from these well-known figures to hear their own local preachers repeat the same sermons. In fact, sermons and sermon collections were so popular that medieval historians refer to them as medieval mass media.[38] A Bible written in Latin might seem incommunicable to an audience, if it even had one, but medieval European society was set up to disseminate these messages effectively. Your average person working the fields in Flanders might never read a word of Aristotle, but he or she would have spent their entire life attending masses where their preacher reported on how Church fathers related Aristotle to the biblical passages they were read every Sunday. Moreover, that person in a field might consider attending a traveling preacher's sermon to be the height of entertainment. Medieval Europeans were steeped in a culture that took these views seriously and sought them out.

If the people on the lowest rung of the social ladder were influenced by philosophy, so were the wealthier people above them. People from merchant or trading backgrounds had their children attend cathedral schools or hired tutors, while the nobles and royalty employed clergy members who taught their children the identical ideas.

While almost every Christian in the medieval period loved sermons, other forms of popular entertainment served a range of audiences and helped to cement these concepts of women. Mystery plays, as their name does not indicate to us now, were theatrical productions that focused on biblical stories, or occasionally the miracles of saints (which we sometimes call "miracle plays" for disambiguation). Since at least the fifth century, mystery plays were performed in churches, with intricate chants, and could go on for days. Often they were put on as a part of large religious festivals like Easter. Eventually, a calendar of mystery plays developed: the story of creation would be performed at the New Year, moving the year through to the Apocalypse at the end.

A play that showed Adam and Eve's expulsion from the Garden of Eden clearly would help cement ideas about women, but mystery plays also showed signs of influence from the ancient philosophers. The incredibly popular English *Corpus Christi* (*Body of Christ*) plays, for example, nod to Platonic and Galenic concepts of the body.[39] Initially, mystery plays were often put on by members of the clergy, the same priests who received classical educations or were reading glosses. They took that knowledge and included it in the plays they were performing for the edification of their parishioners. This practice was stopped in 1210 when Pope Innocent III (1160/61–1216) issued a papal edict (more or less a Catholic cease-and-desist order) that priests should not be acting in mystery plays. The papacy considered that priests should be getting their ideas across on altars, not on stages. By this time, however, the plays were entirely too popular to be stopped altogether. Troupes of actors or members of local guilds (a sort of medieval trade organization) stepped in to fill the gap left by the clergy. The actors and guild members kept these same tropes going, not only because they had learned them from plays themselves but also because guild members were usually well to do and so had the benefit of an education.

As mystery plays moved away from the bosom of the Church, they took on a much more popular character. By this, I mean that they included a lot of sex and fart jokes. Medieval people, while certainly religious minded, absolutely *loved* a good fart joke or chance to moon the audience, and in order to reach more people, and perhaps gain heftier donations from appreciative audience members, some plucky groups of actors came up with a new idea: bawdy parodies of mystery plays. Professional actors, in contrast to priests and the wealthy guild members, were usually not traditionally educated. They were likely to be itinerant entertainers who went from place to place putting on shows and were seen as on par with sex workers. Yes, everyone enjoyed plays, but they were a bit of naughty fun, not high art. In this tradition, the Czech play *Mastičkář* (*The Ointment Seller*) parodied, among other things, Jesus rising from the dead, the story of Abraham and Isaac, and quack doctors.[40] Alongside the requisite fart jokes, it has plenty of gags about the necessity of beating one's wife in order to stop her from mouthing off.

The later medieval popular imagination didn't stop at plays. The bawdy interests of regular people, and their ideas about women, also come to the forefront in works of literature like *The Canterbury Tales*. These celebrated stories, much like the later mystery plays, were a product of mixed society. Geoffrey Chaucer (ca. 1342–1400) was born into a family of winemakers but worked in the households of nobility. He consequently had the ability to write his books down, and he had the sense to do so in English (rather than Latin or French, the common tongue among fancy English people). In order to read *The Canterbury Tales,* a literate person didn't need to know a foreign language. In this collection of stories, women behave in just the ways that medieval society expected them to: they fool their husbands, they have sex with their boyfriends in trees, and they fart in the faces of men that they don't want to sleep with. That alone was encouragement to take up reading as a hobby, and when they did, they were treated to a wealth of stories that highlighted problems with women. The Wife of Bath is a good businesswoman but is greedy and sex crazed. The Prioress, a woman of the clergy, nonetheless wears jewelry (including a broach inscribed *Amor vincit omnia* or "Love conquers all") that indicates she might be up for sex, and her social habits mark her out as grasping and obsessed with mimicking the nobility. All the women in the tales either demand obedience from their husbands, or trick and cuckold them. All in all, *The Canterbury Tales* is a compendium of anecdotes about what was wrong with women.

One might be tempted to think that the finer people that Chaucer wrote for would see a collection of sex stories as outrageous. To us today, people of refined tastes seem unlikely to be interested in long-winded bar stories about the lengths people will go to in order to have sex. But while the fart jokes might not have played at court, the anecdotes about cheating on one's husband were not only tolerated there but were the backbone of the courtly love genre.

Courtly love, as the name suggests, was literature written about

love by and for people at court, from epic tales of bygone kings in
Arthurian literature, to allegorical mystical poems like the popular
Roman de la Rose. As a style, courtly love shot to prominence in the
twelfth century and remained popular into the mid-fourteenth century. Troubadours—itinerant singers who spread out from what is
now southern France into Spain and Italy—expressed it in song. In
whatever expression, what makes courtly love literature courtly love
literature is its focus on the love between a man and a woman who is
likely married to some other man. Arthuriana makes multiple references to the illicit love between the queen Guinevere and the knight
Lancelot, and their sexual liaisons eventually bring down Camelot.
In *Tristan and Iseult,* a romantic tale, the couple's love unfolds as
Tristan escorts Iseult to marry his uncle. Meanwhile Andreas Capellanus's *De amore* (*On Love*) is either a pick-up guide for seducing
women at court or a parody of the ideas of adulterous romance.

This makes sense in context, as medieval people broadly, and
medieval rulers more particularly, did not consider marriage to be
about love. Instead, it was a religious sacrament and a contract about
property. Medieval royals and nobles often married to create alliances between households, enabling great estates. Scores of well-to-
do people lived in those estates, serving the lords and kings present.
Because they were not out plowing the fields like the other 85 percent of the populace, they had much more leisure time. They preferred to spend it hunting, falconing, and writing love songs about
how badly they wanted to have sex with each other.

The upper crust at court, educated to an exceedingly high standard, had plenty of time to impress the man or woman of their
dreams with their very own Aristotelian insights into love and the
nature of women while trying hard not to give in to lust. But they
did give in to lust. Religion can only do so much for a lot of attractive people with time on their hands. Eventually the best courtly
love literature made it out to the masses, who appreciated a story
of impossible love, whether it was told by a wandering minstrel, in

manuscript form, or as an oral story. When courtly love literature traveled, so did its ideas about women.

By analyzing literature, we can learn about the cultures of a period, what people considered important, and what made them tick. We can deduce from their writing that medieval writers were influenced by Aristotle, as they state that women are inverted men. But some writers happily noted the authorities that influenced their worldview explicitly. Those references them helped to consolidate the substance of their writing.

The way literature communicates ideas is never in stasis. Medieval Europeans built on the classical and biblical basis created by their predecessors, but they adapted it to their own world, expanding the classical framework accordingly. In doing so, they influenced the world around them. It is difficult to tell, for example, whether courtly love literature was written to reflect the reality of court life, where married women flirted and traded sexual favors with their husbands' underlings, or if it was initially an invented romantic dynamic which inspired its readers to imitate it after the fact and start extramarital affairs. After a while, though, it didn't matter which came first. People were courting each other, even while some of the lovers involved were married or betrothed, and they were writing poetry about it. Art mimics life, but life also mimics art.

Overall, writings from the medieval period, whether theological, medical, or fictitious, tell us how medieval people understood women. In general, we learn that women were thought of as men who had somehow gone wrong. Whatever stereotypical masculine quality was considered good (courage, strength, intelligence, restraint), women had the opposite quality (cowardice, weakness, foolishness, sexual profligacy). These attributes were seen as an essential part of women's nature, handed down through generations from Eve, who had been created as a necessarily inferior companion for Adam and had driven the world into sin and death. Some feminine attributes, however, were considered good, such as kindness, nurturing,

and well, a lot of matronly stuff. Much as women's bad characteristics were inherited from Eve, their good traits were gifts typified
by Mary—the universal perfect mommy. These ideas about women
were repeated ad nauseam everywhere, from biblical commentary
to the university classroom, and even to escapist romantic fiction.

Medieval and ancient texts share almost exactly the same view of
women, though the reasoning they use to justify it differs. Plato was
not a Christian, no matter what lengths Christians went to in order
to convince themselves that Jesus had saved him. In the same way,
although some medieval attitudes persist in our own society now,
our beliefs about women have changed in many ways to suit our
current understandings of the world. As we will see going forward,
these ideas anchored societal attitudes toward women, including
beauty ideals, concepts about women's sexuality, and women's roles
as family members and workers. One way or another, though, when
we consider the way women are conceptualized in the global north,
we can ultimately start laying the blame back on the ancient Athe-
nians. They have a lot to answer for.

2

MEN LOOKING
AT WOMEN

BEAUTY IS SAID TO BE IN THE EYE OF THE BEHOLDER, AND people throughout time have cautioned about the impossibility of defining what it is. In the thirteenth century, the English philosopher and statesman Robert Grosseteste (ca. 1175–1253) warned that attempting to codify beauty would only prove confusing and sully the very concept. Instead, he advised others that they should "not seek to know what beauty is. . . . As soon as you attempt to do so, the mist of innumerable physical images will cloud your mind. . . . Think of this or that beautiful object. Then, omitting 'this' and 'that,' think of what makes 'this' and 'that' beautiful. Try to see what Beauty is in itself. . . . If you succeed, you will see God Himself, the Beauty which dwells in all beautiful things."[1] Absolutely no one listened to him.

Instead, some of the greatest medieval thinkers set themselves to listing the qualities that all could agree were most pleasing to the eye. In the time-honored medieval tradition, they looked to classical authors for hints at what they should find attractive, hoping to extrapolate from there. Unfortunately for them, a paucity of classical sources describing female beauty existed. So instead they established their own ideals, basing them on literary descriptions of classical characters to get the desired pedigree.

The Ideal

As much as early medieval writers liked to lean on Greek and Roman philosophy, few classical texts specified what made for beauty. That didn't stop medieval writers from assuring us that there were, in fact, rules for figuring out who was attractive. Many early medieval queens, they assured us, were gorgeous. Theodelinda (570–628), queen of the Lombards; her daughter Gundaperga (ca. 591–?) also a Lombard queen; Bathild of Ascania (ca. 626–80), a queen and later a saint; and Judith of Bavaria (797–843) were all praised by chroniclers (or in the case of Bathild, her hagiographer) as beautiful and graceful but very little detail was provided alongside these vague compliments.[2]

These descriptions would certainly have made Robert Grosseteste proud, given that they are fairly light on, well, descriptors. Yet they are still instructive. While we are not told why these women were considered beautiful, their beauty was, in fact, rather the point. Their looks functioned to underline why they were in positions of power. Bathild, for one, had served as a slave but was made queen because of her incredible beauty.[3] In other words, women's beauty functioned as a sort of divine right. They belonged on the throne because of their uncommonly attractive appearance, since beautiful women were rightly elevated.

These writers' reasoning makes perfect sense when we consider that they were in the business of explaining to audiences that they should revere these women. Royal patrons often employed chroniclers to present a history of why the people in their lineage were important. Authors wrote hagiographies, meanwhile, to help get someone elevated to the status of saint, or to spread the extant cult of an established saint. The vaguely detailed but vaunted beauty of these queens was used as a type of publicity, the praise necessary to explain to audiences that these women should be esteemed. Women simply couldn't be considered important, holy, or powerful without also being thought of as attractive.

This concept served not only to aggrandize the wealthy and powerful women whom it flattered, but to also obscure tensions about who got to hold power, which is to say, the rich. While Bathild might have been an outlier, most of the women I named were born into powerful families.[4] They would have been on the throne whether or not they were beautiful. Yet their beauty is still held up as the reason for their power. Bathild, meanwhile, quite literally attracted power through the force of her beauty, which was seen as proof of God's favor. Her husband, King Clovis II of Neustria and Burgundy (633–57) was so overcome by her virtues that he made her a queen, rather than toying with her as a concubine or mistress. Early medieval beauty standards for women were then a conundrum: a woman who was beautiful could rise to power, much as in innumerable fairy tales. If a woman wasn't powerful, however, could she be said to be beautiful? As vague as it was, early medieval beauty was ring-fenced and could be understood as uniquely tied to well-to-do women.

Given that beauty was a key to power, medieval writers gave ever more interest to codifying the criteria for attractiveness. In keeping with the high (post-1000) and late (post-1250) medieval deference to classical thinking, they looked for clues back to Greece and Rome. As if to prove that standards of beauty should be unattainable, the beauties most frequently settled on were no mere historical personages but the ones who inhabited the stories of Hellenic and Roman mythology.

One of the most common destinations for understanding beauty was Troy. Stories of the Trojan War were used to bolster claims to legitimate rule. It was much easier to use the same story to establish who was considered beautiful. Indeed, the same justifications for deferring to the ancients when it came to philosophical knowledge could readily be deployed when discussing beauty standards. If older knowledge was more perfect because it was closer to the divine, then so too were older concepts of beauty.

Medieval authors often looked at *De excidio Troia Historia,* an account of the Trojan War attributed to Dares Phrygius, a Trojan priest at the temple of the god Hephaestus, who lived in the eighth century B.C.E., around the time of Homer, author of the *Iliad* and the *Odyssey.* Dares's tale was translated in the fifth century A.D. and was popular in the medieval period. According to Homer, Dares witnessed the Trojan War, which lent authority to his account, as theoretically Dares could indeed have gazed upon the fair visages of the women involved in that conflict. More important, he took the time to detail the physical characteristics of three particular women: Polyxena, Briseis, and Helen of Troy, who was considered the most stunning woman of that time.

Polyxena was, according to myth, the youngest daughter of King Priam of Troy and his wife, Queen Hecuba. She features largely as a tragic figure. Betrothed to the demigod Achilles, and some-times implicated in his death, she was said to have been sacrificed at his tomb.

Briseis, like many women in classical literature, is less a character in her own right than an object that forced men to act. Her claim to fame is that after Greek armies sacked her city, Lyrnessus, Achil-les killed her entire family in front of her, then enslaved her as his concubine. When he was forced to give her to the higher-up King Agamemnon, he was so incensed (read: pouty) that he withdrew from battle, leading to major losses on the Greek side.

After that long preamble I must unfortunately admit that both Polyxena and Briseis, as they are described in *De excidio Troia His-toria,* had white skin and were blond. They both also sported fetch-ing monobrows. The major point of differentiation between the two was their height: where Polyxena was tall, Briseis was described as "not tall."[5]

One might think that Dares would have been more forthcoming in his description of the woman who launched a thousand ships, Helen of Troy. After all, Helen, a Greek mythological character, was the product of her father Zeus's famous seduction, while in the form of a swan, of her mother Leda. She is important specifically because her parents would have given her incredible beauty. She was married to King Menelaus of Sparta. At the same time, and unknown to her, she was being offered in marriage to another man—Paris of Troy. Paris had been chosen by Zeus to adjudicate a beauty contest awarding a golden apple to the most beautiful goddess, a claim laid by Hera, Athena, and Aphrodite. Although Paris was chosen to judge the contest because of his supposed fairness, his decision on the matter was swayed. All three goddesses promised him a reward for choosing her as the most attractive. Hera, the queen of Olympus, promised that he would become king of Europe and Asia Minor; Athena, the goddess of wisdom, promised to make him the wisest man in the world; and Aphrodite, the goddess of love, offered him the hand of the most beautiful woman in the world. He chose Aphrodite.

Aphrodite hadn't really thought this one through, but she was a goddess of her word. As it happened, Helen wasn't much impressed by Menelaus, who was gone a lot of the time. When Aphrodite appeared and offered to whisk her away to Troy with the handsome young Paris, Helen agreed. Infuriated, Menelaus raised an army, gathered other Greek rulers, and descended upon Troy.

Having seen a beauty so stunning, a theoretical eyewitness like Dares might see fit to describe her in detail, but here too Dares disappoints. He described Helen as "beautiful, ingenious and charming. Her legs were the best; her mouth the cutest. There was a beauty-mark between her eyebrows."[6] That's it.

To be fair to Dares, even if he really did have firsthand knowledge, he was working with the same classical conventions as the other authors in his time. Even Homer's *Iliad* and *Odyssey* provide no detailed description of Helen, simply calling her beautiful or lovely or mentioning her white arms and penchant for wearing white shawls. Fragmentary ancient Greek poems such as *Works and Days* refer to her as having nice hair. Meanwhile the poet Sappho (ca. 630–570 B.C.E.) hardly does better than her male peers, just calling Helen blond.[7] For ancient writers, specificity had nothing to do with poetic descriptions. The point was simply to understand a vague concept of attractiveness, usually linked to white skin and blond hair. Everything else could be left to the reader's imagination.

These frustratingly brief descriptions, and the entreaties of contemporaries like Grosseteste to leave them at that, did little to assuage the interests of the medieval mind. The search for older texts with fuller portraits continued, until the sixth-century elegiac poet Maximianus wrote a far more detailed description of a beautiful woman. While we may consider the sixth century to be medieval, Maximianus made a case for himself as a part of the classical tradition, tracing his lineage to the Etruscans and claiming to have had a friendship with the Roman senator and consul Boethius (ca. 477–524).[8] This was good enough for medieval people, especially combined with the fact that he was the author of one of the first fleshed-out descriptions of a beautiful woman:

> Golden hair, downcast milky neck
> Ingenious features to make more of [her] face
> Black eyebrows, free forehead, bright skin
> These notes often burned my mind.
> I love the flames and little swollen lips
> which tasted me, full of kisses.[9]

This nameless idealized beauty is of note, for while she lacks the mythological pedigree of Polyxena and Briseis, her carefully detailed description was the first to be committed to written record up to to that point. Prospective cataloguers of beauty therefore looked to this description as one of the best possible guides simply because it gave more information.

Maximianus was intensely popular in the medieval period. Indeed, the word *popular* seems hardly to fit here, as he was considered so fundamental an author that his poetry was used to teach Latin in the eleventh and twelfth centuries. Children were therefore taught what a beautiful woman was even as they were learning how to write down an account of one.[10] They learned that the ideal woman had fair skin, dark eyebrows that contrasted with her golden hair, and swollen lips.

It may seem odd that medieval Europeans had so few detailed classical literary portraits of women, but in fact we lack detailed descriptions of women's physical beauty even in the high medieval period (1000–1250). If classical authors preferred to leave beauty in the mind of the beholder, so did early medieval writers, contenting themselves more with copying classical texts than with expanding upon them. Even in the high medieval period and the twelfth-century Renaissance, when poets and thinkers read Maximianus, descriptions of contemporary women are frustratingly limited. Instead, in both the medieval imagination and vernacular literature, Maximianus's description expanded on a classical ideal that could best describe the legendary beauty of Helen of Troy in particular.

In many ways, settling on Helen as an ideal woman made perfect sense. First, a large amount of classical literature praised her beauty but did not detail it, which gave medieval authors a chance to prove their own ability by expanding on the classics. Second, in establishing the supreme qualities of physical womanhood, it is difficult to argue with the woman who was so gorgeous that men started a war for her. Third, linking concepts of beauty to a classical figure gave them the classical cachet that medieval people believed conferred authority, despite the lack of ancient literary portraits to work with.

From the twelfth century on, we are treated to many more thoughts on what a classical beauty was, with added emphasis on *classical*.

The French scholar and author Matthew of Vendôme (twelfth century) penned descriptions of Helen. Matthew is in many ways an ideal author to study for clues about a "medieval" concept of beauty. He was writing about mythological women and modeling his prose on that of the classical authors Ovid (43 B.C.E.–17 C.E.), Horace (65–8 B.C.E.), and Cicero (106–43 B.C.E.), but in a style that was consciously new. His descriptions of Helen of Troy are found first in his *Ars Versificatoria* (*The Art of the Versemaker*), composed around 1175. This was an entirely new type of work: a scholastic guide on how to write poetry and prose in Latin. Here Matthew explained that poems should be written to imbue them with meaning, and he advised how to read them in order to glean said meaning. Readers had to consider four essential but uneven parts: inner meaning; elegance of diction; schemata, tropes, and colors of rhetoric; and treatment of the material. Descriptors of Helen show up in his treatment of the first three categories.

Given that Matthew was discussing tropes and specifically grounded his work on that of previous authorities, he unsurprisingly repeated Maximianus's ideal; after all, none of the classical authorities furnished him with a fleshed-out literary portrait. As a result, his Helen had golden hair and thin black eyebrows on a paper-white forehead. In contrast to her monobrowed forerunners, though, Matthew made much of the "white and clear" space between her eyebrows where "the separated arches [d]o not allow the hairs to run rampant." Her face was bright like a "shining star," as were her eyes. While she was bright and pale, her rosy cheeks gave her a "red and snowy-white countenance." Matthew helpfully described her nose as neither too big nor too small. He gave her smile, in contrast, more treatment than Maximianus provided—it was small, and her teeth were like ivory. Her lips, once again swollen, were honeyed as well, and her breath was like a rose that "pants for kisses." Overall, then,

Matthew gave us several tropes to work with: stars, brightness, snow, roses, and honey.[11]

Later in the same work, as if to hammer home exactly how one created a trope, Matthew had another go at describing Helen. This time he reconnected to two of Maximianus's descriptors that he previously left out. In discussing Helen's forehead, he now said it was white like milk, as opposed to like paper, but also "free" (*libera*) after Maximianus. Most everything else was unchanged. Matthew also waxed lyrical about the meaning of Helen's beauty, "the preciousness of matter, the superiority of figure" that she enjoyed, and the subsequent consequences of her beauty in Troy's destruction and "the ruin of princes."[12] Here the extra description seems to have been more about using showy language and making clear that he was a student of the classics, not just of beautiful women.

Matthew's description of Helen of Troy is compelling because he is absolutely clear that he is teaching his audience how to describe a beautiful woman. He is telling his readers to use these charac teristics in their own work. Hoping to spread his trope, he handily explains that such a description holds the "color of rhetoric" that they should seek when they write. He not only reaches to the past for the guidance of a vaunted writer but also uses a celebrated mythological character, half goddess and half human, to make his point. In so doing, he also expands on his classical knowledge—and stands on the shoulders of giants. Matthew's work proved incredibly influential among his fellow scholarly poets and went on to inspire similar treatises across Europe, all of which kept his same ideal beauty characteristics.

Perhaps the most influential work to build on Matthew's "ideal" descriptors was that of the celebrated poet Geoffrey of Vinsauf (fl. 1200). Geoffrey, like Matthew before him, is an exemplum of how medieval ideas spread. Technically we know very little about the man other than that he worked in Oxford at one time and eventually moved to Rome, where he composed his monumental work, *Poetry*

Nova, as a gift for Pope Innocent III (1160/61–1216). Traditionally, however, these details have been fleshed out to tell us that Geoffrey was born in Normandy, educated in Oxford at St. Frideswide, then took further education at the University of Paris and at various Italian institutions. He was alleged to have been a rowdy intellectual and was forced to cross the English Channel in order to beg forgiveness from the archbishop of Canterbury for disputing a bit too vigorously with his friends.[13]

Geoffrey was also the medieval equivalent of a best-selling author. While *Poetry Nova* was written for the pope, it quickly gained popularity, stayed influential in England and France into the fifteenth century, and has survived to our time in over two hundred manuscripts, making it one of the most widely revered texts of the medieval period. It maintained enough authority that Chaucer quoted it—verbatim—on several occasions.[14] The aim of the book, much like Matthew's before it, was to set out the principles of good poetic construction for contemporary poets. The very title was a challenge to old concepts of classical poetry and to the Latin poet Horace, whose work, initially titled *Art of Poetry,* circulated in the medieval period with the title *Poetria.*

Funnily enough, while Geoffrey's very title promises us new ideas about poetics, we aren't given anything particularly groundbreaking on ideal beauty. "If you want to fully describe the beauty of the female form" he instructs his readers, you do so by speaking of her gold-colored hair, her dark eyebrows with a gap between them in a "milky way," her swelling lips, her snow-white teeth, and her long white neck like a white marble column. As in Matthew's description of Helen, we learn that the ideal woman has long, thin fingers that, again, are Milky Way–colored, as well as short feet, a bit of a descriptive letdown following the Milky Way analogy.[15]

Geoffrey offers a few deviations from Matthew's analogies. He likens women to lilies, the dawn, and crystals and their breath to incense (*thuris*) rather than to honey. He also has a pronounced interest in eyebrows, praising them in six lines of the verse as dark, regular, haughty, arched, and glittering hyacinths. Eyebrows and analogies aside, the overall effect is the same. The ideal woman has white skin, gold hair, two black eyebrows, pouty lips, white teeth, and good breath. The objects to which the ideal beauty's attributes are likened mean that she herself is an object composed of impossible and discrete ideals, and a literary trope *par excellence*.

The beauty that Matthew of Vendôme and Geoffrey of Vinsauf described is an ossified ideal. This makes sense in that it was meant as a uniform poetic model. Implicit within it is that the great majority of women could not possibly live up to it, even if they took these constructs to heart—especially if they were poor. Most obviously, a woman could never achieve a glowing white complexion if she lived her life working outdoors. White teeth were easier for her to come by in a world where sweets were difficult to get hold of, but the brushing that could keep them at their optimal sheen was easier to maintain if she had the free time to worry about dental hygiene. Commoners could be lucky enough to be born with some elements, such as blond hair, pouting lips, or black eyebrows, but these features alone would never allow a woman to be seen as a true classical beauty. Wealth is never expressly mentioned, but fundamentally these tropes were created by wealthy writers who wrote for a similarly wealthy audience. Their own prejudices were therefore baked in even if they might not have been aware of them.

Matthew of Vendôme and Geofforey of Vinsauf had set out to establish a beauty standard about women and to have it disseminated. Both grounded their beauty ideals on that of Maximianus, and they expanded on his premise by giving new analogies while keeping the traits consistent. The concordance in their work signaled to readers that these notions of women's beauty were indeed authoritative, as were their links to Helen of Troy, a classical, and therefore worthy, literary character. It worked. And why would either author possibly care if his great literary success left the poor women of the world behind?

In the thirteenth century, the beauty standard was established enough that it was used, very literally, to describe Beauty (the personification thereof, that is). The French poet and scholar Guillaume de Lorris (ca. 1200–40) populated his epic, allegorical dream vision *Le Roman de la Rose* with representations of various emotions and characteristics. Beauty herself is one such character, with white skin bright as moonlight that outshines the stars, skin (sigh) like lilies and red roses, and blond hair reaching down to her toes.[16] Other women within the novel sport the expected attributes, but with "eyes gray as a falcon" or small mouths.[17] The unimaginative concepts of beauty on display here did little to dampen enthusiasm for *Le Roman de la Rose*. A vernacular story that also functions as a drawn-out metaphor for sex was never going to be held back because of some dull beauty expectations. Its massive popularity and reach across Europe during the rest of the medieval period ensured that its concept of ideal beauty was distributed along with it, including to less scholarly audiences who wanted to read a book with sex at its center.

The ideal blond-haired, black-eyebrowed, milky-skinned beauty eventually made her way from theoretical works into poetic ones. Some of the earliest examples come from poems by an anonymous twelfth-century monk working at the celebrated monastery of Santa Maria de Ripoll in Catalonia. Ripoll was a renowned scriptorium and library for over a century by the time the monk in question decided that he was bored of copying out other people's works and began writing his own love poetry in the blank folios of a manuscript.

The women populating his works are much the same as those proposed by Matthew and Geoffrey. Judith, whom he describes in his poem "When I first saw my love" (*Ubi primum vidi amicam*) has "shining eyes, teeth like snow . . . a white forehead," and smooth skin that "shone like the moon without wrinkles."[18] Later, these tropes reappear in his description of the Countess of Flanders. "Brighter than the sun," she has "glowing white teeth, sparkling eyes . . . legs whiter than snow . . . [and] small artfully formed feet." She is, in short, as beautiful as the goddesses "Venus or Diana."[19]

These descriptions are of note because this monk was working with Matthew and Geoffrey's analogies to describe actual living women. Because there was only one way for authors to write about beautiful women, there was also only one way for women to *be* beautiful women. The general tropes we expect are present (white skin and foreheads, bright eyes, white teeth), but so are a number of descriptors (blond hair, black eyebrows, swollen lips) that Matthew and Geoffrey set down that these two beauties are not praised as having.

This may indicate a sort of literary airbrushing. The monk wishes to convey to his audiences that these women are beautiful, so he lists all the traits in common with the poetic beauty standard that he is following. Because they are real women, though, he will not lie about their real characteristics. Instead, he paints an abstract of a beautiful woman.

By the time Chaucer was writing in the fourteenth century, the ideal beauty as an entrenched trope was strong enough that he was able to parody it. In "The Miller's Tale" of *The Canterbury Tales*, he depicts Alisoun, who is a common woman, which is to say she is neither noble nor even a member of the wealthy merchant classes who belong to guilds. She ends up cheating on her much older carpenter husband. Despite her status, Chaucer describes Alisoun in similar terms to the idealized woman: "Her mouth was sweet as ale and honey or mead, / Or a hoard of apples laid in hay or heather."[20] What makes this satire is that he mentions common ale and the perhaps slightly putrid sweetness of a clutch of hidden apples alongside the traditional honey and mead that we would expect. Moreover, we are meant to understand that compliments like these are ridiculous, since Chaucer lavishes praise originally used for demigoddesses on a woman who is willing to have sex with her suitor in a washing tub and so cuckold her husband.

While this beauty ideal could be found from England to Spain, throughout France, and into Rome, outside Western Christendom some of these iconic details didn't hold sway. In Constantinople, the poet John Tzetzes (ca. 1110–80) wrote the *Antehomerica,* in which he recounts the events in the run-up to the Trojan War. Here is his description of the princess Briseis: "Tall and white, her hair was black and curly; she had beautiful breasts and cheeks and nose; she was, also, well-behaved; her smile was bright, her eyebrows big."[21] Clearly, then the medieval imagination still had room for brunettes with bushy eyebrows to be hailed as beauties. Perhaps Tzetzes bent the ideal slightly to incorporate the more prevalent dark hair of Anatolian women.

While it is liberating to see even this small deviation from the standard script, Tzetzes conforms to expectations when portraying Helen of Troy, whom he describes as having "skin so white and bright as if it was made of snow . . . long, curly, blond hair; . . . a lot more beautiful than all the other women, just like the moon is brighter than the stars in the sky."[22] In other words, while variations within the beauty standard were possible, the hierarchy remained, and blondes were firmly at the top. Brunettes might be imbued with the sort of beauty that changed battles, but blondes were the ones that men fought wars over. Ideally, in either case, the Eastern Roman Empire liked women with curls.

We see a marked lack of interest in blondness in other cultures, such as those of the Iberian Peninsula. There poets were happy to celebrate hair ranging from blond to black, curly or long, but in general they praised it as being soft. Overall, however, many Arabic texts—including *Historia de la doncella Teodor,* a thirteenth-century Spanish translation of an Arabic fairy tale, and even the fifteenth-century sex manual the *Speculum al foderi,* or *Mirror of Coitus* (literally, "a mirror to fuck")—state a categorical preference for black hair.[23] Interestingly, those on the peninsula who did seem explicitly to prefer blondes seemed to frequent the more well-to-do circles of Iberian society.[24]

Clearly, most medieval European writers accepted the same way of describing a beautiful woman, even if some outliers disagreed. The exceptions seem to prove the rule more than provide evidence for any widespread pushback against the blond, white-skinned ideal. However, it is important that—especially within communities outside Western Christendom—there was room for variation on these themes.

Body Shape

The idealized beauty of literature by no means ended at the glorification of specific facial features and hair. The male gaze was more than happy to wander down a woman's body. Not surprisingly, the beauty ideals for the body were as rigid as those for the head. As medieval literary scholar Edmond Faral has pointed out, these descriptions followed a top-down order, almost as though checking features off a list:

1. The hair
2. The forehead
3. The eyebrows and the space between them
4. The eyes
5. The cheeks and their color
6. The nose
7. The mouth
8. The teeth
9. The chin
10. The throat
11. The neck and its nape
12. The shoulders

13. The arms
14. The hands
15. The breasts
16. The waist
17. The belly
18. The legs
19. The feet [25]

This makes some sense, given that medieval writers loved guide-lines, and that this list follows a generalized pattern of recognition of how people look at one another. Notwithstanding those gentlemen who occasionally need to be reminded of where, exactly, a woman's face is, most people scan other humans starting with the head, given its proximity to their own, and working their way down to the feet, should they be interested enough to learn more.

So we too now find ourselves moving to the body, in the order of the medieval list. We begin with the neck, which is often described in vague terms. Matthew of Vendôme used the whiteness of snow for a neck's beauty.[26] Geoffrey of Vinsauf used an architectural analogy, seeing the feminine neck as long and white like a column.[27] Most other neck descriptions agree that they be long and white.[28] By the later medieval period, some poets expanded the repertoire of simi-les to note that a beautiful woman has a neck "like a swan."[29] Iberian writers, instead, sometimes compared it to that of a heron or even an antelope, but white and long it remained.[30]

We can move quickly past the shoulders, since once again they are almost universally praised for being white and smooth, and move on to arms and hands. Never let it be said that medieval liter-ature offered no diversity in women's bodies. The French poet Guil-laume de Machaut (ca. 1300–77) was for "arms long and straight," but Chaucer interchangeably praised "small," "slender" and "plump" arms.[31] Perhaps arms weren't high on the medieval list of sexy things.

What seems to have been most important was that a woman's arms be white and soft like the rest of her body.

There might have been more room for diversity in arms, because hands and fingers were more often the focus. Hands were uniformly spoken of as white and were often said to be soft and long. The emphasis on whiteness and softness is again a clue about which women might be able to live up to such a literary beauty ideal. Soft white hands were the province of wealthy women who were not planting the fields in all weather, hand-washing clothes and dishes, and wrangling farm animals. Having said that, many writers simply didn't care enough about hands to dwell on them. Geoffrey of Vinsauf, for example, was happy to rush past them, expressing more interest in how his beauty's arms flowed into hands with long fingers.[32] Matthew of Vendôme's Helen of Troy, on the other hand, simply had hands that did "not shake with flabby flesh."[33] All in all then, hands were meant to be noticed, but provided they were white, soft, and long, there was wiggle room in how one could write about them.

The relatively scant discussion of arms and hands landed medieval writers somewhere that our own society (and certainly the legions of evolutionary psychologists) likes to place emphasis—the breasts. If you as a modern reader are excitedly hoping for tales of heaving bosoms spilling from gowns, I am afraid I have disappointing news for you. Medieval men were uniform in their description of the perfect set of boobs as decidedly small and white. Matthew of Vendôme praised the "dainty" breasts of Helen of Troy, which lay "modest on her chest."[34] Geoffrey of Vinsauf meanwhile wrote that the ideal beauty's breasts were like gems and were only a "brief handful."[35] Machaut, adding more adjectives to the discussion of a young woman's chest, nonetheless took pains to emphasize that while they were "white, firm, and high-seated/pointed, round," they were also "small enough," perhaps indicating that in an ideal world her cups would overflow a bit less.[36]

An interest in small breasts is of note because this ideal too was easier for the wealthy to live up to, as they could opt out of breast-feeding. Most mothers undoubtedly nursed their own children, but wealthy women could employ wet nurses to do so in their stead. Women of the nobility and royalty simply bound their maternal breasts up, to ensure that they shrank back down to a pleasing size, and left it to the lower-class women in their employ to feed any and all screaming mouths. The wet nurse as the preferred method of keeping breasts small is testified to in the *Trotula,* a twelfth-century medical guidebook, in a segment called "On Conditions of Women," which devotes an entire section to "Choosing a Wet Nurse." Funnily, any good wet nurse should have the preferred beauty attributes found among the nobility, "redness mixed with white . . . who is not blemished, nor who has breasts that are flabby or too large . . . and who is a little bit fat."[37] In this way, well-off women had the ability to keep the dainty breasts that were so preferred, while also ensuring the beauty benefits of a good night's sleep.

While our culture might not share medieval writers' interest in small breasts, we do have a tendency to feel the way they do about waist size. Medieval people appear to have preferred a smaller one, although they tend not to be lavish in their descriptions. Matthew of Vendôme assured his readers that Helen of Troy's "sides were narrow at her waist."[38] Later, Machaut's gave beauty this rundown: "in proportion . . . amply fleshed, long, straight, pleasing, resilient, agreeable, and svelte."[39]

If the desire for women to be both "amply fleshed" and "svelte" seems like a contradiction, it is resolved as the theoretical eyes of the writer and reader scan downward. From the waist they light on, per Matthew, "the luscious little belly."[40] Modern readers might think that this is a reference to a flat belly to match the small waist. Instead, Matthew and his cohort were speaking of their delight in a pot belly, which "rises" outward, hearkening back to Machaut's reference to his beauty being "amply fleshed." Elsewhere the same preference for a belly is referred to as a softness or a swelling. When poets made no specific reference to bellies, they often expounded on the long torsos of the beauties that inhabited their minds. One way or another, medieval writers were emphatic that they in no way favored women skipping lunch.

Once again, an interest in protruding and enlarged bellies was indicative of a preference for the looks of the rich. Most women, as peasants, were involved in doing manual labor and breastfeeding their own kids. As such, they had ample opportunity to burn off any calories that they ingested. A refined life at court, or indeed in a merchant's household, was much more sedentary. Women certainly worked in those contexts, but that work had much more to do with diplomacy or keeping accounts or indeed sewing, which could all be accomplished comfortably with their feet up. Moreover, rich women were more likely to have the sort of food on the table that helps cultivate a belly. Sweets, white bread, and fatty meats were much easier to come by with money. All in all, then, wealthy women had a head start in the belly stakes.

As writers moved on to the legs, they tended to treat them in two separate parts. They almost universally agreed that a leg should sport a "fleshy," "well shaped" thigh.[41] Interestingly, at times this preference comes across as an oblique hint at genitalia. Matthew, for example, referenced the "sweet home of Venus . . . made hid" by the "festive adjoining areas," which is to say the thighs.[42] This description wouldn't be misplaced in any modern bodice-ripper and serves as a reminder that while in theory such descriptions of beauty resemble an academic exercise, they still carry a sexual charge. Then as now, when writers explained beauty, they meant for their audiences to *believe* their descriptions and to acknowledge their expertise with such charms. Geoffrey seems to have seen the inflamed passions of his audiences coming and instead pointedly declined to describe the thighs, or what was between them, because "say[ing] nothing of the parts below . . . more aptly speaks the language of the heart."[43]

Both authors absolutely knew that the images they conjured were *sexy*. The only difference was that Matthew wanted to connect that to a specificity, whereas Geoffrey left his audience to fill in the blanks, even if he risked opening himself to criticisms about a lack of first-hand knowledge on the subject.

Legs were a less sexy endeavor. Authors uniformly praised their length, their fullness, and sometimes their straightness as well. Geoffrey's coyness fell away when he asserted the fine length of his beauty's shins.[44] Machaut felt a need to mention the legs as a body part separate from the thighs, but he happily called them "well shaped" and let his audience do the rest of the heavy lifting.

After the titillation that the thighs provided, the feet were anticlimactic, as authors systemically, to a man, dutifully described the ideal—small—foot. Some called it dainty, or praised long, straight toes. However, just when you might conclude that descriptions of feet lack the giggling poetic excitement of thighs and legs, Machaut swoops in to call out "the feet, [a]rched, plump, and well formed, [c]unningly shod with exquisite shoes,"[45] of his ideal beauty, spending more time there than on the thighs, legs, and hips combined.

Age

While the ideal medieval woman had a certain set of characteristics that we can even arrange on a checklist, one final factor was occasionally voiced as well: age. We certainly identify age as a generalized "young," but for medieval people, years on the planet didn't serve to convey the meaning that they were attempting to indicate. Men who were engaged in conjuring the ideal beauty into existence thought a woman, in order to be truly beautiful, had to be not just young but also sexually inexperienced. In other words, she had to be that medieval construction: a maiden.

In the medieval period, the term *maiden* referred generally to the stage of life that loosely maps to our own concept of the "teenager."

Maidens, much like teenagers, were no longer children but had not yet attained full adulthood. Maidenhood, like the teen years, was a transitory stage. But the term also implied a sexual maturity that had not yet been acted on and as a result was a "perfect" sort of femininity.

This state of "perfection" was in turn linked to a totally different way of considering aging in humans. Contrary to some of our more persistent myths about the medieval period, "maidens" were quite young not because of a short medieval life expectancy. Medieval people lived about the same life span as we do now, provided that they managed to survive infancy and (in the case of women) child-birth. The idea that the "average medieval person lived until 32" is a misreading of what *average* means. About 50 percent of medieval people died as infants, an incredibly sad statistic that remained largely true until the development of vaccines and modern medi-cal interventions. So if half of the population died before the age of one year, then in order to get an average life span in the thirties, the other half of the population had to live into their seventies (if you remember your basic math). And this was indeed the case! As a result of a fairly long life, the majority of people married in their twenties, much as they do now.[46] So it would be incorrect to refer to an eight-year-old as a maiden, as she was still simply a girl. A maiden was young and a virgin, but she was also, in theory, of marriageable age.

According to the late fourteenth-century scholar Bartholomaeus Anglicus (1203–72), a maiden "is called *puella* as it were clean and pure as the black of the eye. . . . For among all that is loved in a wench chastity and cleanness is loved most. . . . *Puella* is a name of soundness without wem [flaw], and also of honesty [honor]. . . . A maid has that name *virgo* of cleanness and incorruption as it were *virago*, for she knows not the very passion of women."[47] Maid-ens, then, were more likely to be beautiful women, and vice versa, because they were, as Kim M. Phillips has noted, "possessed of all the attractive qualities of femininity but [were] free of the faults."[48] They were beautiful, kind, calm, chaste, pure, delicate, modest, and humble. Also, and very crucially, they were sexy, but they weren't *sexual*. This is remarkable, because it's difficult to conceive of a form of young womanhood that clashes so wholly with our concept of teenage women. Moreover, it perfectly encapsulates how (like the studious inventory of beautiful women) the very concept of maidenhood was invented purely in the heads of men. Maidens were everything that a woman could be without all of the inconvenience of being an actual person with needs, opinions, and complaints.

This concept was not simply a conviction in the minds of lascivious men writing impossible women into existence. Rather, it was fostered from the revered minds of philosophers. Maidenhood was considered to be the "perfect age" for women because they were not only mentally developed and feminine but also, crucially, like men in terms of humoral composition. All children were thought to be hotter and dryer than their older iterations. Advancing age, and death itself, were both associated with wetness. As a result, girls were more masculine than older women because they had not yet become cold and wet. This hot and dry characteristic helped girls burn off their superfluous humors with ease. The sign that they were becoming cold and wet was menarche, when the hot and dry character wore off and the body had to expel excess blood instead of burning it off. Maidens were then perfect, because they were women enough to be distinguishable from men but not so cold and wet that they became deathly.[49]

That this was the optimum age for women was echoed in theological works. For example, in the End Times, when the dead would rise from their graves for the Final Judgment, they would do so in bodies that reflected their perfect age. This understanding was gleaned from a parsing of Ephesians 4:13: "until we all meet into the unity of faith and of the knowledge of the son of God, unto a perfect man, unto the measure of the age of the fullness of Christ." This perfect age was considered to mimic that of Jesus at the time of his death, so thirty-three or so.[50] But for women, it was maidenhood. This belief is underlined in the epic poem *Pearl,* wherein a father who lost his two-year-old daughter has a dream in which he is reunited with her. Instead of the toddler the man lost, he meets a beautiful maiden with every perfect attribute, from blond hair to gray eyes to white and rose coloring. As she is in heaven, due to her innocence, she is able to enjoy the perfect body that she never attained on Earth.[51] Again, a perfect and constructed idea of what a maiden could be is presented here with very little reference to what the actualities of the theoretical mourned two-year-old were. In death, the little girl became perfect, and there was exactly one literary way to express that fact.

At the same time, the virginity that was required of a maiden was tied to religious concepts about sex in general. As we will discuss in more depth in Chapter 3, ideal women were those who avoided the pitfalls of sex and retained a holy chastity. To have sex was to surrender to the corruption of the mortal world. Virginity, in contrast, was proof of moral purity and a spiritual ability to focus on the next life. The virginity of the dead Pearl is one reason she is in heaven and proof that she belongs there and can enjoy her unsullied and beautiful older body. Granted, no one would expect a two-year-old to have experienced sex, but we are meant to understand that one of the few benefits of losing a beloved daughter at a young age was that she was never corrupted in life and could proceed directly to paradise after death.

While it is easy to focus on the ideal, maidens lived with the weight of all these expectations on their shoulders. Not only were they expected to exemplify all of the best and most positive things about women, but a timer was ticking. The moment that they lived up to the promise of their maidenhood and became wives and mothers, or even worse *sexual* but unmarried, they would lose the status that made them desirable in the first place. Even if a woman navigated this particular tightrope by cleaving to her virginity, there was no hope for her. The march of time would see to it that coldness and wetness, the essence of her femininity, crept in, sweeping her toward decrepitude and eventually death. Still, eschatologically speaking, any virtuous woman would be rewarded at the Apocalypse by a return to her ideal stage and could then look forward forever to being surrounded by perfect men who appeared to be in their thirties.

Despite the perfection of the maiden, women could still be beautiful after that stage. The archetypical beauty Helen of Troy, who was married to Menelaus, was not a maiden. Guinevere, as well as Alisoun and May (the beautiful young wives in Chaucer's "Miller's Tale" and "Merchant's Tale," respectively) were all rather conspicuously married, which is to say that they were emphatically *not* maidens. More to the point, marital status was the nexus around which their dramas swirled. All these women were wives and also extravagantly, outrageously, even dangerously beautiful.

For all these women, their status as wives in no way hindered their beauty, and their husbands were often conspicuously older. Helen, famously, didn't have much say in being given to Paris after the whole apple contest thing, but in some tellings, she did fall in love with the youth afterward. The fact that Paris was a lover not a fighter made him a foil for the scorned Menelaus, who was skilled in battle but generally less so in turning his wife's head. Guinevere, in turn, was married to King Arthur, who is often depicted as older than she was, and he was certainly no match, in looks and youth, for the gallant Lancelot. Meanwhile, Alisoun and May are both markedly beautiful and married to men much their senior.

While these women were said to be beautiful, their married status marked them as *not* ideal. In fact, they were more like femmes fatales, women whose beauty was dangerous and led to destruction. To whit: Helen's love of Paris led to a war; Guinevere's flirtation with Lancelot, to the downfall of Camelot; and while Alisoun and May didn't exactly bring about the fall of kingdoms, they certainly did humiliate their doting older husbands. Overall, what these women's beauty did was highlight the fact that in marriage a beautiful woman always and essentially became *dangerous*. She retained her desirability, but because she had become attached to a man, any man's pursuit of her, or her pursuit of any man, would have consequences. Maidens didn't come with such an immediate obstacle. A man could at least approach the father for marriage, even if the father rejected him. Married beauties could never be ideal because they were already owned.

Art

Artists gave visual form to the same tropes that poets laboriously constructed in their literary portraits. The ideal beauty shows up in medicval art with regularity, most obviously in depictions of one woman: Eve.

Eve was handy as a stand-in for beautiful women partly because of her pivotal role in Christianity. Many of the pieces of medieval art that have survived are elaborate and accomplished, meaning that they were made for wealthy people, and a lot of those people were in the Church. You will likely be unsurprised to learn that when the Church asked for art, it meant religious art. As a result, the beautiful women whose depictions survive are usually women in biblical stories or are worthy martyrs of the late antique or medieval eras.

To be fair, any religious woman depicted in Church art would, by definition, be shown as beautiful, since beauty was synonymous with virtue. Christian, Jewish, and Muslim thinkers agreed that all physical beings had the potential for beauty, and that they achieved beauty when they were in harmony with nature. Because nature was conceived of as divine, those who were holiest and therefore closest to God were also in harmony with nature. Thus, they were necessarily beautiful. As a result, images of a pre-fallen Eve were portraits of the most beautiful woman that it was possible to be.

In terms of popularity in art, Eve edges out other beautiful religious women for another reason as well: it was okay to depict her naked. While medieval Europeans often ignored religious strictures when it suited them, bending the rules was probably not going to cut it in making art for religious audiences. If you were an aspiring fine artist and wanted to try your hand at depicting full nudity, then you headed straight to the Garden of Eden. Eve, therefore, held the same place in art as Helen of Troy did in literature. She was the go-to hottie, the beauty against whom all other beauties could be measured. While naked.

Over and over, artworks show an Eve that could well be mistaken for literary descriptions of Helen. Whether she is being drawn from her husband's side as he sleeps, deep in conversation with a snake, or is fleeing Paradise in shame, she is a certifiable babe. Eve stares at us from fifth-century floors with blond hair and high small breasts. Her round belly opens the book of Genesis in ninth-century Bibles. Her skin gleams white in books of hours and on cathedral ceilings, wherever audiences needed to be reminded that, if not for the fact that women were fundamentally untrustworthy, everyone would still be gorgeous and naked right at this very moment.

More to the point for our interests, women would have been beautiful and naked in exactly the same way. While the styles of art that represent Eve changed over the course of the medieval period, the way she was depicted varied little. She is always blond and always has arched eyebrows, a high forehead, white skin, pink cheeks, red lips, white teeth, a long neck, small breasts, a pot belly, and thick thighs. Over time, these features only became more pronounced, and by the fifteenth century, portrayals of Eve show her skin not as metaphorically white but as actually so. She glows like the snow that all medieval women aspired to be compared to. No woman could ever be that beautiful, either physically or morally.

The same tropes repeat for other beautiful women. The Virgin Mary, the only woman who managed to avoid the curse of Eve's sin, was gorgeous: white, blond, and iconically beautiful. The popular

Eve from *The Adoration of the
Mystic Lamb,* by Jan van Eyck,
1432, Ghent Altarpiece, Sint
Baafskathedraal, Ghent.

virgin saints, who often attained sainthood through their willingness to reject suitors, also made appearances, from church frescos
to the insides of Bibles. Some saints could plausibly be depicted as
naked, like Saint Agatha, who miraculously regrew her breasts after
pagan Roman torturers cut them off. Her legend allowed artists to
portray a beautiful young woman bound to a pillar whose chest was
naked and sometimes wielded instruments of torture. As artistic
subjects went, it was fairly popular.

The Martyrdom of St Agatha of Catania, by Jean le Tavernier, 1454, KB,
National Library of the Netherlands, The Hague. THE HAGUE, KB,
NATIONAL LIBRARY OF THE NETHERLANDS, 76 F 2, FOL. 278 R.

In some paintings, like the Ghent Altarpiece, armies of beautiful martyrs march to the Adoration of the Mystic Lamb at the end of the universe. They are barely distinguishable from each other, except by their iconographic details. Saint Barbara carries her tower and Saint Agnes her lamb, for example. Otherwise, a mass of white-skinned blondes advances, carrying the palms that signify their martyrdom, as Eve looks down from an upper panel. Their beauty is not only interchangeable but also nonnegotiable from an artistic standpoint.

These images were objects of religious devotion and veneration; people would pray with them, focusing their minds on them, or being reminded of what they had lost with the Fall of Man. While the women *had* to be beautiful to make the religious point that they were holy, these images were also considered sexy.

We know that from decidedly hostile witnesses: Protestants. In

The Virgin Martyrs, from *The Adoration of the Mystic Lamb,* by Jan van Eyck, 1432, Ghent Altarpiece, Sint Baafskathedraal, Ghent. IANDAGNALL COMPUTING / ALAMY STOCK PHOTO.

the early modern period, when a number of Christians broke from the Catholic Church, one of their myriad complaints was about religious images in churches. In 1520 one Protestant in Strasbourg complained, "I often had base thoughts when I looked upon the female saints on the altars. For no courtesan can dress or adorn herself more sumptuously and shamelessly than they nowadays fashion the Mother of God, Saint Barbara, Katherine, and the other saints."[52]

The fact that this unnamed man was turned on by church statues is not only a testament to the human erotic imagination but also funny and instructive. As we have seen, the medieval concept of beauty was painstakingly constructed and repeated ad nauseam down through the centuries, which can make it difficult to ascertain whether the average medieval individual agreed with it. Did most people think small-breasted women with big thighs and pot bellies were beautiful, or was this was just a literary and artistic conceit? This unnamed Protestant's religious complaint shows that not only did individual men agree with the artistic beauty ideal, but it also turned them on in church.

To be fair, this particular reminiscence does come, as stated, from an antagonistic source. The gentleman in question was trying to make a point about the Catholic Church and the sins that it inspired with its excesses. Protestants were extremely fond of painting churches white and removing all statues. Implying that you used to get distracted and even turned on by images of saints during Mass was a great way to make a point about why it was time to break out the whitewash. However, if he had said he found the church frescos sexy in a social climate that disagreed, it would have been tantamount to admitting a strange fetish to his congregation. As a result, we can take this gentleman at his word and assume that the religious art was, indeed, titillating.

Sexy images did not remain entirely within the realm of religious art, however. Later medieval art, which enjoyed a higher rate of survival, shows similar images of sexy women in secular contexts.

Interestingly, the hot women are sometimes retrofitted into older sources. Fifteenth-century editions of *Le Roman de la Rose*, still popular two hundred years after its initial composition, are often filled with images of lovely nude women accompanying its classical stories. Pygmalion is shown alongside his living naked statue, or the Greek painter Zeuxis (fifth century B.C.E.) is pictured with an easel and a bevy of nude models. Beyond the novel, books of hours, in an interesting nod to artistic license, sometimes depict the zodiac sign Aquarius as a naked woman, rather than a man, gathering water. Some versions of Christine de Pizan's *City of Women* also boasted images of classically beautiful nude women. The muses, for example, were sometimes pictured bathing when Christine first encounters them, an excellent opportunity to show a number of women naked from the groin upward.

Elsewhere, images of women who were meant to be taken as pagan or to have dubious morals were now also suddenly shown as beautiful, despite clearly being out of God's divine grace. A fifteenth-century copy of Augustine's *City of God* took the opportunity to picture the foolishness and excess of pagan societies as typified by nude men and women dancing around a wizard casting spells. Similarly, a fifteenth-century painting by an unknown Rhenish master shows a beautiful witch casting love spells, naked apart from a pair of really gorgeous shoes with stilettos coming out of the tips.

In all these cases, new opportunities were opening up for artists to depict beautiful (and crucially, naked) women. Luxurious editions of epic romance poetry do, admittedly, lend themselves to accompanying beautiful images. A patron who had the money to employ someone to make beautiful and sexy images in a private edition of a book might very well wish to see women who resemble those described in the book's prose. More to the point, private art had more of a possibility to *be* erotic without bringing any untoward attention toward the artist. It was one thing to try to get away with painting an attractive female saint in a church. But if you didn't have

Liebeszauber/The Love Spell, by the Lower Rhenish Master, ca. 1470–80,
Museum der bildenden Künste, Leipzig. THE PICTURE ART COLLECTION / ALAMY
STOCK PHOTO.

to smuggle a sexy image past a priest, you had much freer rein. Even when nude images appear in religious texts like *The City of God,* they are excusable because they are being used in an instructive way. The artist implies that the frolicking naked women are foolish, making them acceptable.

While the better survival rates of medieval private erotic art allow us more of a glimpse into it, these images differ little from the previous religious ones. They show same interchangeably beautiful women. Whether she is a witch, a muse, a pagan, or an unnamed model, she displays the expected attributes, from blond hair down to dainty feet. It doesn't matter who she is, or even really what her context is—she is a pale, blond, pear shape with a coy smile. Only the names attached to the beauties in question change. The beauty itself remains static.

Beauty Interventions

While being attractive was largely beyond the reach of aspiring beauties, women could still tweak their appearance in certain ways. First and foremost, they could at the very least be clean. The interest in cleanliness may come as a surprise because of the long-standing myth that medieval people did not bathe.

In fact, medieval people subscribed heartily to the adage "cleanliness is next to godliness." Much as they considered physical beauty to represent spiritual purity, they considered hygiene the same way. If one's body was impure, it would by definition be unattractive and out of harmony. If it had any imperfections, one would best address them through cleansing.[53]

The average medieval woman's beauty routine held cleanliness as one of the very highest virtues, though what women had access to in order to accomplish it varied. Lower-class women probably had the most pressing interest in cleanliness given the physically taxing nature of their everyday work. The most likely scenario for these women is that they would wash daily by collecting water in a ewer, heating it, then pouring it into a large basin from which they would wash.

This daily scrubbing could be augmented by baths in a wooden bathing tub. Baths would happen less often, given it was a world without plumbing. Water is heavy, and collecting it, heating it, and then getting it from the kettle into the bathtub was difficult. Moreover, uninsulated wooden tubs lost heat much more quickly than our modern ones do, so the tub would be drawn near a hearth to keep the water warm. And in order to have a big bath, not only would you have to schlep buckets of water, you also needed space, which was at a premium in most households.

Luckily, there were a few ways to bathe outside the home. In warmer months, you could simply bathe in local water sources. Find a pond or a lake, and you were good to go. But in January this could be a problem, and that was where bathhouses came in. Bathhouses took the laborious and difficult work of drawing and heating water and monetized it. Most towns boasted at least one professional bathhouse, while cities played host to a number of competing establishments. In Paris, a guild for bathhouse keepers (which we will learn more about later) set rules that bathkeepers had to abide by. Much like modern spas, they offered customers a cheaper "steam bath [for] two deniers; and if he bathes, [he] should pay four deniers."[54] To stand out in a crowded field, Parisian bathhouses employed criers to drum up business from women eager to put their best foot forward.[55]

Rich women had a major advantage over their common peers in that they could afford to have others do the hard work of making the bath for them. They could send servants to fetch and heat water, and more luxurious households sometimes had rooms dedicated to bathing, rendering the necessity of public bathhouses moot. Those with extra income sometimes even traveled to famous bathing spots. Particularly celebrated were the baths of Pozzuoli outside Naples, a destination so famous that entire poems were written celebrating its virtues.

Outside Christian contexts, this emphasis on cleanliness was echoed in the bathing practices of Muslim communities in Sicily and on the Iberian Peninsula, and the Jewish communities that were spread across medieval Europe. Bathing was an explicitly mandated part of Jewish custom and was required before the sabbath. Women could bathe either in a public bathhouse, which would include steam and hot water, or in a cold-water *mikveh*, which was used for ritual purification. The religious necessity of the *mikveh*, and the not quite as pleasurable practice of cold-water submersion, meant that such bathing places were usually limited to use by Jewish women and found near synagogues.[56] Meanwhile, Muslim women's interest in the *hammam* is evidenced by the astounding number of surviving baths as well as by some pointed polemical tracts wherein Muslim men wondered what exactly women were getting up to while they were bathing, away from the prying eyes of men.[57]

The emphasis on cleanliness also lead to an advancement in bath products and in particular to the great medieval invention: soap. We are unsure how long people had been making soap at home, but most medieval people did. The earliest surviving written description of soap in Europe dates to the fourth century, when Theodorus Priscianus, a physician in Constantinople, describes a French product that was used for washing, especially the head.[58] In the Italian-speaking lands, soap was being produced professionally and in great enough quantities that guilds of soap makers existed by at least the seventh century. By the eighth century, soap was being made across the French-speaking lands and in Spain. Ninth-century Carolingian documents mentioned soap makers, and by the tenth, soap was known and used even in the farthest-flung reaches of Christendom, the backwater of England. In the twelfth century, the fine "hard" soaps of the Middle East began to be imported to Europe. *Hard* here indicates that they were made with higher-quality ash, which yields lighter bars of soap, in contrast to darker "soft" soaps made with wood ash and lye, which was the norm in the earlier medieval period. These nicer soaps encouraged Europeans to up their game, and soon Marseille and Castile were major centers of soap production, as they are to this day. The Italian city-states of Genoa, Venice, and Bari also shared in the art of soap making, as all had excellent access to olive oil and barilla, a plant that makes excellent soda lye.

Unfortunately for aspiring commonplace women, especially those living away from the Mediterranean lands, well-made soaps were a luxury that many would never know. To fill the gap, women made their own cleansers at home, and they had a range of types to choose from. Soap recipes were common and included in books of secrets—manuals for women to make various beauty products, as well as medicinal items. While most would simply find a good recipe for soap and use it, specialist cleansing products were also available. Hildegard of Bingen, for one, had her own recipe for barley-water face cleanser, which she recommended for "skin, made harsh from the wind." She assured worried women that after its use, "the skin will become soft and smooth, and will have a beautiful color."[59] Enterprising women were also advised to scent bathwater with herbs, or even concoct what we would call deodorants from hyssop and bay leaf. Such small luxuries were likely in wide use, given that herb-scented water and homemade soap were not in short supply to those who made their homes on farms.

If the means of getting clean were available to everyone, women from wealthier backgrounds nonetheless had an easier time *staying* clean in their day-to-day lives. Peasant women were, after all, engaging in manual labor on farms all day. They were in contact with farm animals. They baled hay and dug in crops. They got messy. They could scrub up as soon as they came in from the fields, but a significant portion of their day still involved physically demanding dirty work. Women from merchant or noble backgrounds therefore always had an edge. Doing the books for your family company was arduous mentally, but you were unlikely to come into contact with the same amount of dirt as a laborer. When physically laboring women strived for a clean ideal, they were attempting to emulate women from the sedentary classes.

After the bath, beauty routines were divided more explicitly along class lines. The medical and beauty guide *Trotula* advocated that after bathing women should "wear musk in their hair, or clove, or both, but take care that it is not seen by anyone."[60] But these instructions warned readers that scenting the hair was expressly a joy to be experienced by "noblewomen."[61] Despite this warning not to imitate their theoretical betters, some women, at least among the merchant elite, saw no problem with availing themselves of a bit of perfume.

Outside the bath, medieval women could cleanse their ears more thoroughly, using ear scoops, shaped like miniature ice-cream scoops, to remove wax. These multiuse objects put our own disposable cotton swabs to shame and show up in the archaeological record across Europe, proving that no crevice was too small for medieval women to attempt to clean. Almost any medieval woman could have these tools. Peasant women were likely to use wooden ear scoops, while their wealthy counterparts could use horn or, even, silver ones.

All in all, even medieval women of modest means had ways to live up to at least one beauty ideal, and they very clearly considered it a serious undertaking. They couldn't give themselves gray eyes or blond hair, nor could they reverse the aging process. However, they could strive to wash their face and hands, and even working women could luxuriate in a weekly bath, safe in the knowledge that they would be celebrated for doing so.

Limitations

Ideally, a woman would be beautiful but also totally unconcerned with that fact. This studied indifference to their own appearance was a point of literal instruction for young women. In 1371–72 Geoffroy, the fourth chevalier of La Tour Landry, took it upon himself to write a guide for his daughters, the somewhat unimaginatively named *The Book of the Knight of La Tour Landry for Teaching His Daughters* (*Livre du Chevalier de La Tour Landry pour l'enseignement de ses filles*).[62] Within it he repeatedly warns his progeny about the evils of any sort of vanity. In his opinion, courtesy and good manners were far more important than physical beauty, and any true gentlewoman would concern herself far more with these considerations than with her looks.

This tension is found throughout the medieval period: women were simultaneously told to be beautiful but, very crucially, to do absolutely nothing at all to highlight it. Women were warned in the Bible, in sermons, and in manuals like the Chevalier's against employing any sort of beauty intervention that would allow them to meet the exacting beauty standards that had been set in literary and artistic works but that they didn't *naturally* have. Women were particularly warned against using cosmetics and depilation, which would allow them to achieve the arched eyebrows and rosy cheeks that they had been told they must possess from almost their first day on earth.

Cosmetics occupied a dark place in the medieval imagination for a number of biblical reasons. First and foremost, they were *not natural,* and naturalness was the benchmark of anyone truly beautiful. The moment a woman resorted to cosmetics, she was attempting to embellish the work of the divine. This in turn led to the second concern, a conflation of makeup with dark magic. Both concerns were combined in the biblical story of Jezebel, which was trotted out to warn women who were thinking about trying a new recipe for rouge.

Jezebel, the wife of King Ahab of Israel, was a fairly terrible person. Aside from being foreign (which we are meant to understand was automatically bad), Jezebel had engaged in some light murder. She and Ahab had a neighbor, Naboth, who owned a thriving vineyard next door to the palace. After he rebuffed their offers to buy the land, Jezebel conspired to have him falsely accused of blasphemy. He was executed, and the lands passed to her and her husband (1 Kings 21:1–14). Subsequently, justices closed in on Jezebel, whereupon she "painted her eyes and adorned her head and looked out of a window." She was later thrown from that window, her blood splattering everywhere. Her corpse was eaten by dogs (2 Kings 9:30).

While most of us would probably say that the thing that marked Jezebel as the wrong sort was, you know, the murder, medieval biblical exegetes disagreed. For them, the worry was the eyeliner and the hairdo. As a result, Jezebel makes a return in the New Testament, in Apocalypse 2:20–23. In Apocalypse, which you might know by the decidedly less cool name Revelation, John of Patmos (ca. 6–100 C.E.) got extremely angry with Jezebel. According to John, God had complained to him that she "calls herself a prophetess and is teaching and seducing my servants to practice sexual immorality and to eat food sacrificed to idols. I gave her time to repent, but she refuses to repent of her sexual immorality. Behold, I will throw her onto a sickbed, and those who commit adultery with her I will throw into great tribulation, unless they repent of her works; and I will strike her children dead." Biblical scholars considered the references to "sexual immorality" and "adultery" here to be directly linked to the whole eyeliner thing, given that murder was decidedly less attractive to the average man. The fourteenth-century Czech preacher Jan Milíč of Kroměříž (d. 1374), for example, announced that during the Last Days, Jezebel would arise from the dead to lead "all who paint their faces" to their Last Judgment and subsequently to Hell.[63] Jezebel's use of makeup thus was more than just throwaway vanity. It is an overtly sexual act that could be conflated with large-scale and vaguely magical seduction, and that had a clearly delineated role in the Apocalypse. In other words, it was not good.

Meanwhile, Jewish and Christian communities could turn to Genesis for their concerns about women using makeup for the purposes of seduction and bringing about the end of the world. Some scholars' commentaries on Genesis warned against the daughters of God who had used cosmetics to disguise themselves and seduce a group of angels, "the sons of God." These women explicitly attempted to improve on God's natural creation and bring themselves up to the level of the divine. Luckily for the hussies in question, they didn't manage to bring about the Apocalypse, as Christian mystics were concerned they would. They were instead blamed for the Great Flood—their sinful nature being one of the things that God allegedly wished to wash from the earth. While cosmetics didn't manage to completely destroy the world in this instance, they came close. Makeup and the dangerous seductive power that women could wield as a result of it were clearly best avoided.[64]

In case Jezebel's dangerousness and the Flood were not enough of a warning, medieval writers set out to underline the diabolical possibilities of eyeliner. Enter, again, the concerned father of daughters, the Chevalier of La Tour Landry. This time he shared the tale of a beautiful princess, whose looks brought her acclaim, admirers, and riches. Rather than remaining a pure emanation of the will of God, however, this princess was augmenting her looks with makeup. As she aged and her beauty faded, she attempted to keep her looks by using yet more makeup, but her face began to wither. The Chevalier assured his daughters that "I heard tell from many that when she was dead, her face became such that one could not know what it was, nor what type of deformation; because it did not seem at all to be the face of a woman, nor did anyone take it for the face of a woman, so hideous was it and horrible to see. So, I think indeed that the layers of paint that she put on it were the cause of this phenomenon."[65]

Some theological scholars saw fit to consider the *real* victims of the use of cosmetics: men. In the twelfth century at least two theologians, the French Peter the Chanter (d. 1197) and his likely student the English Thomas of Chobham (ca. 1160–1236) tackled the hard question of what, exactly, men should do if they engaged a sex worker in good faith, only to find out later that she had been wearing makeup. Both enlightened minds agreed that in such a case, the clients who hired such women would have in effect been duped. Any woman who was found to be using cosmetics to entice clients was essentially selling falsified goods and should have to return any money that she received for sex.[66]

In the Muslim lands, the seductive power of cosmetics stirred similar concerns, especially perfumes. Jurists grappled with the question of what women could anoint themselves with and came to the conclusion that while it was fine for women to use tints to enhance their faces, these substances shouldn't be heavily perfumed. A light perfume, which could be perceived only by those in close physical proximity to a woman (namely, her husband), was acceptable. What was not acceptable was a perfume that left a trail of scent and therefore seduction. Women who ignored such rules faced legal consequences, as "a perfumed woman who passes by a group of men in order that they will notice her smell is an adulteress."[67]

Women who were tempted to use cosmetics, then, faced condemnation from a number of camps. They faced theological and legal consequences should they decide to enhance their looks through outside help. These concerns were not necessarily for the women but for the men whom they could defraud and seduce thanks to their contrivances. Furthermore, made-up women could cause an honest-to-God Apocalypse, or at least a fairly major flood. Either way it was clear that, in order to ensure the social order, women had to be threatened with legal repercussions.

Despite all these warnings, medieval women still seemed to be interested in using cosmetics. How-to guides for makeup and hair dye survive in great numbers. The *Trotula* was a boon to the beauty-conscious woman attempting to emulate the ideal. Her hair could be dyed blond, the *Trotula* informed her, giving no fewer than seven ways of doing so, which she could pick and choose from given the products she had at hand.[68] Her face could be whitened in seven different ways, and she was also offered a recipe to protect against sunburn. To achieve the necessary red cheeks, she could apply a

rouge made of brazilwood, rosewater, and alum.[69] Want the red honeyed mouth of a man's dreams? Well, mix honey with cucumber and
rosewater, then boil it to a reduction.[70] Men might not like it, but one
way or another women were going to live up to the standards men
had set.

Again, concerns about cosmetics had a class element. The women
who might be able to enjoy white skin naturally were those who
worked indoors. Peasant women worked outside in all conditions,
without SPF. Keeping a perfectly snow-white countenance simply
wasn't going to be possible for most women, who had to milk cows,
feed chickens, and bring in harvests. To condemn skin whitening,
then, was to push back not only against a theoretical moral failing
but also against poor women who didn't know their place.

If the cosmetics-based moral panic seems a bit extreme, it wasn't
even the greatest concern that men seem to have had with women
altering their appearances. That title was awarded to depilation, the
moral dangers of which dozens of men wrote ardently against. Their
focus was less the legs and underarms than the face. Those arched
eyebrows and wide clear foreheads were highly desired, so men were
fearful of their being achieved through machinations.

The Chevalier of La Tour Landry fittingly had stories for his
daughters on the dangers of a well-plucked face. He recounted the
tale of a knight whose wife had died and whom he mourned greatly.
To connect with her and ensure that her soul was at rest, the knight
employed a hermit to pray for her soul. The faithful hermit prayed
so hard for the dead wife that he was granted a vision of her in the
afterlife by an angel—and was surprised to find her being tortured
by demons:

> He saw that a demon held her by her hair and by the tresses with one
> of his claws as a lion holds its prey, . . . and then he put daggers and
> burning needles into her eyebrows, and into her temples, and into her
> forehead all the way to her brain, and the poor soul cried out each time

that he put the burning dagger in. . . . And after she had suffered this
martyrdom, which lasted a very long time, another very hideous demon
came who had huge hideous and sharp teeth, to take her by the face
and grind and chew it, and after that he came with great firebrands to
burn her and thrust them into her face so horribly and painfully that
the hermit shook all over with fear and revulsion.[71]

The reason she was being tortured? She had plucked hair at each
point where a demon was now stabbing her with a dagger, a punishment that the angel categorized as "well deserved." Little wonder then that the concerned Chevalier would warn his daughters
against the folly of falsifying their beauty to encompass societal
expectations.

Even those who weren't specifically concerned about the religious
implications of women plucking their eyebrows nevertheless saw
fit to mock the practice. Chaucer made much of the fact that Alisoun, the beauty in "The Miller's Tale," "thinned out carefully her
eyebrows two, And they were arched and black as any sloe."[72] That
indicated that Alisoun was common and lower class, since a natural
beauty would have had no need to pluck her eyebrows, and a woman
from a better background would have been raised to avoid such van-
ities. Today's equivalent might be wearing too much fake tan, or
indeed overdrawing one's eyebrows. Alisoun might be good for a
short-term romp or a lighthearted tavern story, but she was not the
classical beauty that she was striving to be.

Clerics too were concerned about hair removal. In a fifteenth-
century confessional guide, Antoninus, the archbishop of Florence, instructed priests to ask a woman in confession if "she has
ever plucked her neck, or eyebrows or beard because this is a mortal
sin."[73] The Catholic Church verified that hair removal, as the Chevalier had written, was a sinful practice that could lead to Hell.

If religious men warned against hair removal, medical men
theorized that hairy women might be unhealthy. Hair growth was

conceptualized as an offshoot of impure humors generated in the liver. Men processed them by growing excess body hair, whereas women were meant to purge them through their menses, and hence were less hairy than men. Any woman with what was considered undue facial hair thus risked being read as having a poisonous womb. As the historian John Block Friedman has pointed out, women who dutifully followed advice not to remove their hair ran the risk of being seen "as poor bets for marriage because of probable infertility and a potential for domineering behavior."[74]

So despite the protestations of religious men, hair removal was common among women, sometimes posing real dangers to their physical health. To achieve the preferred high hairline and arched eyebrows, the *Trotula* offered women recipes for depilatories with such components as quicklime. It admitted that leaving such preparations on the face too long could cause "excessive heat" and burn the skin. For women who injured themselves in this manner, it advised using rose or violet oil, or the juice of houseleek.[75] The fact that depilatories injured women is further testified to by Arnold of Villanova (1240–1311), a physician who recommended that "if, because of the strength of the depilatory, the lady's face was peeled, burned, roughened, or blistered, she should wash it with a mixture of rooster blood, honey, and camphor."[76] If cosmetic use could lead to chemical burns, little wonder that the Chevalier of La Tour Landry warned that it could cause a woman's face to collapse over time.

Besides the use of cosmetics, women could also use fashion to enhance their looks and their body. Fashion is trickier for us to understand, as it is by its very nature in flux. While we can decisively identify the medieval beauty standard for faces, it is much more difficult to say with certainty what an entire continent found fashionable for over a millennium. Medieval fashion, as a marker of taste and distinction, changed as our own industry does. And the fact that the medieval economies of Venice, Ghent, Florence, and London were built around the production of fabrics meant that individuals were attuned to the demands for new styles.

Having said that, we can trace some medieval fashions through art, literary descriptions, and eventually late medieval "costume books" that purport to show us the popular fashions in various locations. Medieval literary works increasingly described what people and characters were wearing. As a result, we are able to make some generalizations. Prior to the twelfth century, much fashion was about what was easiest to sew; people favored T-shaped garments that could be sewn quickly and augmented with details. Tailoring became progressively more complex over the period, however, and during the twelfth century garments got tighter across the chest, revealing more body shape, with long trailing sleeves. The thirteenth century saw tighter armholes; regularly spaced decorative cuts in the fabric of hems, a technique known as "slashing"; and sleeveless overgarments worn over a long-sleeved tunic or dress. By the fourteenth century, most dresses had shorter sleeves, but with tails hanging from the backs of them.[77]

While such changes in women's fashion abounded over time, some similarities persisted. Women consistently favored clothing that emphasized the ideal pear-shaped body. Even the T-shaped garments of the eleventh century included cinching just under the bust, the better to highlight the ideal small waist and exaggerated belly. The fourteenth century saw an interest in slashed or cut-in detail work and cinching that drew attention to wide hips. Women in the late fourteenth and early fifteenth centuries preferred fashion that bared the shoulders, the better to show off their milky whiteness. The other thing consistent about fashion throughout the period was that men got angry that women took an interest in it.

Women's concern for what they wore was as much of an existential threat as cosmetics. Consider representations of the Whore of Babylon, who, like Jezebel, appears in the Book of Revelation as an existential warning against vanity. Revelation 17:5 helpfully identi-

fies her as the "mother of harlots and abominations of the earth."
She rides the seven-headed beast at the end of the world, drunk on
the blood of saints and absolutely dressed to kill. John of Patmos
stated that she wore purple and red (two of the most difficult and
expensive clothing dyes to produce) and was bedecked in gold, precious stones, and pearls, which medieval artists enjoyed giving their
personalized spins on.

When biblical warnings were not enough, literary condemna-
tions could help. Books of vices and virtues were a popular form
of literature that catalogued what ideal Christians strove to avoid
and to emulate. They warned readers that many fine ladies, despite
lives of virtue and charity, were often, after death, surprised to find
themselves in Hell simply as a result of their fashion choices. For
"certainly they sin well grievously, for they make and be the cause
of loss of many souls, and where-through many men are dead and
fall into great sin. . . . For she has no member on her body that is
not a grin of the devil, as Solomon says, wherefore they must yield
accounts at the day of doom of all the souls that by reason of them
are damned."[78]

Similarly, when the Black Death spread across Europe in the fourteenth century, many were quick to identify the cause of the pesti-
lence as an overabundant interest in fashionable dress on the part
of both men and women, for which God was punishing the world.
The monk John of Reading (d. 1368/9) wrote in *Westminster Chroni-
cle* that the plague was visited on the earth because "women flowed
with the tides of fashion in this and other things even more eagerly,
wearing clothes that were so tight that they wore a fox tail hanging
down inside their skirts at the back, to hide their arses. The sin of
pride manifested in this way must surely bring down misfortune in
the future."[79]

Even gentler texts such as Christine de Pizan's *City of Ladies*
warned its readers that well-meaning women were on dangerous
ground when they engaged with fashion. In one conversation, the

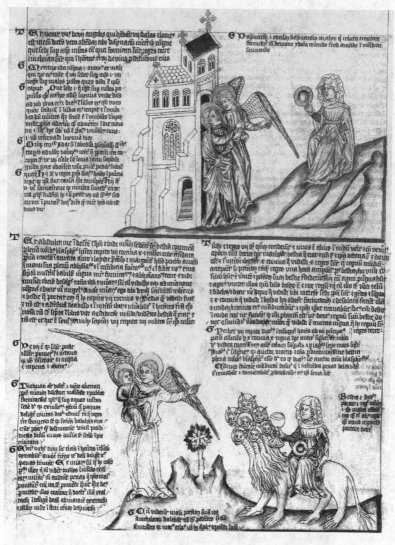

The Whore of Babylon, holding a mirror and chalice, riding the seven-headed beast, from *Wellcome Apocalypse*, ca. 1420, Wellcome Collection, London. WELLCOME APOCALYPSE, WELLCOME COLLECTION.

embodiment of Rectitude tells Christine that some women, as well as men, are naturally predisposed to taking pleasure in "elaborate clothes." It's therefore not really their fault if they find it difficult to resist dressing fashionably.

But some women genuinely needed to dress well. Women at court were expected to, and those who were unable to maintain a high enough standard of dress would not be taken seriously as courtiers and risked being sent away. Unfortunately for them, the cost of clothing oneself for fashionable court settings, particularly in the later medieval period, could be ruinous.[80] Anne Besset, a young English lady who was sent to live with the aristocratic de Riou family in the Somme, beseeched her mother for new and more lavish clothing: "Madame, I would earnestly entreat you that if I am to pass the winter in France I may have some new gown to pass it in, as I am out of apparel for every day. Madame, . . . there are so many little trifling things which are here necessary which are not needed in England."[81]

While such a letter might simply have been a teenage daughter's histrionic plea for nicer clothes, it still reflected the reality for women at court. Women were kept in aristocratic homes not only to help with tasks but also to act as ornaments. They were meant to be beautiful and to dress beautifully—to be seen and provide evidence that the family with whom they stayed was indeed very fine. In these situations, it was all very well to say that women shouldn't care about the way they dressed, but in reality their positions depended on maintaining a fashionable wardrobe and displaying themselves in a style befitting a woman of refinement.

The aristocracy's pursuit of high fashion was a way of underlining their place in society and was by and large an exercise in conspicuous consumption. Wearing cloth of gold or red velvet such as could bankrupt even the wealthy was a way of showing status, while wearing ridiculous clothing that would interfere with heavy labor was a way of ensuring that everyone understood that the wearer did not have to engage in physical work. The high-heeled shoes that irate wealthy women in Italian city-states fought to wear had no place on the farm. Not only would mud ruin a perfectly nice shoe, but you needed sensible shoes if you were working on your feet all day. That was why peasant women wore heavy wooden overshoes. Whether consciously or not, clothing replicated the social hierarchy. A poor girl might be born beautiful, but she was unlikely to be able to dress like a beauty.

Wealthy women were thus in a constant moral and social quandary about how to dress. They had to show what part of society they belonged to, but not tip over into sinfulness. Likely some well-dressed women simply did not care about religious calls to austerity. The warnings in books of virtue and vice and in *The City of Ladies* were aimed at persuading these unrepentant fashionistas. More spiritually minded women, in contrast, would consciously limit embellished designs and bright colors and show their status through the quality of the cloth, the stitching on the garments, and long sleeved and tailed dresses that precluded manual labor. Extreme cases, especially wealthy women hoping to become saints, would square this circle by secretly wearing rough and irritating hair shirts under their fine clothing. That way they lived up to social expectations but punished themselves for doing so.

If certain women were expected to dress well, many more were prevented from doing so. In the later medieval period especially, "sumptuary laws" were passed to make sure that women weren't dressing above their perceived station. These laws were billed as a means of condemning profligate spending when money could instead be put to better more charitable uses, but in reality, they were used to ensure that people of the lower orders would not be mistaken for nobility or "live nobly" (*vivre noblem*).[82] They commonly mandated that the lower social orders could not wear velvet or silk. Particular colors, such as green and purple, might also be reserved for the upper classes. Fine furs such as ermine were allowed only to those at court. Some sumptuary laws regulated whole styles of clothing. In Bruges, in what is now Belgium, where wealthy citizens enjoyed a comparatively swank style of life, sumptuary laws forbade nonnobles from wearing "jerkins, cornets, and robes, etc."[83]

Women did not necessarily conform to such limitations. In Bologna, after a 1453 law from Cardinal Giovanni Bessarion limited women's fashion, Nicolosa Sanuti, a matron from a wealthy merchant family, wrote a treatise demanding of "the Bolognese papal legate, that ornaments be restored to women."[84] Other women wrote in groups, insisting that high fashion was necessary both for married women, to please their husbands, who enjoyed seeing their wives ornamented, and for unmarried women, to enhance their looks so they could entice men into marriage.[85]

The fact that sumptuary laws existed is testament to the fact that those who ruled jealously guarded access to finer clothing. Even when women pushed back against legal limitations on their fashion choices, they came from the loftier realms of society. The merchant women who were literate enough to pen defenses of their clothing choices, and who had the money to afford the high-heeled shoes and trained dresses that sumptuary laws forbade, were undoubtedly wealthy if not noble. The fact that such petitions were made by monied women is evidenced in the answers that the women received to their complaints. While overall the laws were not lifted, rulers allowed women to buy licenses to continue to enjoy expensive styles.[86] Even if women from common backgrounds could afford the clothes that were considered attractive, they likely could not afford to buy the license to wear them.

All this condemnation of women who dared to take an interest in their appearance may seem a bit over the top. After all, it's only fashion. However, a woman's interest in cosmetics, perfumes, plucking, and clothing showed not simply an unbecoming interest in oneself but hints that she harbored deadly vices. The seven deadly vices or sins were classified as particularly troublesome transgressions because they could give rise to other immoralities. As a result, they were seen as specifically "deadly" for the soul, which is to say that they were likely to result in one's damnation. They were also unique in that their sorts of sinfulness were encouraged by a person's temperament. Someone who indulged in them, therefore, clearly had something intrinsically unbalanced in his or her character.

The sin that was most often connected to women's interest in their appearance was *superbia*, which we often translate as "pride" but can also mean "vanity." Vanity was a sin because it meant that a woman was overly concerned with her mortal and outward appearance, rather than with her immortal soul and her religious duties. Moreover, the vanity that led a woman to interfere with her natural countenance through plucking, shaving, or cosmetic use was an affront to God's chosen plan. Vain women were telling God they could do a better job than he could, which was completely unacceptable. Pride in appearance was also an issue because when a woman gave in to it, she inevitably sparked in the hearts of others yet another deadly sin: lust, or *luxuria*. Women who used cosmetics and dressed fashionably, who took an interest in their appearance, were thought at best to be stoking lust in men and at worst entertaining their own interest in rampant sexuality. Indeed, Chaucer's description of his beauty means that she is up for sex with pretty much anyone other than her husband. Overt narcissism led to deeds of overt sexuality and in turn stoked lust in the hearts of those who were subsequently seduced into transgression. It was a self-propagating sin, leading more and more innocent souls into damnation.

All in all, medieval society spent a long time concocting a beauty ideal for women that was possible only for wealthy women to live up to, and then furiously policing it when commoners tried to emulate it. At every opportunity women were told that they must be beautiful, and that that made them desirable, lovable, and holy. However, attempting to live up to this rigid standard, especially if one was poor, was called sinful and at times was illegal. The Church thrust women into an impossible quandary: If they were not born with looks that accorded with the beauty standard, should they lose status and perhaps remain single? Or should they use subterfuge to get closer to that exacting standard, even if it meant they might face an eternity in Hell?

3

HOW TO LOVE

TO SAY THAT OUR OWN SOCIETY HAS COMPLEX FEELINGS about relationships and sex would be, as we historians put it, a massive understatement. Our own tensions surrounding concepts of sexuality and love mean that only until very recently has sexuality been accepted as a legitimate field of study, whether that be historically, psychologically, or even biologically. Sadly, on the whole, we have yet to approach the subject without resorting to snickering. This collective unwillingness to take a sober look at sexuality means that we can be forgiven for thinking that sex was invented during the 1960s to pass the time.

Luckily for those still clinging to this idea, this chapter will focus on medieval ideas about women, sexuality, and love. In contrast to our modern distaste for the contemplation of sexuality, medieval thinkers were much less burdened by such qualms. Sexuality was a topic of lively debate among theologians, philosophers, physicians, and poets. It sparked its own genres of wildly popular literature and underpinned marital advice. Indeed, sexuality was considered to be at the very heart of medieval concepts of women because it was generally agreed that women were impossibly, insatiably, and over-whelmingly horny.

In order to understand their ideas, we have to begin with the concept of sex itself and where everything in the Christian imagination began: the Garden of Eden.

Sexual Theology

As we have seen, medieval theologians considered that sex in and of itself was sinful, because its very existence was bound up with the doctrine of Original Sin. That's not to say that sex was entirely absent in the Garden of Eden. After all, God had bidden Adam and Eve to "go forth and multiply," and he hadn't provided an alternative way of doing that besides sex. However, prior to gaining the knowledge that they were naked, Adam and Eve would have been able to have sex, it was agreed. The major distinction was that before the Fall of Man, when they got around to having sex, they would have done so without it being *sexy*.

Augustine devoted himself to the contemplation of sex within the Garden, insisting that "they would not have had the activity of turbulent lust in their flesh . . . but only the movement of peaceful will by which we command the other members of the body." In other words, if Adam and Eve wanted to have sex in order to procreate, they could simply will their genitals to work, much as we might decide to move our arms or legs. While they could have had innocent sex prior to the Fall, "they incurred the penalty of exile from paradise before they could unite in the task of propagation as a deliberate act undisturbed by passion."[1] The jurist Gratian (ca. 1101–59) concurred, stating in his *Decretum*, "The first institution of marriage was effected in Paradise such that there would have been 'an unstained bed and honourable marriage' [Hebrews 13.4] resulting in conception without ardour."[2] That is to say, Adam and Eve were so innocent and peaceful before the Fall that they never actually got around to any of that wholesome nonlustful sex.

Instead, as we all know, they ate from the Tree of Knowledge and realized their nakedness, at which point everything changed. Of course, a major issue with the whole nakedness thing was that Adam and Eve felt shame at it and covered themselves with fig leaves. Augustine argued that this shame was not simply about being without clothes, but about being *turned on* by the fact that they were naked. In his words, "They turned their eyes on their own genitals, and lusted after them with that stirring movement they had not previously known."[3] No longer having perfect control over their genitals, Adam and Eve's bodies were as disobedient as they had been toward the Lord's commandments. As Augustine wrote:

Human nature then is, without any doubt, ashamed about lust, and rightly ashamed. For in its disobedience, which subjected the sexual organs solely to its own impulses and snatched them from the will's authority, we see a proof of the retribution imposed on man for that first disobedience. And it was entirely fitting that this retribution should show itself in that part which effects the procreation of the very nature that was changed for the worse through that first great sin.[4]

Sex was an inherently sinful action and was tied, in the minds of theologians, to women. Since Eve was tempted into eating the fruit from the Tree of Knowledge, it was her fault that humans had realized how sexy their genitals were. Eve's temptation was often discussed in sexual terms. For example, in 2 Corinthians 11:3, Paul states that "the serpent seduced Eve by his craftiness," a passage that Augustine later used to illustrate the concept of perverted love that was tainted by possessiveness and lust.[5] Ambrose (ca. 340–97), a theologian and bishop of Milan, concurred, stating that "if Eve's door had been closed, Adam would not have been deceived and she, under question, would not have responded to the serpent. Death entered through the window, i.e. through the door of Eve."[6]

Women, even in their perfect state in paradise, were simply more susceptible to caving to seduction and sexual depravity. And Eve, as the model for all femininity, passed her own unseemly interest in sexuality down to all women, making them responsible for the sinful nature of sex.

Women were also seen as inherently lustful because of the sin's illogical nature. Women were thought to be incapable of the rational and logical thought that men could achieve and were therefore more likely to give in to the urges of their genitals. Men had the ability to master themselves and confront the sinful nature of such stirrings. Women, however, were weak and base creatures, lacking the capacity for disciplined self-mortification. Instead, they were led by their passions, and their minds were every bit as disobedient as Eve's, and so they would have given in to the temptations of the serpent.

Because sex was sinful, it was thought, the ideal human—whether man or woman—would not have sex at all. The best possible thing that people could do was devote themselves to God and religious contemplation, eschewing all lustful thought. For this reason, the clergy, as God's servants on Earth, were to be celibate. Yet clerical celibacy had not always been a part of Christianity. The fourth-century Council of Elvira wrote the regulation stating that "bishops, presbyters, deacons, and others with a position in the ministry" were to "abstain completely from sexual intercourse with their wives and from the procreation of children" or face being removed from the clergy.[7] This provision was heavily debated, however, and the Eastern Church often interpreted it as meaning that a clergyman could not marry after ordination, but if a man was already married before taking holy orders, he could still become a member of the clergy. Even in the West, many Latin clergymen were married. But then in 1123 the First Lateran Council announced that it "absolutely for-

b[ade] priests . . . to associate with concubines and women, or to live
with women" and "to have concubines or to contract marriage."[8] Sixteen years later the Second Lateran Council, reaffirmed the rule,
and thereafter people were encouraged not to attend Mass led by
married clergy.

The pushback against marriage and sex among the clergy was
linked to the theological concept of chastity as the highest state for
humans. Chastity was laudable because it meant that one mastered
their disobedient body and overcame the curse of original sin. It
also had knock-on benefits, such as allowing one to sever themselves
from the ordinary world. Vows of chastity were required of priests,
monks, and nuns, but they were also a popular option among many
lay orders as well as heretical movements. In the most spectacular
cases, it catalyzed a person to the holiness of martyrdom. As we saw
in Chapter 2, the celebrated Virgin Martyrs—such as Saint Agatha,
Saint Lucy, and Saint Barbara—all preferred chastity and death to
lives of riches and sex. They were also seen as some of the sexiest
possible women *because* they were both beautiful and resisted car-
nality. It was richly dressed images of these women that men like the
disgusted Protestant in Chapter 2 were viewing in church, making
the situation even more confusing.

So concerned were theologians with keeping the theoretical
purity of celibacy that an entire category of scholarly debate surrounded the concept of "nocturnal emissions" or "nocturnal pol-
lutions," which is to say wet dreams. As the word *pollution* indicates,
sex was seen as so sinful that even unpartnered, involuntary ejacula-
tion was a source of concern. In the fifteenth century, Jean Gerson
(1363–1429), a preacher and humanist, was inspired to write the
tract *On Pollution* to argue that priests who had experienced nocturnal emissions were not in a state of sin and could celebrate the
Mass in good faith.[9] This was in agreement with Thomas Aquinas,
who dedicated a section of his *Summa Theologica* to the question, "Is
nocturnal pollution a mortal sin?" He found that while a man was

asleep, his reason and judgment were hindered, and he therefore had little way to stop himself from ejaculating.[10]

Unfortunately, as all those considering the finer points of sexual sin would readily admit, sex was necessary. After all, just because Adam and Eve had been expelled from the Garden for getting turned on, they couldn't renege on the whole "be fruitful and multiply" thing. Humans were tasked with continuing to populate the Earth and creating new Christians to worship God. Sex was sinful, but if the human race were to continue, it had to become *acceptable*. Hence the ritual of marriage.

Medieval Europeans cited 1 Corinthians 7:9 to explain the acceptability of sex within marriage: "It is better to marry than to burn." Here the word *burn* can be interpreted to mean the fires of Hell. If sex is sinful but you absolutely cannot handle living without it, then you should marry and thereby sanctify the sex you have. But *burn* can also be a reference to undue lust. If you, as a weak sinner, find yourself preoccupied with thoughts of sex, it is better for you to get married than to burn with and be distracted by lust. Marriage would give you a licit sexual outlet and you would be able to focus your mind on the logical and spiritual. In this way, marriage was conceived as a sort of sexual pressure valve, allowing people a necessary outlet so they could lead more productive and focused lives.

From a theological standpoint, sex was approved within marriage because marriage was, first and foremost, a sacrament. According to medieval philosophers, God had decreed that marriage should exist. However, even if sex was fine within marriage, it was still subject to limits within those bounds. Marrying simply to assuage one's lust for someone was in and of itself sinful. As far back as the fourth century, after all, Jerome (ca. 342–420) had warned Christians that "a man who is too passionately in love with his wife is an adulterer."[11] The fourteenth-century canon lawyer William of Pagula (d. 1332) softened this stance saying that it could be all right for a man to be really hot for his spouse, provided that he didn't marry her *primarily*

for sex.[12] Being too sexually attracted to anyone was never a great
idea, and God would know if you took a sacred vow just to get some
sexual kicks.

Even if you were an upstanding Christian who was barely attracted
to your spouse, the only time sex was okay was if you were actively
attempting to have children. Otherwise, you were simply trying to
dodge the fact that it was sinful. Peter Lombard (ca. 1096–1160), a
theologian and bishop of Paris, underlined this point, stating that
"when these goods are absent, namely fidelity and offspring, it does
not seem that intercourse is defended from being a crime."[13] Moreover, while attempting to get pregnant, married couples also had to
have the least amount of fun possible. Sex, as a necessary evil on the
way to children, was to be perfunctory. As Augustine put it, "Surely
any friend of wisdom and holy joys . . . would prefer, if possible, to
beget children without lust," just as Adam and Eve would have done
before the Fall of Man.[14]

Having too much fun during sex was wrong because it might dis-
tract people from the holy mission of creating children and make
them fall prey to lust. If the entire point of marital sex was to channel
sexual feelings into one approved outlet, it simply wouldn't do to go
around getting all hot and bothered and subverting the pure beget-
ting of children. Therefore, couples had to avoid doing anything to
heighten sexual pleasure. For Thomas Aquinas, this included "lascivious" kisses and caresses above and beyond what was strictly necessary for procreation, for "when these kisses and caresses are done
for this delectation, it follows that they are mortal sins, and only in
this way are they said to be lustful."[15] Further, Aquinas believed sex
could be classified on a spectrum of "rational" to "irrational," and it
was irrationality that contributed to sinfulness.

Another problem with people having too much fun during sex
was that it would simply restoke the lust that their wholesome procreative martial sex was meant to be satisfying. Jerome warned
that an abundance of pleasurable sex "enervates a man's mind,

and engrosses all thought except for the passion which it feeds."[16] Experiencing too much pleasure during sex therefore had exactly the opposite effect for which theologians were aiming. It was paramount, therefore, that married couples attempt to restrain their ardor during sex so as not to remain aroused afterward.

Sexual Practices

Theologians warned people that they could slip into lust in multifarious ways. One way was to have sex in any position other than what we now call the missionary position. Interestingly, medieval thinkers elaborated on this preoccupation at much greater length than classical ones had done. When Jerome repeatedly insisted that "there is nothing blacker than to love a wife as if she were an adultress," historians think he might have been warning people of the dangers of nonmissionary sex positions.[17]

According to medieval theologians the missionary position highlighted the appropriate relationship between the genders and what was "natural." Men, as the superior gender, had their role as leaders and dominators affirmed and were taking an "active" approach during sex. Women, in contrast, were meant to be "passive" and their place as the inferior gender was reinforced by their position under their husbands. This belief was repeated *ad nauseum* throughout medieval sex-think writings, with major proponents, including Thomas Aquinas.[18]

Medieval theologians were also happy to go into detail about what sex acts people should not indulge in. They were against *retro* sex— which is to say sex from behind, or what we would call doggy style— a term repeated by medieval writers. Burchard (ca. 950–1025), the bishop of Worms and a major enthusiast of compiling penitential literature, stated that married couples who indulged in its excessive pleasures should do penance for ten days on bread and water.[19] Here the "unnaturalness" that concerned theologians was an excess of pleasure, which Aquinas categorized as "bestial."[20]

While theologians had an overwhelming consensus on the right sex position, there were naysayers as well. The twelfth-century theologian Alexander of Hales (ca. 1185–1245) and the fourteenth-century moralist William of Pagula both argued that nonstandard sex positions, such as sex standing up or seated, could be acceptable for physical or health reasons. For example, obesity could prevent a married couple from having sex in what some by now referred to as the "standard fashion." However, they too had limits. Alexander emphasized that in no instances would doggy-style sex, "the fashion of brutes," be acceptable, and it should be considered a mortal, or damnable, offense.[21] Further, if couples used other positions for any reasons other than absolute physical necessity, they were still engaging in a sin of "extraordinary voluptuousness" (*extraordinaries voluptatis*), as the anonymously authored twelfth-century tract *Fragmentum Cantabrigiense* declared.[22]

On top of attempting to control how much fun married couples had during sex, medieval theologians found it unacceptable for them to engage in sex during particularly solemn religious times of the year, such as Lent and Advent. Some warned that sex on Wednesdays and Fridays was out of the question because they were traditional days of penance. Similarly, they should avoid sex on Saturdays in case they became too aroused and couldn't concentrate during church on Sunday. Meanwhile virtually all agreed that Sunday was off-limits for sex as it was a day of holy reflection.[23] Because prospective sex-havers were to have sex only when the woman was able to become pregnant, sex was unacceptable when a woman had her menses or when she was pregnant. Ideally, couples would also avoid sex if a woman was breastfeeding.[24]

If all this wasn't enough, a lot of rules seemed to restrict visual stimuli during intercourse. Sex was, preferably, to take place clothed.

Similarly, couples should have sex at night in the dark. Essentially they should do everything possible to ensure that they could see as little of each other as possible, and to spare any incidental onlookers the same sight, a not unusual concern in a society in which most people didn't have the luxury of private bedrooms.

Placing all these limits on the pleasure of a married couples had to do with curbing excessive lust. To be too enamored of one's spouse or too interested in sex was a sin all too readily fallen into, especially when married couples might think that now that they were safely ensconced within the realm of marriage, anything went. Excessive voluptuousness and sensual pleasure were a slippery slope on the way to sex for its own sake.

Theologians were further concerned that if married people enjoyed procreative sex a bit too much, they might slip into another and much more dangerous sin: sodomy. Today we use the term *sodomy* to refer almost exclusively to anal sex, more specifically to anal sex between two men. However, medieval people used it to mean any form of sex that could not result in procreation. So a whole host of sexual activities, indeed most of them, were mortal sins. Whether you were talking about mutual masturbation, oral sex, interfemoral sex, or a round of rousing dry humping, you were talking about sodomy. Of course, anal sex perfectly met this definition, as did any sort of same-sex sexual contact.

But a bunch of professional thinkers could not simply leave it at "sodomy can't result in pregnancy, so it's bad." Instead, theologians elaborated in florid prose on why it was bad. Gratian declared that acts of sodomy constituted "extraordinary sensual pleasures" and likened them to "whoreish embraces."[25] For Aquinas, it was just *illogical*. Everyone knew that sex was supposed to be about procreation. To engage in a sort of sex that had no way of doing that was to knowingly commit the sin of lust. Perfectly acceptable sex was readily available to married couples. Why would they damn their souls instead? In the thirteenth century, Johannes Teutonicus

(d. 1245) announced that the trouble with sodomy was that it was "unnatural."[26] What was natural was that which was divine, which meant engaging in the least sexy sex possible, getting pregnant, and moving on.

Sexual Interest

The stringent theological structure that defined which sex was acceptable meant that most people who had sex were unlikely to do it in a perfectly acceptable manner. However, the rules and regulations put women at a particular disadvantage. That women would break these very important theological rules was obvious. Women— patterned on the easily seduced and sinful Eve—were simply more sexual and sensuous beings. As the theologian and sometime archbishop Isidore of Seville put it, women's libidinousness was a part of their very nature, and they were even named for it. According to him, "the word *femina* comes from the Greek derived from the force of fire because her concupiscence is very passionate: women are more libidinous than men."[27]

The proofs were manifold, but many of them were directly linked to what was seen as women's "unnatural" and irrational interest in sex. Much was made of the fact that women were interested in having sex while they were having their periods, when it was impossible for them to become pregnant. According to the physician, philosopher, and theologian Albertus Magnus (ca. 1200–80), "A woman never desires sex so much as she does when she is pregnant," a condition that makes absolutely no sense if we accept that the only reason one would be having sex at all was to get pregnant.[28]

Even women who had sex at the "correct" time were suspiciously horny. A woman could still be interested in having sex even after her husband dutifully ejaculated his semen into her, at which point logically she ought to be aware that the purpose of sex was over and lose interest. Jerome warned of women's insatiable interest in sex, claiming that "women's love in general is accused of ever being insatiable; put it out, it bursts into flame; give it plenty, it is again in need."[29] The lust of women was a sort of perpetual-motion machine. The more sex they had, the more sex they wanted.

Medieval people believed that women's lust was insatiable for several reasons. First, a medical standpoint sometimes put forward that women enjoyed sex more than men, a view that derived from natural philosophy. In the medieval mind, pleasure, which we would call orgasm, was specifically linked to the expulsion of reproductive matter, given that this was the "logical" endpoint of any and all sexual interest. There were two competing medieval ideas of how this expulsion occurred. According to the Aristotelian one-seed model, women's wombs acted mostly as incubators for men's active seed, which did all of the growing into a baby on its own, so long as it was provided with fertile ground. In contrast, the slightly more prevalent "two-seed" theory considered that both men and women expelled semen, which when mixed together produced offspring.[30]

Constantine the African was a proponent of the two-seed theory. In his tract *On Coitus*, he wrote that women were more interested in sex because "women experience twofold pleasure: both by expelling their own sperm and receiving the male's sperm, from the desire of their fervent vulva."[31] Avicenna detailed that the pleasure that women received, from both their own and men's ejaculate, was as a result of the "motion of the seed that is in them," meaning that sperm could be considered something like small internal vibrators.[32] As a result, sex was way more fun for them than it was for the men they slept with. Why wouldn't they have sex on the brain?

The second scientific rationale was based on humoral theory. The thirteenth-century anonymous treatise *The Prose Salernitan Questions* sought to address the question, "Why does woman, although she is of a colder and moister nature than man have a more burning desire?"[33] One answer was that women's cold, wet nature meant that they took longer to heat up, but once they did, they burned much hotter than did men. Using this analogy, women were likened to a wet forest that is lit on fire and becomes more difficult to put out than a dry fire, or to a dense metal like iron, which takes longer to heat than gold but retains its heat longer.[34]

Moreover, women's cold quality meant that they yearned for the heat that was generated during sex simply because they lacked it. In this view, women were likened to cold-blooded creatures like snakes, who were said to seek the heat emanating from human bodies.[35] By the thirteenth century, this explanation was elaborated on and made more expressly misogynist. The medical treatise *The Secrets of Women* said that a woman's desire resulted from the fact that she had "a greater desire for coitus than a man, for something foul is drawn to the good."[36] Women's despicable nature meant that they were innately drawn to men and desired contact with them and their presumably not "foul" semen.

A third reason for women's oversexed nature was that they were, well, stupid and passive. A healthy skepticism of sex and a desire to engage in it only when it was logical and acceptable was the preserve of the untarnished male. Women were simple and childlike creatures, unable to engage in anything properly. Their inability to differentiate right from wrong, and their susceptibility to being swayed into sexual sin, had been evident since the time of Eve. Because of this stupidity, according to Albertus Magnus, women were unable to relate to the pleasure that they experienced in a rational way. Women experience a greater *quantity* of pleasure during sex, he said, but men's pleasure was of a higher *quality* because of their ability to sense it in a rational and refined way.[37] Because women experienced more pleasure of a lower caliber, they were constantly desirous of more, unable to act in order to receive it, and just as unable to be sated. Even those who subscribed to the Aristotelian one-seed theory could get on board with this idea, given that it explained women's immoderate interest and pleasure in sex, but also firmly established that they contributed nothing to the procreative act.

Overall then, women by their very natures were simply too horny to function. The thirteenth-century Dominican Vincent of Beauvais (ca. 1184–1264), convinced that women were basically stupid, cold sex monsters, looked to the first-century Roman satirist Juvenal for confirmation of his ideas. Juvenal provided assurance that woman was a creature "always ready for coitus" but who was afterward "tired, but never satisfied."[38] That sexual contact left women exhausted and wanting more was, these men assured each other, absolutely their own problem.

While men were busy discussing why women were obsessed with sex yet bad at enjoying it, their conceit wasn't necessarily universal. The women we are able to hear from did not exactly share the idea that women are stupid, horny, poisonous creatures. Once again Hildegard of Bingen emerges with her own way of relating to women's sexuality. She concedes that "woman is colder and moister [than man], but it is these characteristics which make her fertile: she is more spacious and her passions milder, and these characteristics allow her to conceive, carry, and give birth to children. . . . Since her desire is less violent, a woman is more able to contain herself— because of the moistness 'where the pleasure burns' and because of either fear or shame."[39]

This counterpoint shows us that although woman's assumed nature remains the same, not everyone likened women to a stupid, horny forest fire. Further, it recasts as beneficial the humoral attributes that men used to make critiques about the sinful and exasperating nature of women. What might look to some like a less focused passion could seem to others like a nurturing one.

Going further, Hildegard decided that women's sexuality, far from being something "foul," counteracted men's harmful sexual output. According to her, "the strength of man in his genital member is turned into poisonous foam, and the blood of woman is turned into a contrary effusion."[40] Hildegard can perhaps be credited as the first person to commit the concept of toxic masculinity to the written record. All the strength and virility that men liked to boast of in order to prove their theoretical superiority could just as easily be framed as poisonous, requiring the sexual intervention of women to quench.

While Hildegard's voice gives us a sense of how to relate to sexuality in a different way within the same framework, the idea that women were not evil sex harpies was sadly not a widespread one. If the idea that women's humoral nature made them overly interested in sex was prevalent among the intellectual elite, it was accepted across the social spectrum.

Sexual Demands

One twelfth-century French *fabliau* (a rhyming tale aimed at court audiences, generally written anonymously) focused on a young, newly married fisherman and his wife. The fisherman is convinced that his wife is interested in him only for sex. She takes that as a grave insult, insisting that she loves him because he lavishes her with gifts. While the husband is out fishing, he comes across the corpse of a priest who had run from a jealous husband and drowned. Sensing an opportunity to trick his wife, the fisherman removes the corpse's penis and returns home. He shows it to his wife, saying he was attacked by a group of wives who castrated him. His wife declares, "I pray to God you soon will die! / Your body is the thing that I / now most hold in abomination." The husband then reveals his intact penis and claims that God has intervened to preserve his member. His wife is delighted and exclaims, "My darling husband, truest friend, / today you gave me such a fright! / Never since I first saw the light / of day has my heart known such pain!"[41] Her sinful nature is thereby revealed: she is interested only in sex, not in her husband's ability to provide for her.

Fabliaux such as this one may have been influenced by intellectual concepts of gender, given that they were aimed at elite readers who had the benefits of education. Yet the same themes played out throughout the medieval period ad nauseam. Chaucer's Wife of Bath picked up where the fisherman's wife left off, but with the benefit of a few centuries to consider the nature of women. Her character decides that it is time to put an end to the pretense that she and other women marry for any other reason than to obtain ready access to sex. On a quest to right this historical wrong, she regales the other pilgrims with tales of her several husbands, exclaiming:

> Blessed be God that I have wedded five!
> Of which I have picked out the best,
> Both of their nether purse [testicles] and of their strongbox.
> Diverse schools make perfect clerks,
> And diverse practice in many various works
> Makes the workman truly perfect;
> Of five husbands' schooling am I.
> Welcome the sixth, whenever he shall appear.
> For truly, I will not keep myself chaste in all.[42]

She still mentions that, as the fisherman's wife insisted, she is also interested in a man's wealth. However, through her entire and extended prologue (which is longer than the main text of her tale), her focus is on the pleasure that she takes in sex and the several marriages that she had to secure it.

The reason the prologue is long is that the fictional Wife is engaging in a defense of her five marriages to any would-be theologians. After all, using marriage to get sexual pleasure was theologically condemned. As a Frankish church council in 829 put it, "Marriage is ordained by God and should be sought not for the sake of lust, but rather for the sake of offspring. . . . Carnal connection . . . must take place for the sake of offspring, not pleasure."[43]

However, while the kinds of sex that could be had in marriage were limited, sex was still an obligatory part of the institution—a concept known as the marital or conjugal debt. The idea within a Christian context is based on Paul's first Letter to the Corinthians 7:3–4: "Let the husband pay the debt to his wife, and the wife also in like manner to the husband. The wife does not have power over her own body, but the husband; likewise, the husband does not have power over his own body, but the wife." Conjugal debt codified this exhortation to an expectation that any married person had the right to request sex from their partner provided that the request was "reasonable." As Aquinas put it, "In marriage there is a contract whereby one is bound to pay the other the marital debt: wherefore just as in other contracts, the bond is unfitting if a person bind himself to what he cannot give or do, so the marriage contract is unfitting, if it be made by one who cannot pay the marital debt."[44]

Whether a request was "reasonable" hinged on any number of factors, from a woman's likelihood of pregnancy from said sexual encounter, to the appropriateness of the day and time. It would not be "reasonable," for example, for a partner to demand sex while the woman was menstruating on a Sunday morning during Lent. Barring any reasonable theological or physiological impediments, however, spouses were completely within their rights to demand the sex that they were "owed" by the marriage contract.

A wife's inability to perform sexually and pay the conjugal debt to the satisfaction of her husband could well mean that she ended up divorced against her will. Having a small or injured vagina, being intersex with morphological variance, or experiencing painful sex causing trauma could all make entry sex either difficult or impossible. If a husband wished to secure a divorce for this reason, a panel of experienced medical matrons could be called on to examine his wife, and she could find herself divorced. This fate, of course, worried men very little.

Men were, however, greatly concerned about being unable to perform penis-in-vagina sex due to what we would call erectile disfunction—and women's ability to denounce them for it. In England, a man could be called before an expert witness who would test the ability of his genitals. In the later medieval period, that might mean a physician, as in the case of Jean Carré, an unlucky husband whose "incapacity" (*inhabilitas*) was affirmed by Masters Guibert de Serseto and Guillaume Boucher in fourteenth-century Paris.[45] When a medical professional could not be found, however, there was recourse to other expertise. In England, a jury of sex workers could be appointed to see whether a married man was unable to rise to the occasion. They would then report their findings to the court.

Such a pressurized situation might not be the most conducive to a man proving his ability to have sex with his wife, but that was not considered. After all, the pressure to perform under threat of divorce was present in any sexual encounter between spouses. Similarly, the fact that the sex workers who tested the man roundly scolded him afterward "for presuming to marry a young woman, defrauding her if he could not serve and please her better than that," was humiliating. Yet the average man could expect to hear much the same from a disappointed wife demanding her sexual appetite be satiated.[46] After all, women were not simply sex crazed but quarrelsome and given to scolding. A man who did not satisfy his wife could thus expect to hear about it.

A man might also worry that his wife took delight in his pain and humiliation and indeed was behind it. Constantine the African, in his chapter "On those Who Cannot Unite," wrote about malicious women who cast an evil spell, roasting beans over a fire, then placing them in their target's bed or near the entrance to their bedroom. The hardened bed beans apparently caused impotence, which "must be cured by divine aid rather than by men."[47]

Women interested in casting spells on men's penises, through beans or otherwise, were thought to be those who had been scorned by the men in question. In the thirteenth century, Thomas of Chobham noted that in Paris, a sorceress cast a spell over a man who had broken up with her, so that he wouldn't be able to have intercourse with the woman that he had left her to marry. She chanted a spell over a lock with a key in it, then threw the lock and key into two different wells. As a result, the man became impotent. Eventually the sorceress was confronted and admitted what she had done. The lock and key were then retrieved, and as soon as the lock was opened, the man was able to have sex with his wife.[48] The sexual desires of women even outside extant relationships were thus a threat to men's reputations and bodies.

Sexual Infidelity

Even a man whose penis was in "good working order" couldn't necessarily keep up with his wife's sexual desire. As a result, men were concerned that women would look outside marriage for sexual gratification. After all, as Boccaccio put it, "whereas a single cock is quite sufficient for ten hens, ten men are hard put to satisfy one woman."[49]

That women were, in general, both open and looking forward to cheating on their spouses was a matter of general conceit. The sexually rapacious woman was bound to seek out lovers where possible in order to assuage her appetites. This was often bound up in the medieval mind with women's perceived interest in their own looks. As we discussed previously, women's interest in finery and adornment was linked to their perceived lust. When they dressed themselves up or did their hair, they were presumably trying to attract sexual attention, more particularly extramarital interest. One spurned husband in the *Roman de la Rose* lamented this inarguable truth:

Is it for me that you amuse yourself?
Is it for me you lead so gay a life?
Who do you think that you're deceiving now?
I never thought to see such dressing up
As that with which you waken the desires
Of ribald lechers . . .

To dances and to church alike they wear
Their finery, which surely they'd not do
Did they not hope the men who see them there
Would thus be pleased—more quickly to be seduced.[50]

Little wonder, then, that concerned fathers warned their daughters against wearing makeup. If they wished to advertise their progeny as worthy marriage prospects, they would want to emphasize their chastity and lack of interest in sex outside the bounds of marriage. Best then to ensure that they did not adopt the latest fashion as well as the lustful intent that came along with it.

If men were concerned that the women in their lives were taking too much of an interest in their personal appearance, and therefore signaling their interest in unacceptable or extramarital sexual activity, they had a remedy: preachers suggested that men render their wives, sisters, and daughters unattractive to prevent them from leaving the house and undertaking affairs. The English preacher Odo of Cheriton (d. 1247), for example, advised that for attractive wives and daughters "every paterfamilias ought to knot up the hair of these women into a bun and scorch it. And he ought to dress them in skins rather than in precious garments. For then they will stay at home."[51] Inflict some casual abuse, and your female relatives would simply be too embarrassed to pursue the sex that they were so clearly desperate to have.

The fear of sex-crazed women was serious enough that it, at times, led to legislation. Bologna, starting in 1288, created laws against adultery. Men paid fines depending on their station in society and their wealth— either thirty or fifty pounds. Yet "an adulteress is condemned to pay one hundred pounds and in order to pay such a large amount it may be deducted from her dowry."[52]

Women's infidelity was a much larger concern than men's. Not only was no consideration given for a woman's background, but her punishment is twice that of a wealthy man. Moreover, the fine was to be taken directly from her dowry, the money that she brought into a marriage and that was generally earmarked for her own disposal.

Since women were more sexual than men, they needed the greater fine to ensure that they stayed on the straight and narrow. And since an unfaithful woman might bear a child that was not her husband's, her infidelity was an existential threat to the explicit point of marriage. Punishments like this high fee were seen as necessary to hammer home the seriousness of women's sexual profligacy, not only because women were lustful but also because marriage wasn't meant to be the sexiest institution going. Wealthy women and women of the noble classes, the group to whom such large fines would apply (lower-class women were not usually punished since they didn't have large dowries), were particularly suspected of interest in sex outside marriage for the same reasons that they had entered marriage in the first place.

For medieval Europeans, marriage was a familial institution and a religious sacrament, as we will see in Chapter 4. And because marriage largely existed to create children, it became an arrangement for the families involved to broker and contract.

The most extreme examples of bringing two families together were royal marriages, undertaken to secure alliances and to create heirs who would continue dynastic lines. The role of women as the bearers of children first and foremost and of marriage as the means to that end was especially upheld in royal and noble houses, whose wealth and power had to be secured so it could be passed down intergenerationally. In medieval Europe, marriages among powerful individuals had nothing to do with romance or love. They were business deals sealed through a religious sacrament.

Marriages had to be consummated sexually to cement the religious-business pact and potentially produce heirs. Sex in such a pressurized and transactional situation wasn't necessarily something that either spouse was excited about, though. If your parents had decided that this was the person you were going to have sex with to the exclusion of all others, you might not be thrilled either.

That isn't to say that people didn't have some choice in marriage. Indeed, prospective grooms and brides were both usually given a right of refusal; as we saw in Chapter 2, the Chevalier de La Tour Landry insisted that bridegrooms were turning down women for not keeping their gaze straight.[53] Still, marriage, especially among the upper classes, was not considered primarily a romantic institution. Instead, medieval people thought romance was to be found almost exclusively outside the marriages of the wealthy. That was where families were uninvolved and individual choice could come into play. Indeed, extramarital affairs were the backbone of one of the most popular and enduring genres of medieval literature: courtly love.

Courtly love as a form of literature focused on the romantic intrigues of, well, courts. As a genre, it held a mirror up to an extant form of romance in a rarefied society and helped to establish, affirm, and spread these ideals as a convention throughout medieval Europe. As an ideal, it might have belonged most properly in the homes of the powerful, but the literature that it produced was massively popular across social strata. Think about the way bodice rippers now often focus on lords and ladies in the past but are read by people who are not nobles, and you have a fairly good grasp of the idea.

Courtly love literature sought to record the romantic and sexual conditions of those at court. There the rich and relatively idle spent their days in splendor, surrounded by the huge retinues of the house. Any given royal or noble court supported great numbers of young people. Young women were employed as ladies-in-waiting or *domicellae*, better known to us now as damsels, and young men as squires and knights. The women's expected duties included carrying the lady of the house's train as she made her way to chapel and helping with embroidery. The men's might include being called to war or sent on diplomatic missions. For both sexes, their positions at court were a chance to establish their reputations and hopefully secure good marriages. The extraordinarily stylized manner in which the members of the court lived expressed the power and wealth they enjoyed. It also meant that a number of people milling about in close quarters might be interested in others more than in their current or prospective spouses.

The result was a form of romance that was almost exclusively focused on love affairs between married women and the unmarried men they lived alongside. Denizens of the court created an intricate form of romance with carefully delineated rules, infused with a healthy dose of the theological and philosophical concepts of gender that were carefully imparted to young courtiers through extensive and lavish private tuition. They couldn't just go around having affairs willy-nilly. There were formalities as to how they had to comport themselves and also who and how they could love. The best example comes to us from Andreas Capellanus, the twelfth-century chaplain who wrote *De amore* (*On Love*), presumably for the Countess Marie of Champagne (1145–98), daughter of Eleanor of Aquitaine (1122–1204). The work is an interesting one as it can be read as either a satire or in earnest. Which interpretation the author intended makes little difference to those of us interested in medieval sexual mores. Andreas might have been writing about a court world where stylized love was prevalent enough that a guide to it was required, or he might have been making fun of a culture that was prevalent enough that his readers understood the humor embedded in his guide. Either interpretation means that we are able to learn about a dominant romantic culture.

However, the possible humor of the guide is hinted at in the very name of the author. If Andreas was a chaplain, he was a clergy member, and so he should probably not have been the first person you went to for ideas about love. Andreas himself had no such qualms.

He assured his friend Walter, to whom the book was addressed (and who may or not have existed), that man of God or not, he "learned from experience" what he termed "the art of love."[54] After all, "the life of the clergy is, because of the continual idleness and the great abundance of food, naturally more liable to temptations of the body," and so apparently Andreas managed to pick up a thing or two about love along the way.

The guide was a set of rules and vignettes, not unlike the pick-up artist manuals of our own time, that explained to men how to court women. Andreas first instructs his audience that love is "a suffering derived from the sight of and excessive meditation upon the beauty of the opposite sex, which causes each one to wish above all things the embraces of the other." He then explains the various types of love that are possible and who is capable of enjoying them, that is, heterosexual relationships, in which "love is always either decreasing or increasing," between people with money as "poverty has nothing with which to feed its love." The peasantry instead should simply copulate "like a horse or a mule." So far, so classy.[55]

Andreas, consummate gentleman of the clergy that he was, also sets time limitations on lovers that prevent love after sixty for men and fifty for women "because at that age the natural heat begins to lose its force, and the natural moisture is greatly increased." He specified that boys could not love until after their fourteenth year, and girls their twelfth, as they had not settled into maturity. This romantic love is specifically for the able-bodied, with the blind excluded as they cannot see their lovers. Similarly, one should not love nuns, though male clergy members such as himself can take on the challenge; nor should one love sex workers, for "a woman who you know wants money in return for her love should be looked upon as a deadly enemy."[56]

But Andreas does more than set out boundaries; he also tells readers how to court. He imagines various dialogues between a pursuant man and a pursued woman, specifying how best to flatter women of various classes in combination with men of various classes: the middle class, the nobility, and the higher nobility. In every case, men control the situation, and the women they are pursuing respond in predictable ways. The trick is for a man to pitch his flattery in the right manner based on the power imbalance, to ensure that the targeted woman will grant him her love and her "embraces." For a man imprudent enough to be stirred by the sight of a peasant girl, Andreas (who considered peasants almost subhuman) disturbingly advises the man to "not hesitate to take what [he] seeks and to embrace them by force." In this way, Andreas gives his approval to rape.[57]

Besides being a seduction guide, Andreas dealt with the setting by imagining a series of "Courts of Love" overseen by Eleanor of Aquitaine and her daughters. While we don't know if the queen and her family ever oversaw such courts, we know that by the fourteenth century, Andreas's work was being used as a guide in the Court of Love in Barcelona, which was overseen by Juan I of Aragon (1350–96) and his wife Violant of Bar (ca. 1365–1431). Because numerous copies of On Love survived into the fifteenth century, many after them used Andreas's guide to while away the hours and pronounce on exactly who should be having sex with whom.[58]

Love courts, in practice and in theory, might lead to a number of romantic issues. On Love advised what a knight wooing a woman should do if she fell in love with the messenger rather than himself (shun both her and the messenger from polite company); whether a love affair can continue if it is discovered that the lovers are related (it can't, although the woman involved might want it to); and whether a woman should take back her lover when he lies to her and says he wants to see another woman as a test of her devotion (she should despair when he says he is leaving her and welcome him back when he reveals the ruse).

Of particular interest to us is case seventeen, in which a knight is in love with a woman who is in love with another man. The woman tells the knight that "if it should ever happen that she lost the love of her beloved, then without a doubt her love would go to" the knight. Soon afterward the woman and the man she loves marry. The knight maintains that she should now love him, since she is not supposed to be in love with her husband. She rejects his logic and him. Eleanor of Aquitaine allegedly weighed in to say that "love can exert no power between husband and wife. Therefore, we recommend that the lady should grant the love she has promised."[59]

There is no clearer indication of the nature of marriage in the highest echelons of medieval European society. Even if someone was lucky enough to marry for love, the institution of marriage itself would annul the emotional bond that drove them toward the religious and legal one. What was more, love could be compelled from a woman. Her desires were no matter, as she could not be trusted to bestow her love on the right person. Instead, she could be pointed at the correct man and was malleable enough to go with the appropriate lover. If she was foolish enough to think her love would and could continue after marriage, luckily she had the court to set her right.

Indeed, in all the model cases in the guide, women seldom are allowed to decide on the objects of their love. A rare example is case eleven, wherein a woman is allowed to choose "whether she will listen to the good man or the better one" when her love is sought by a "good and prudent man" followed immediately by one "still more worthy."[60] In all other cases, the love and sexual attention of the women is treated as something that can be assigned without their input, and something that *must* be assigned outside their marriages.

Throughout Andreas's imagined dialogues and court cases, one thread is clear: women are sexualized pawns, with very little to say for themselves. He stresses repeatedly that they must freely grant their love to their suitors, and he assures his friend that they will freely provide that love (and the subsequent desired sex) provided that the men who approach them use the correct formula. Women at court are algorithms, responding in a regulated way to proffered inputs. They are so sexual and so feeble intellectually that they will fall for whichever man flatters them in the right way, as an escape from their dull duties to their husbands.

Even after writing a book about seduction and its rules, Andreas insists that men should eschew courtly love and extramarital sex for their own benefit and that of the simple sexual women they would entice. He reminds his male readers that "not only does love cause men to lose their celestial heritage, but it even deprives them of all honor in this world." While men may enjoy themselves at the time, they and the women they target stand to lose their reputation if it is found that they have "given [their] love to anyone." The men must take control and resist the temptation to seduce women who are unable to "restrain [their] passion like a man."[61] Men are ultimately the keepers of women's chastity. They either restrain themselves and refuse to offer up praise and presents, staving off sex, or they engage with women in romance, and both they and their targets inevitably fall.

Overall, Andreas advises his male reader that "every woman in the world is . . . wanton, because no woman, no matter how famous or honored she is, will refuse her embraces to any man, even the most vile and abject," who is good at romancing her.[62] Still, he is going to end up unhappy since she will always remain unsatisfied, for that is the nature of women, and she will leave him for someone else since she is inconstant. The same ideas fill the pages of every major courtly love work after it, such as the Arthurian legends and *Tristan and Iseult*. In *Guigemar*, a Breton *lai* or romantic narrative poem by Marie de France (ca. 1160–1215), the plot revolves around the eponymous hero's love for a married woman who has been imprisoned by her husband out of jealousy. Consummation of their adulterous love results in a harsher imprisonment for the lady, as well as a war, with terrible casualties on both sides, after she manages to escape her husband but is captured by yet another amorous lord. Even in Chaucer's *Troilus and Criseyde*, where the woman is not married, she is still inconstant. Criseyde betrays Troilus's trust, electing not to elope with him after consummating their relationship. She instead decides that she will be courted by Diomede.

In some courtly love works, the women are constant in comparison to the men, such as Marie de France's *Eliduc*, a *lai* in which the titular hero has a faithful wife at home and a new lover across the English Channel. However, examples of faithful women are few enough that they serve more as exceptions than as a robust argument for the constancy of women's love.

To say that women are unfaithful in works of courtly love is an understatement. While courtly love literature might have been written to reflect the circumstances of an elevated part of society, it did not stay within those circles. The stories spread throughout society, with some changing as they were recopied by various scribes, then were performed as songs or poems to eager audiences. As a result, the same attitude toward women crops up in less elegant literature. The thoughts on display in Chaucer's highbrow *Troilus and Criseyde*, for example, replay throughout his bawdy *Canterbury Tales*. Unfaithful wives form the backbone of "The Miller's Tale," "The Merchant's Tale," and "The Shipman's Tale," and are alluded to in "The Cook's Tale" (an unfinished fragment about the exploits of a wife who makes a living as a sex worker). Even among commoners, women were depicted as undertaking marriage not for love but for safety and maybe sex.

The literature that survives stands alongside the scientific and theological complaints of the period to give us a consistent picture of the average woman as an unintelligent creature driven more by her sexual desires than by intelligence or spiritual fervor. Smart men, then, guarded their daughters and their wives alike. Preserving women's purity was a job for a level-headed, logical, and faithful man. Women simply couldn't be trusted to do it themselves and would wind up imperiling their marriage prospects, their marriages, and their immortal souls as a result.

Men guarded women not simply for the women's sake but also to ensure their own reputation. A man kept an eye on his daughter so he could trade her for maximum value into a marriage that would meet neither her sexual needs nor her interest. And he kept watch over his wife to ensure that his honor and reputation were upheld and that any children were his own. Ultimately, the sexual behavior of women was about the men in their life.

Sexual Pleasure

Worries about women's sexuality and procreation did not begin and end outside the bonds of marriage, however. The tension around women's sexuality was always high. The two-seed theory (see page 102) had introduced a conundrum: if a woman's and a man's seed were both necessary for conception during sex, then the woman had to experience orgasm in order to release her seed, just as men did. This is not a difficult problem to solve from a theological standpoint. A couple would simply have the necessary penis-in-vagina sex, everyone would orgasm, and voilà—baby. In a divinely ordered world where the only reason sex existed was to respond to the desires of God, then the orgasms necessary for procreation would simply appear.

Then as now, however, penis-in-vagina sex in no way guaranteed that a woman would orgasm, no matter how much Thomas Aquinas wanted it to be true. As Avicenna noted, "women's pleasure" had to be considered as a factor in reproduction, because "when the woman does not emit any sperm, conception does not take place."[63]

From a modern perspective, one straightforward answer to this conundrum is clitoral stimulation. But in the medieval context this was much trickier, because the clitoris had yet to make its debut as even an observed part of the vulva. Partially, this oversight seems to have come from the concept of the female body as an inversion of the male (see Chapter 2).

To be fair, human genitals are remarkably similar. Ovaries are more or less analogous to testicles. However, in their desire to identify reproductive organs as perfect mirrors of each other, ancient and medieval physicians incorrectly identified the womb "as the penis turned around" and the vagina as the "neck hollow within as the penis." Instead, it is the clitoris that is analogous to the penis. Both the clitoris and the penis have a glans; both are made of spongy tissue and harden when blood is trapped within them during arousal; and both have a skin covering that protects them from becoming sore. The major differences between the clitoris and the penis are that the clitoris lacks a urethra and that penises, in general, protrude farther than clitorises.

As the sex educator Justin Hancock notes, "there aren't analogous body parts for everyone (and we don't want to replace one ideology with another), but there are more similarities than people think and the differences aren't always to do with gender or binary notions of sex."[64] The desire to find an exact mirror image of one body in another led to the state of confusion surrounding the most sensitive sexual organs up until the modern period. However, given the generalized similarities that are observable, some of the medieval confusion around the function of the clitoris is understandable.

The inability of medieval physicians to identify what a clitoris does was not particularly surprising given their context. First, they were trained to take the word of classical thinkers such as Galen seriously. They could add to Galen's knowledge, but to question his authority was an impossibility. Moreover, in a Christian context, the body was seen as a divine design wherein each part had a dedicated role to play. With sexual pleasure explicitly linked to sin and the Fall of Man, the very idea that a part of the body could exist for the sole purpose of sexual arousal was unthinkable. God would never deign to create something that was there just to make sex a bit more fun. During this time, anatomical descriptions are devoid of observations about how bodies actually work.

Yet observers could see that women seemed to really like it if you rubbed them there. In the thirteenth and fourteenth centuries, Pietro d'Abano (ca. 1257–1315), a professor of medicine at the celebrated University of Padua, noted in his *Conciliator* that women were sexually aroused "by having the upper orifice near their pubis rubbed; in this way the indiscreet, or curious [*curiosi*] bring them to orgasm. For the pleasure that can be obtained from this part of the body is comparable to that obtained from the tip of the penis."[65] When medical thinkers employed observation, they were entirely able to identify the orgasmic potential of the clitoris.

Pietro's accurate account of the usefulness of the clitoris for some women does not wholly recommend the practice. Labeling those who rely on pubic stimulation to achieve orgasm as "the indiscreet" or perhaps "the curious" was likely a condemnation of the practice. In an ideal world, women would be orgasming through penetration alone. Curiosity about anything beyond procreative activity was unseemly and was even linked to the curiosity that drove Eve to bring about the Fall of Man. Medical authorities saw that clitoral stimulation (or more precisely, pubis stimulation) was efficacious in arousing women, but they usually left it simply as a technique for arousal, then moved on to the appropriate intercourse.

Avicenna advocated just this method, telling his audiences that "men . . . should caress [women's] breasts and pubis, and enfold their partners in their arms, without really performing the act." Only after women's desire was aroused in this manner should men consider penetrative sex. While Avicenna might have understood that women enjoy clitoral stimulation, he was as likely to state that problems for women during sex were linked to small penises that were "often a hindrance to climax and emission in the woman."[66] The finest medical minds of several centuries might have been able to identify what women find pleasurable, but they also sought immediately to return to conversations about how to have acceptable, procreative sex.

Most medieval discussions of the clitoris were written by men, largely for an audience of other men. In this context, discussions of orgasm and how women experience it are entirely focused on the ends that men require: progeny. They are not about sex for pleasure but about how to elicit a specific bodily response. Hence we can understand why the clitoris would be overlooked in medical manuals, because the only time anyone really needed to consider what women experienced during sex was as a medical hurdle to be overcome. Orgasms existed to make babies, and you needed to start worrying about that only when the babies didn't arrive. Until that point, why consider how a woman might orgasm at all?

The theory that orgasm is required for conception has truly disturbing and dehumanizing aspects. When it came to women making their livelihoods as sex workers (about whom we will speak more in Chapter 4), it was often said that they could not become pregnant.[67] That idea had a doubly deleterious influence for the women in question. First, it encouraged men to not consider the paternal implications of penis-in-vagina sex with the women they hired. Second, it classed sex workers as individuals outside the bonds of ordinary sex. Incapable of pleasure and driven solely by an interest in money, such women could safely be ignored, as they had jettisoned even the grasping lustfulness of the usual woman.

Medieval thinkers admitted that in some rare cases, sex workers did manage to find love with a man. In these cases, romantic love was said to rekindle her sexual interest and therefore her ability to procreate. Still, the women in question were wholly sidelined. They are passive sexual beings, waiting either for money from their clients or for romantic solace from any man who deigns to have them and let them once again become "real" women, a state determined by their ability to have children.

Equally distressing were the implications for victims of rape that orgasm was required for pregnancy. Rape was largely thought of as a property dispute between men, with the aggrieved party being the man who lawfully held the woman in question as a part of his house. The wronged party could therefore be a father (or other male family member) or a husband. With this understanding, for rape to be made right, the woman must simply be returned to the man whose authority she is designated under, be that her father or fiancé, and "pay the price of her purity," which is to say a fine to the man in question.[68] This concept makes the very definition of rape malleable. Aquinas does not differentiate, for example, between an unmarried woman who is taken from her parents' house and forcibly raped, or a woman who is taken from her parents' house and subsequently decides to have what we term consensual sex, and what Aquinas calls the "act of fornication." Further, if a woman is taken from her parents' house and decides to marry her abductor without the consent of her parents, that too is rape.[69] The key to the definition is the consent of the man who is perceived as controlling the woman in question.

Medieval thinkers generally agreed that rape was a grave crime and that women who were attacked could not have pleasure from the sex act. However, women who had been attacked, and were by all discernible means greatly distressed, sometimes became pregnant. The philosopher William of Conches (ca.1090–1155/70) came up with an explanation for why pregnancy could happen: "although raped women dislike the act in the beginning, in the end, however, from the weakness of the flesh, they like it."[70] In other words, if a woman became pregnant following her rape, it meant she had ultimately enjoyed herself.

This sneering approach to the distress of women certainly has roots in the general concept of humans as sinful creatures driven by base instincts, the hallmark of Christianity as a whole. It also speaks to the fact that women were understood to be much more prone to such weakness than were men. Attributing "pleasure" to a woman during sex could as easily be turned into a tool to shame her after a traumatic event, as it could be used to encourage loving men to consider the needs of their partners during sex.

All of this speculation about women orgasming, and their ability to do so outside the bounds of what both the Church and medical practitioners considered "normal," left women's real sexual preferences up for scrutiny. It was all well and good for medical professionals such as Avicenna to advise methods by which to make orgasm more likely. But from a theological stance, such interests were dubious at best. At what point did couples kiss to prepare for acceptable marital sex, and at what point did they trip into "lasciviousness"?

Sexual Health

The disordered passion of women could spell health problems further down the road—both for the women and the men who engaged in sex with them. A matter of great curiosity for medieval people was that women seemed interested in sex even when they had their periods. Here was proof of women's lustful nature, as no other animal attempted to have sex when a resulting pregnancy was impossible. Considered sodomy, as previously mentioned, and thus a sin, sex during menstruation was, at the very least, "illogical" to Aquinas, who enjoyed categorizing things. Beyond sin, men who were fooled into having sex with menstruating women had to consider that they were opening themselves up to one of the most dreaded medieval diseases, leprosy.

Leprosy is a bacterial infection caused by *Mycobacterium leprae* or *Mycobacterium lepromatosis*. It is a treatable condition, but without medical intervention it can lead to extensive damage to the skin, eyes, respiratory system, and nerves. It is first recorded as having occurred in Alexandria in the third century B.C.E., and you may have seen its cameo appearances in the Bible. Leprosy was endemic across medieval Europe, and in a world without antibiotics, its effects were often quite debilitating. The rashes that it causes can make sufferers more susceptible to secondary bacterial and viral infections that sometimes lead to loss of limbs. Medieval people lived in fear of contracting this difficult and painful condition, which was thought to be highly contagious. Those with leprosy were often separated from the general community and forced to live in what were called lazar houses, which wealthy people funded as a sign of their piety.

People with leprosy were targets simultaneously of pity and disgust. Many healthy people were moved by their obvious pain and distress. Those with the disease survived through a combination of charitable donations and begging. On the other hand, leprosy was often linked to sinfulness. The Dominican minster-general Humber of Romans (ca. 1194–1277) offers us a glimpse at the poor regard in which people with leprosy were held: "They blaspheme God like persons in Hell . . . they fight among themselves . . . [and] putting aside any rein on the fires of their desire they abandon themselves to lust and filthy behavior."[71]

The identification of people with leprosy as being particularly horny seems to be linked to the idea that leprosy was contracted through sexual contact with a woman suffering with leprosy, or even one who had her period. In either case, men could get leprosy, and it would doom a child as "from the seed corrupted fetus is born."[72]

The authors of these texts might have used the term *leprosy* to speak about what we would deem sexually transmitted infections like herpes or gonorrhea. Leprosy was so firmly linked to sexual profligacy and had such an outsized place in medieval fears that it made sense, from their perspective, to categorize these infections together.

The risk of contracting leprosy from sex with a menstruating woman was linked to ideas about menstruation itself. In Galenic theory, menstrual blood provided nourishment for embryos. The tenth-century Persian Galenist 'Ali ibn al-'Abbas al-Majusi (d. ca. 982) argued that menstrual blood formed "the liver and the other fleshy parts, with the exception of the heart," which was formed by arterial blood.[73] If a woman was not pregnant, however, menstrual blood built up as a malign humor. Being cold and wet, they were forced to expel it.

Menstruation, then, was a natural bloodletting, wherein women's bodies rid themselves of the excess blood that would otherwise corrupt them. The tainted nature of menstrual blood was thought to be what led to leprosy through sexual contact. It also allegedly caused a whole host of ills, including wilting crops, dulling mirrors, and even in extreme circumstances killing people either through contact with the blood, or merely through the gaze of the menstruating woman.

Poisonous though menstrual blood assuredly was, even more worrisome were women who had ceased to menstruate. Women in menopause were not seen as having overcome the humoral imbalance that necessitated menstruation. Instead, it was thought, the malign blood was now building up inside them, because they were too cold and wet to burn off its excess. As a result, they were so corrupted by poison that they might kill children in the cradle with a glance. If someone was depraved enough to have sex with a postmenopausal woman, for whom pregnancy was impossible, they risked disease and sudden death even as they risked their soul for committing sodomy.

William of Conches, one of the most widely read medieval medical authorities, took it upon himself to answer one of the great questions about sex and leprosy: "Why is it that if a leper lies with a woman she is not infected, and yet the next man to lie with her becomes a leper?" He credits it to the fact that "the warmest woman is colder than the coldest man. Such a complexion is harsh and resists corruption. . . . Nevertheless the putrid matter, coming from the coition with the leper remains in the womb. So when a [second] man enters her his male member . . . by virtue of its attractive force, draws the corruption to it and transmits it to the parts adjoining."[74]

Here the nature of women is being debated on a number of levels. Their cold and wet nature leads their wombs to build up toxins that can spread leprosy during sex. They can even kill with a glance if they can no longer expel their toxins. This same cold and wet nature also means that they are impervious to contagion themselves. After all, they are able to build up putrid menstrual blood without it giving *them* leprosy, so it stands to reason that they are also impervious to leprosy if it is transmitted to them sexually.

Luckily for men who contracted leprosy because of the sexual wiles of women, there were, in theory, some medical ways to prevent infection. John of Gaddesden (ca. 1280–1361) recommended that whether exposed to menstrual blood or leprosy, "if you wish to preserve your organ from all harm, should you suspect your partner of being corrupted, purify yourself, as soon as you have withdrawn, with cold water in which you have mixed vinegar, or with urine."[75] Most medieval thinkers agreed that the best way to avoid leprosy was to abstain from sex, but men might find it impossible to resist the siren song of the lustful women who preyed upon them.

While men were given ways to improve their chances against leprosy, I haven't found any medical advice for prevention designed for women. Recipes for helping women prepare medications to deal with genital lesions and pustules take their place. In the *Trotula* are two recipes for medicines, called Hieralogodian and Theriac, that boast that they can "bring on the menses" and improve "leprous lesions."[76] Such recipes hint at the connections between the dangers of retained menstrual blood and leprosy, though both also claim to cure a range of ailments including retention of black bile, migraines, and in the case of Hieralogodian, demonic possession.

The matter-of-fact way the *Trotula* refers to the treatment of leprosy's symptoms seems to indicate that the individuals who compiled these sections sensed that women would inevitably get the disease. Since the process of aging could bring it on naturally, odds were that women might need to know how to treat the symptoms. Luckily, the same ointment used to treat women's migraine could be used against leprosy. Women seem on some level to have accepted the medical warnings about them as carriers of leprosy, and they responded by resolving to do their best and make do when they were afflicted.

If sexual contact with women was considered medically risky, women who *did not* have sex could also suffer from resulting maladies. From the high Middle Ages on, physicians warned of the scourge of *suffocatio* or *prefocatio matricis,* a "suffocation" of the womb. According to the *Trotula,* it could manifest as loss of appetite, fainting, low pulse, contractions that resulted in doubling over, loss of vision or voice, and jaw grinding, among other issues.[77] A worrisome condition with a number of uncomfortable symptoms, *suffocatio* afflicted women in general but especially widows who were used to having sex regularly but then subsequently lost their partners, as well as virgins who were old enough to marry but had not yet done so.

Constantine the African noted that widows and virgins suffered this malady because their wombs were being suffocated by an "abundance of sperm or its corruption . . . [which] occurs when women are deprived of union with a man." This excessive sperm would putrefy into a poison that turned into a smoke and rose to the diaphragm, suffocating the uterus.[78] The best cure for the disease was for women to find an acceptable sexual outlet or, as John of Gaddesden prescribed, to get married.

Suffocation of the womb is of note because it meant that women who were sexually inactive lacked immunity to their own sperm. The venomous qualities of sexually active women turned inward if women lacked a sexual outlet. Either way, at their core, women were thought of as poisonous beings.

Some women were not married, such as maidens, women who took religious vows, and widows who refused remarriage. They all potentially suffered from suffocated wombs, but medical solutions were available. The *Trotula* recommended that women anoint their vaginas internally and externally with warm, sweet-scented oils and ointments, which should bring on menses. Failing that, they could apply cupping glasses to the pubic area. Alternatively, they could consume a powdered fox's or roebuck's penis internally, by means of a pessary.[79] John of Gaddesden instructed that midwives should coat their fingers with the oil of lilies, laurel, or spikenard, then insert them into the sufferer's womb and vigorously shake them around.[80]

These medical interventions look suspiciously like what you and I might call fingering. We are not alone in this supposition, as the medical luminary Albertus Magnus addressed that concern in *Commentary on the Sentences,* saying, "the hand which defiles leads to flabbiness or sodomy, but the hand that cures does not. . . . The hand does not defile nor corrupt these women, but rather cures them."[81] Because of the way women were built, it was sometimes medically necessary to masturbate them, and it was imperative to draw a distinction between medical intervention and sodomy. It was much better that women receive disinterested intervention, lest they turn to *actual* sodomy with each other or "the solitary vice" of masturbation.

Solo Sexuality

The overtly sexual nature of women, and the perceived health risks posed by abstinence, gave rise to a fear that women might at any moment have sex with themselves. Albertus Magnus considered that pubescent girls in particular could suffer from such agitations and would fantasize about men and their genitalia "and often rub themselves strongly with their fingers or with other instruments until, the vessels having been relaxed through the heat of rubbing and coitus, the spermatic humor exits . . . and then their groins are rendered temperate and then they become more chaste."[82] Physicians then seem to have approached masturbation, at least among young women, as a response to a medical issue and bodily necessity. The young women behaved much as a medical professional would in order to ease the discomfort of excess sperm. Albertus's response is largely clinical, giving a medical version of "girls will be girls" to the question of solo sex. If women were sexual beings who medically required the release of sperm, it was understandable, if not laudable, that they would do so in a pinch.

Theologians, on the other hand were not so quick to excuse profligate sexual activity. Many felt it necessary to curb the twinned scourges of what we would call masturbation and lesbian sex. The medieval mind, especially when pondering the sexuality of women, usually linked partnered sex and solo sex. In the eighth century Bishop Theodore of Tarsus (602–90) recorded in *Penitential of Theodore* that:

12. If a woman practices vice with a woman, she shall do penance for three years.
13. If she practices solitary vice, she shall do penance for the same period.
14. The penance of a widow and a girl is the same. She who has a husband deserves a greater penalty if she commits fornication.[83]

Theodore didn't distinguish between women having sex with each other and women having sex alone, but he did gauge that such sins were more serious if a woman who had the acceptable sexual outlet of a husband chose to neglect him in favor of illicit activity.

Similarly, Burchard of Worms in *Decretum* nudged priests to ask the women who came to confession if they used a strap-on to have sex with another woman or if one was used on them. The punishment? "Penance for five years on legitimate holy days." And women who masturbated had to do penance for "one year on legitimate holy days."[84] Burchard saw a clear link between two women having sex and women having sex with themselves, but sex with another woman carried a higher penance, indicating that it was more sinful.

The grouping of lesbian sex and masturbation seems to have been born from the idea that both activities arose from women being oversexed and lacking a marital outlet for their desires. But sex between women or by themselves simply didn't "count" the way sex with a man did. Many theological arguments framed lesbian sex as a question of the misuse of objects for the pursuit of sexual pleasure. Hincmar of Reims (806–82) was alarmed by the insertion of objects as a substitute for a penis.[85] Here even though a woman had a partner, such sex was considered masturbatory and a sin against "one's own body."

Understanding solo or lesbian sex was difficult within a system in which a heterosexual couple doing the missionary position was the definition of sex. Even Albertus Magnus, who wrote more of "rubbing" than insertion when discussing women masturbating, insisted that during the act, the girls in question "imagine men's private parts." The implication was that, given the opportunity, women would always prefer to have sex with a man, but in a crisis, they would make do. Whether that meant alone or with another woman was up for interpretation.

Sexual Magic

While women's overt sexual nature was in turns a danger to the institution of marriage, a danger to the health of men, a danger to women's own health if bottled up, some worried that women's sexual preoccupations could cause them to turn to the occult. Buchard instructed priests to ask women whether, to increase their husband's passion, they "take a live fish and put it in their vagina, keeping it there for a while until it is dead. Then they cook or roast it and give it to their husbands to eat." This time the woman was supposed to "do two years of penance on the appointed fast days."[86]

To be honest, the likelihood that medieval women inserted live fish into their vaginas and then fed them to their husbands was probably low. It cannot be ruled out, but all in all it seems unlikely, no matter how lacking their sex lives might have been. However, actual practice mattered less than the fact that Burchard found such behavior plausible and enough of a worry that he advised clergy members to interrogate female parishioners about it. The idea that women were horny enough to suffocate a fish in their genitals if it meant more and better sex was one thing. It was another that they were willing to do occult magic and endanger their soul.

Theologians were concerned about attempts to meddle with the phenomenal universe through the application of magic. In general, they thought someone who tampered with the theoretical divine/ natural order of the world must have done it by demonic means. They regarded plenty of magic natural (such as electric eels or magnets), but they had to consider how a magic spell worked and wrote long and scholastic arguments about whether it could be achieved through angelic intercession. Sweeping changes through divine intervention were miraculous in nature and would not happen as a result of spells. But if the nature of reality were changed to aid sex, then women were likely meddling with demonic powers. These women's sexuality endangered their souls and theoretically those of the people in their communities as well. After all, the forces of hell, much like women, were seldom satisfied.

Burchard worried that demonic practices could leak to the rest of the community. Women were naturally prone to gossip and lascivious talk, and given their outsize interest in sex, and the evil influence behind spells involving sex, surely women would share such information. Women had to learn about the beans that prevented erections, or how to promote love through unorthodox recipes for fish from somewhere.

Even beyond their concerns about casting spells, theologians sensed that women's sexuality was demonic in quality. They frequently accused women of enchanting or bewitching men with their sexuality. One Franciscan saint, Gerard Cagnoli (ca. 1267–1342), boasted several miracles that led to his posthumous canonization. One was his ability to exorcise lust from men who had become "occupied with an accursed woman." A mother once told him that her twenty-one-year-old son had "been bewitched and taken away by a woman who ha[d] been unfaithful to her husband." She begged him to intervene and swore she would walk barefoot on pilgrimage to Pisa if God freed her son from what she characterized as the "snares of the Devil."[87] Long story short, Gerard came through, and the son was able to overcome the lust of the enchanting woman.

Similarly, in the north of the continent, Saint Bridget of Sweden (ca. 1303–1373) was called to intercede when a priest fell under a sorceress's spell and "burned with carnal temptation like a fire, so that he could think of nothing except foul carnal thoughts." He beseeched Bridget to make him resist her. Bridget prayed for the priest, and the happy ending to the story is that the sexy sorceress "took a knife and cut her own groin with it, and shouted to all who were listening, 'Come my Devil, and follow me.' And thus, with such a horrible cry she put an end to her life in a wretched way."[88]

In both of these instances, the power to enervate men's minds, and in one case to alter the course of his life to sin, came from the devil, but women's sexuality was the intermediary. In both cases, there is no concern for the women who, in theory, might also have been poisoned by demonic forces. Instead, intervention and concern are reserved for the "victims"—the men who were sexually bewitched by them. No one cared whether the women in these stories were later able to turn their lives around. In the Swedish case, the woman's grisly death was celebrated. The message was clear: women's sexuality was a demonic force against which men had to invoke God's protection. Men were not responsible for their obsessions or demonic possessions. Women were. They invited their own damnation and inflicted it on fully grown men who apparently still needed their mothers' protection.

In the late fifteenth century, concerns about women's occult interests and demonic sexuality came to a head. The witch hunter's manual, the *Malleus Malificarum,* or *Hammer of Witches,* centered on such fears. Written by at least one concerned Church inquisitor, Heinrich Kramer (ca. 1430–1505), the *Malleus* was meant as an argument that witchcraft existed as well as a guide on how to stop it.[89] If the *Malleus's* readers wondered why such a document was needed, it had a handy answer for them—women's sexuality.

The *Malleus* contains a chapter entitled "Concerning Witches who copulate with Devils. Why it is that Women are chiefly addicted to Evil Superstitions."[90] It presents manifold reasons for that addiction, in a parade of the typical medieval concepts of women: they were credulous, "impressionable," bearing "slippery tongues," unable to hide the dark magic they knew from each other; "and since they are weak, they find an easy and secret manner of vindicating themselves by witchcraft. . . . To conclude. All witchcraft comes from carnal lust, which is in women insatiable."[91] Women had any number of faults, but the primary one was their lustfulness, as it meant they were ripe for seduction by the devil and thus were conduits for demonic magic.

According to the *Malleus,* witches gained their powers through demonic pacts with the devil that were consummated through sex. The witches then went on to perform magical spells that often dealt with having sex, preventing sex, or preventing procreation when they became jealous because men they desired were having sex with other women. The *Malleus* considered such important points as whether witches could prevent generation or obstruct sex from happening; whether the witches who were midwives performed abortions or offered newborn children to devils; and whether witches could work illusions that would make it seem as though men's penises were no longer attached to their bodies.

This latter spell affected only the man, making it seem as if he had been castrated. Everyone else would be able to see that the man in question had a penis, but he wouldn't be able to see or use it.

Meanwhile the illusory missing penis would appear elsewhere, to the delight of witches who "sometimes collect male organs in great numbers together, and put them in a bird's nest, or shut them up in a box, where they move themselves like living members and eat oats and corn."[92] The spell worked through the power of illusion, but it was potent enough that distraught men allegedly turned to the Church for counsel and dropped their trousers when they couldn't find their penises.

The *Malleus* followed up with witches preventing erections, which they could do because sex was the source of sinfulness.[93] Witches' ability in this area hints at the general tension around sex in the medieval and early modern mind. Theologians had agreed that sex was allowed when performed in the appropriate context so that the human species could continue. Even then, having sex was problematic. The ideal Christian would forsake sex altogether, so God didn't mind allowing a little light sexual frustration from time to time, to hammer home the point.

Worse than stolen penises and frustrated erections, the *Malleus* warned that witches, no matter their age, slaked their lust with each other and with the powerful and well-connected. Having seduced lawmakers and even churchmen, they would be able to command them to shield them from harm or to elevate their standing in society. From these secret, sexual political alliances arose "the great danger of the time, namely, the extermination of the Faith."[94] Women's sexuality was not just excessive or unpleasant. It was a supernatural threat to the very fabric of Christendom and any hope for fair rule.

If all this seems overwrought to us now, the first readers of the *Malleus* agreed with us. They largely laughed at it. Indeed, Kramer's insistence in the introduction that witches existed and that that was a Catholic tenet indicates the fact that such a case had to be made.[95] It wasn't that medieval people didn't believe women were engaging in magic, as Burchard's *Decretum* shows. Rather, the type of magic that women got up to subtly shifted.

In the ninth century, Burchard attempted to dissuade women from believing in the idea of the night flight of witches and that witches participated in ritual *sabbats*—midnight meetings with demons and each other. Kramer, in contrast, argued explicitly that "it is shown in various ways that they [witches] can be bodily transported."[96] The *Malleus* therefore asked readers to consider that women were capable of magical acts like flying; and rather than picking up magical practices here and there because of their nature and through gossip, they were making clear choices to enter sexual pacts with the devil. In other words, medieval people believed that women were prone to magical intervention and were using it for sexual purposes. The differences between Burchard and Kramer were in what they saw as the scope of the problem and the veracity of individual stories told about such women.

For most of Kramer's contemporaries, this shift to seeing witches everywhere was rather too much to concede. In 1484 the industrious inquisitor was prosecuting witchcraft cases in the Tyrol region and losing them. Frustrated with his antics, the local bishop asked him to leave Innsbruck, as he was causing a scene. Kramer was facing legal troubles and accusations that he had brought Helena Scheuberin, one of his accused, to trial because he was obsessed with her sex life. When he composed his magnum opus three years later, some perceived it as an apologia for his failed prosecutions and an attempt to save face. At its first publication, most of those who read the *Malleus* considered it ridiculous and its assertions unprovable. However, Kramer continued to argue his case, and the book slowly gained popularity.

By the second half of the sixteenth century, the qualms that Kramer's contemporaries held had faded away. Now the book seemed to hold gravitas, given its longevity and wide circulation, and the unfortunate exploits of its author had faded into the past. A new class of would-be witch hunters accepted it and used it in what would become the witch panics of the seventeenth century. While the *Malleus* was one of the most comprehensive works to discuss the dangers of women, witchcraft, and sexuality, it built on some thousand years of thinking about sexuality more broadly and women's sexuality in particular. The idea that women were practicing magic combined with specific sexual undertones was a general medieval theme. What the *Malleus* did differently was to put a modern gloss on the medieval conceit. It advised that the sexual magic of women was *organized*. Witches knowingly worked directly with demons and flew together to strange sexual *sabbats*. They were a collective that had to be stopped by the full Church rather than by individual intervention during confession.

The other modern aspect that the *Malleus* and later witch hunters introduced was the idea that this magic had to be met with physical violence. Among the remedies for witchcraft the guide recommends applying to a woman is "winding a towel tightly around her neck, and chock[ing] her" until "her face [is] swelling and growing black."[97] Apparently such violence compelled witches to restore the illusorily removed penises of the men they ensnared. Contrast this solution with earlier medieval remedies of telling women to stop, fast, and do penance. What remained similar was that men were responsible for dealing with sinful women, if possible before they damaged their bodies, their family's reputations, their souls, and society as a whole. And as time passed, instead of people finding women's encounters with demons to be more unbelievable, in many ways men become more hostile, more organized against, and more violent toward women.

4

HOW TO BE

MODERN SOCIETY BY AND LARGE TREATS WOMEN AND WORK as a new phenomenon. Before the twentieth century, we are told, women did not participate in the economic life of their household, or at least they didn't bring money home. Women in the past lived within the confines of their home, tending to the needs of their families, and were either uninterested in or prevented from doing nondomestic work. Only today are they attempting to "break into" the professional world and "break the glass ceiling."

This is nonsense. To be sure, raising children and looking after a home is crushing and thankless work. Anyone who has ever been responsible for multiple children while attempting to do household chores will be able to confirm that it is not something they would take up as a hobby. Domestic labor is and was very much labor, as is confirmed by the fact that well-to-do people hire others to take care of it whenever possible. To be fair, domesticity was the major expectation that medieval Europe had for women. They would marry. They would become mothers. They would look after their children and homes. However, ideas about women and work did not begin and end at the hearth.

Women have always been a part of the world's economy writ large. In fact, women's work in the premodern world is generally ubiquitous. The idea that women largely existed in a domestic bubble wholly removed from the realities of labor and work would have seemed laughable to medieval people. In all classes of society, women worked and were expected to do so.

Medieval women's work differed depending on their status and place of birth. Women in the countryside were more likely to work as peasants or laborers if they were from poorer backgrounds, or if they were from lofty families, to work in great households as ladies-in-waiting or even as heads of households. In the cities, meanwhile, women worked at any number of occupations, from the backbreaking labor of laundry work, to the middling and variable profitability of work in brewing or baking, to the rarefied esteem of guild work. Women from the very highest echelons of society also, of course, worked at court and were even involved in high-level diplomatic and ceremonial pursuits. At the same time, some women who chose the religious life and became nuns or joined secular religious communities such as the Beguines, where they worked as they prayed.

This chapter will shine a light on the working lives of medieval women in order to better understand how the medieval world functioned and who exactly was doing all the work. It will explain how labor functioned in a world before the introduction of large-scale industry and will reflect on our ideas about what counts as work. Most of the structures we take for granted now are extremely modern, but our willingness to overlook the work of women as unimportant simply because women were doing it remains the same.

Motherhood and Marriage

Part of the reason that we don't tend to think of medieval women as workers is that the major expectation for them was that they would be wives and, crucially, mothers. A young woman, no matter her place in society, spent much of her time preparing for her eventual role as wife and mother in the household of her husband's family. Her parents wanted to ensure that they brought up their daughter in such a way that she would not "be a sore vexation to her bridegroom," as the Church father and theologian John of Chrysostom (347–407) put it.[1] So when a young unmarried woman did receive, say, an education, it was largely tied to investing in her theoretical value as a bride. Well-educated women made for good wives since they could later educate their own children, as we will see. They would also be expected to run their own households, a job that involved fiscal acumen, and in the case of larger households, to manage staff. When a medieval girl was educated, it wasn't necessarily an altruistic activity to better her for her own good. It was a calculated marketing strategy and a means of marking her as an excellent potential mother.

The focus on motherhood and the getting of heirs existed for a number of reasons. As discussed in Chapter 3, for the rich, it was a way of ensuring that the property that a family had amassed would be passed down to a younger generation and their interests would be protected. Poor families needed children not necessarily to safeguard property but to have help on it. In an agricultural society, extra hands to help on the farm were in demand, especially when they didn't have to be paid wages. But regardless of whether you wanted kids to carry on your legacy or to help on the farm, you had to contend with one significant barrier: infant mortality. Children died at an incredibly high rate, not only in the medieval period but up until the twentieth century. At the very lowest, somewhere between 20 and 30 percent of all medieval children under seven died, though some put the mark as high as 50 percent. As a result, families required many more births of children than we are accustomed to in order to ensure viable heirs.

Producing all the heirs that their male relatives demanded put women's lives in real danger, but this danger was an accepted part of their position and calling as wives. The *Hali Meiðhad* or *Letter on Virginity*, which was written in the English Midlands, acknowledged the pain, danger, and worry of mothers, stating that "in carrying [a child] there is heaviness and constant discomfort; in giving birth to it, the cruelest of all pains, and sometimes death; in bringing it up many weary hours. . . . By God, woman, . . . you should avoid this act above all things, for the integrity of your flesh, for the sake of your body, and for your physical health."[2] The danger and pain—the real *labor* of childbirth and child rearing—were thus not lost on medieval commentators. This was *the job* that medieval women were expected to carry out, and it sucked.

Beyond childbirth and -rearing, the position of wife in and of itself implied work. According to Jerome, "Men marry, indeed, so as to get a manager for the house, to solace weariness, to banish solitude."[3] The *Letter on Virginity* likewise directly challenges the idea that women benefit from subsuming themselves into marriage and motherhood. When a submissive would-be wife states that men's strength is needed for help with work and to secure adequate food, and that wealth is the result of marriage and several healthy children, the *Letter* asserts that such a picture of marriage deliberately misleads women, and that any advantages that they experience from marriage and motherhood come at too high a personal cost. Marriage, the *Letter* insists, is not a way of forming a team and enjoying a family but is "servitude to a man."[4] Sugarcoat it one might, but marriage was not a romantic partnership but a contract, in which women signed themselves up for a life of grinding maternal labor as well as work alongside their husbands, for which they would not be acknowledged in historical records.

Medieval women appear as parts of households, or "wives of"

named men in historical records. But wives were expected to take on the role of helpmeet and coworker alongside their husbands. Even those who heeded the warnings of the Church and turned from a life of motherhood toward God would find themselves working away inside nunneries. Similarly, single laywomen had to work to get by, and society marked out positions specifically for women who, for whatever reason, were not attached to a household. All these women are worth seeing as workers.

Peasants

To discuss medieval work is mostly to discuss the peasantry. The majority of medieval people were peasants, which is to say farmers who worked a small share of land, whether they rented it or owned it outright. At this time about 85 percent of Europe's population were peasants. Most peasants had landlords, who could be either local lords or clergy.

Of the peasants, the vast majority—roughly about 75 percent of the overall population—were serfs. A serf was tied to the land and was viewed as a part of it. Serfs were obliged to stay within the area held by their landlord—they could not elect to move to a new area. Serfs had to pay fees upon reaching particular life events, such as when they married or inherited land. Many serfs were required to use the facilities that their landlords owned, such as mills, to the exclusion of all others.

In this system, peasant women sometimes had a claim to farmland that was linked directly to them, though not at the same rate that men did. Across Europe and throughout the medieval period, several inheritance systems were in effect: primogeniture, wherein the eldest son inherited everything; ultimogeniture, wherein the youngest son inherited everything else or lands customarily associated with the family, while the eldest son inherited anything that his parents had purchased. In other words, women could miss out on inheriting the land they grew up on in several ways. If a family had no sons, any daughters would then be their parents' inheritors, and if there were a number of daughters, the land would be divided equally among them. In the case of just one daughter, she would often be the sole inheritor.

However, women could also own land before marriage or inheritance. In the Brigstock village in England, Cristina Penifader's father gave her land grants in 1313, 1314, and 1316, well before her marriage in 1317.[5] Parents could also give their daughter land as a dowry, which meant it would pass to her when she married—often with the express instruction that it could not be alienated from her person, regardless of her husband's wishes. All in all, land transfers to daughters seem to have accounted for about a quarter of land transactions in Brigstock. While this is a much lower rate than that at which sons inherited, serfs were still interested in ensuring that their daughters were safe and had land that could support them.[6]

In either case, in order to sell land that had been given to them under these circumstances, women had to testify that they were doing so freely. This didn't rule out coercion from husbands but does show us that women had at least some say over the land they owned. Moreover, the administration of such lands was usually overseen by a woman's husband, so while a woman was nominally its owner, it wasn't necessarily under her control.

The obligations on serf women remained the same as on any other landholder. A thirteenth-century survey of the duties of peasants in Alwalton, where the landlord was the abbot of Peterborough, listed the yearly fees that applied to eighteen separate serfs, including "Emma at Pertre . . . [and] Eda widow of Ralph." Six more women, all widows, had the same obligations for their cottages and crofts.[7] These records show that women were more commonly named as the subjects of their landlords' taxes when they were widows. Only Emma at Pertre, whose relationship to a man wasn't noted, seemed to hold her own land. Thus, while women serfs weren't necessarily landholders in their own right, they certainly might be, and when it happened, it does not seem to have been worth comment from their landlords.

Women and indeed men could also be free peasants. While most of those engaged in farming and owning land were serfs, a good 10 percent of Europe's total population owned their own lands and could, more or less, do with it as they chose. It was entirely possible then for a woman to be a farmer, endowed with her own lands, and unencumbered from the requirements that serfs were. If she chose, she could sell her land and move from the area. However, a nice piece of land, especially one near or adjoining her husband's land, would have been difficult to walk away from, even if the city sounded like more fun. Given such advantages, most free peasants stayed on, with fewer rules and regulations restricting them.

Medieval peasants worked in what historians refer to as the open field system. Most landlords would hold two to three extremely large fields, grazing pasture for animals, perhaps some woodland, and fishing or mill ponds. In this system, the land was apportioned to serfs in long strips of field. These had varying names—in England, they were referred to as *selions*. In the high to late medieval period, peasants, especially in northern Europe, would use the three-field system and divide their *selion* into three sections. On one, they would plant barley, rye, or wheat in the autumn; the second would lie fallow, growing over with weeds that animals could graze on; and the third would be planted with legumes, oats, or barley in the spring. The next year the use for each section would change places. Cereal crops massively depleted the soil on which they were grown, but the legumes re-enriched it with nitrogen. The fallow period allowed the soil to be further enriched by the manure of the animals grazing there, making it ready to take on a new crop of cereals after resting. This system helped to insulate peasants against the disaster of a bad harvest, because there was always a new crop coming through.

Regardless of whether women peasants held their own land, they were always farming. Peasants worked to feed themselves, certainly, but also often grew excess, not just for the tithes that they owed their landlords but to sell at market for ready cash. In this system a peasant—serf or free—could live a comfortable life or even become well off. In the thirteenth century, some 174 families lived in the farming village of Halesowen in England; about forty (23 percent) were wealthy, sixty-four (37 percent) were managing well, analogous to middle-class families now, and the remaining seventy (40 percent) were poor.[8] The odds of being comfortable, then, weren't great but they also weren't impossible. Peasants had slightly more chance of being classed as rich or middling than of being poor. It is just that more people were poor than were in the middle or top of the social ladder. When we speak of peasants, then, we shouldn't be too quick to assume that they lived miserable lives of poverty. They worked very hard for a living, but that living could be fine.

Women's Work on the Farm

Whether peasants were poor or well off, their life involved a lot of work, and that labor was not necessarily gendered. With a surfeit of work, it made no sense to rigidly partition. If it needed to get done, it would, by whoever was there to help. Huge tasks, like bringing in the harvest, required every available pair of hands, woman or man, young or old. Jobs that required more brute strength, such as handling teams of oxen, and later horses, to plow the land, were more often assigned to men, but women could perform them too. Similarly, some tasks saw more women at the helm.

We have a lot of ways to ascertain what work was being done on farms, but one of the more delightful is to look at the common "labors of the months" illustration cycles that show the work that people conducted in each month of the year and give us a great idea of what that looked like. The illustrations show up in manuscripts, in stone carvings at Chartres cathedral, and in fountains in Perugia, and as stained-glass representations at Notre Dame in Paris and the Basilica of St. Denis. They are idealized representations of a mix of activities, some of which show the life of the nobility, but most of which show peasants at work. January is reserved for feasting, given its inclement weather. Most of the Christmas liturgical calendar takes place in that month, but still firewood must be brought in and animals tended. February often shows people warming themselves at a fire, after shivering their way back from the same activities. March shows tree pruning, plowing, and digging. In April, peasants plant the harvest or tend to their livestock, driving the animals back to the fields, while nobles pick flowers and court one another. In May the well-off hawk or hunt. In June the hay harvest comes in, and in July and August the wheat. July also sees sheep shearing in some cycles. September is the grape harvest and wine making. In October the crops that grow in autumn and winter, like winter wheat, are plowed and sown. In November flax is treated, and pigs are fattened on acorns in the woods. And in December the pigs are slaughtered. In these various cycles, women appear, time and again, alongside men doing their part to keep the farms running.

Women in these images can usually be read as the partners of the men, except where groups of people labored for the wealthy. Although women regularly appear in "labors of the months" cycles, in smaller images that show only one person performing a task, it is invariably a man. Because these scenes are idealized representations of farming, women are not considered lead agricultural laborers, or indeed default and archetypal peasants, no matter how much hay they raked, or how many sheep they sheared. Instead, they are presented as appendages to the men.

A wealthier peasant woman might hire a serving maid or a dairy maid to help with the work. The serving maid would oversee the laying of hens and feed the poultry and the dogs. She also cared for ill or orphaned lambs and for calves that had not yet been weaned. She would also help to feed other workers.[9] Meanwhile, dairymaids would

Peasant women making hay in June, from *Les Très Riches Heures du duc de Berry*, by the Limbourg brothers (active 1385–1416), Bibliothèque du Château, Chantilly. HISTORIC IMAGES / ALAMY STOCK PHOTO.

look after milking, make cheese and butter, and keep accounts of the dairy. They would deal with bailiffs and any audits of the premises. They managed tools and helped out with farm animals and any other odd jobs in whatever spare time they might have.[10]

Women's Work

While women worked in the fields, often in the same occupations as men, within the home they did work slated for women, directly connected to the home itself and child rearing. The *Letter on Virginity* encouraged women to lead lives of virginity and faith, but to achieve that goal, married peasant women did difficult, exhausting work. The *Letter* asked its readers, "What kind of position is the wife in who when she comes in, hears her child screaming, sees the cat at the filch and the dog at the hide, her loaf burning on the hearth and her calf suckling, the pot boiling over into the fire—*and* her husband complaining. Although it may sound ridiculous, it ought, maiden, to discourage you from it all the more, because it is no joke to the woman who tries it."[11]

This passage is a great example of the domestic tasks that women were in charge of, and that complaining husbands apparently had little desire to help with. Women were mostly in charge of smaller domestic animals, so cats and dogs thieving in the kitchen, and calves needing feeding fell under their purview. (Peasants commonly lived in the same building with their livestock so all could keep warm and to save on the cost of grander outbuildings, though purpose-built barns were not unusual.) In a rural setting, bread would have to be made in house, and the wife would have to bake it. Similarly, women did the cooking—hence the overboiling pot in this cautionary tale. Finally, women reared the children in these circumstances. Presumably a screaming child was simply not worth looking into by its father.

On top of this, many other jobs fell to women, especially in the rural economy. Women drew the water for domestic use. In the British Isles and the lowlands, which were wetter, this chore might be shorter but was still heavy. Women drew water from wells, springs, rivers, and any nearby source. In the drier climates of southern Europe, however, the drawing and carrying of water involved longer trips and sometimes influenced municipal architecture. In Castile bridges over water that acted as exits from towns had to be large enough to allow women carrying water jugs to pass.[12] Though not as difficult as washing, this everyday activity chipped into the busy lives of women, both rural and urban, at the modest end of the social spectrum, and was a very real and physically taxing form of work.

Medieval society, similarly, saw washing as an explicitly feminine task, although it was intensive work. The medieval world, like a great part of the modern one, lacked running water. As a result, water not only had to be laboriously carried for bathing, it had to be lugged and heated for washing. This difficult manual process fell to women. So deeply feminized was washing that the men who wrote the sources explaining the work often condemned the gossiping that women were said to engage in as they worked. In Brittany, the sites where women gathered to wash clothes together were referred to as women's courts. There, as the women washed, rinsed, twisted, and beat their laundry, their "tongues [were] quite as active as the washerwoman's beetles; it is the seat of feminine justice with little mercy for the men-folk."[13] Washing clothes was a several-day process. First dirty laundry was soaked, usually overnight. It was then layered into tubs, with the dirtiest items on the bottom, covered by a sheet that suspended soaking agents, such as a layer of wood ash, sometimes mixed with nettles, eggshells, and soapwort. Boiling water was then poured over this concoction, and any overflow collected, reheated, then poured back over the top repeatedly for anywhere from ten to twenty hours. The next day the soaked laundry was carried to a source of running water, be it a washhouse or the local river. There it was soaped, scrubbed, beaten, rinsed, and wrung out before drying on bushes or lines.[14]

Like washing, cloth making was a fairly universal task for medieval women, and most knew the rudimentary processes of both spinning and weaving. First they had to turn the shorn wool into yarn or thread through carding. They combed the wool through two large brushes that removed dirt and also aligned the fibers to make the creation of yarn or thread easier. If they wanted colored thread or yarn, they would dye the wool at this point. Medieval people were partial to colored fabric and grew plants used for dyeing, like weld for yellow or woad for blue, in small gardens. They would grind or mash these plants together, dry, then boil them into a paste, requiring yet more water, as well as firewood. Alum, a metal salt that helped colors fix, could be added directly to the dyeing agents or used to pretreat the yarn. Either way, the yarn would eventually be tossed into the dye and left to soak. It would be retrieved sometime later and dried, ready to be made into cloth. This relatively straight-forward but labor-intensive process meant that even peasant women likely sported colorful clothing.

Women then spun the material, usually wool or flax. Before the thir-teenth century they used a distaff and spindle. They took the prepped fiber and wrapped it around the distaff, then twisted the fibers around the spindle manually, stretching it out and creating thread. In the thir-teenth century, the spinning wheel was invented, speeding up the entire process; but spinning wheels were specialist equipment, more likely to be used by women spinning professionally rather than for their household. Once women made the thread or yarn, they wove it into cloth on a loom.

So fully feminized was the work of cloth making that Buchard of Worms (the dildo-panic guy in Chapter 3) advised priests to ques-tion women in confession about whether they were doing any casual magic while they were making textiles. He bade them ask women whether they had ever witnessed or taken part in incantations over cloth as it was woven to intentionally create a knotting pattern so dif-ficult that the weaving would fail unless "diabolical counter-incan-tations" were employed to fix it.[15] Informal accusations of diabolic magic aside, Buchard's concerns about what women were up to while weaving tells us something of the detailed and difficult nature of cloth work. So painstaking was the process that men could believe women would use magic to be spared the work of making it.

The time-consuming nature of making and washing clothing meant that peasant women with means elected to skip it altogether. Wealthy women often employed household help from the local area, and one of the most common jobs for poorer women seeking to bring in extra money was washing. Larger peasant households could employ women as chambermaids who, as twelfth-century English scholar Alexander Neckham (1157–1217) prescribed, were

A queen and her ladies carding, spinning, and weaving, after miniature, fourteenth century. INTERFOTO / ALAMY STOCK PHOTO.

to have charming faces that would put people to ease as they made silk thread and knots, sewed and mended linen and woolen clothes, knitted garments, and also did embroidery and feather stitching.[16]

Any poorer woman would do this sort of work on her own holdings if she lacked the funds to hire someone else to do it. While the less wealthy peasants were probably not going to spend much time worrying about silk thread and embroidery, they likely sewed or knitted the clothes that their families wore. Even for rich women, a chambermaid would likely reduce the work she was doing rather than take over the entire job.

Women were also regularly employed in brewing, at least as much as men. Medieval peasants drank rather a lot of small (or low-alcohol) beer and ale. In the tenth-century *Ælfric's Colloquy*, which records theoretical dialogues between a teacher and his students, one young man states, "I drink ale, usually, if I drink at all, and water if I have no ale. . . . I am not rich enough to be able to buy myself wine: Wine is not a drink for boys or fools but for old men and wise men."[17] By the late medieval period, in brewing centers such as České Budějovice, from whence the name Budweiser comes, beer was being made on a large enough scale that it was being exported to Bavaria.

Medieval people desired to drink beer and ale not because water was unsafe, but because farmwork is extremely hard. Small beer and ale added additional calories to their daily uptake in an enjoyable way. Although the wealthy were probably able to procure professionally made and imported beers, most people, especially in the earlier medieval period, made their own ale or bought it from nearby producers. Ale was brewed primarily from barley and did not include the hops of beer, which meant it could not be stored for long before going off. As such, those who wanted ale had to be constantly brewing it to ensure a steady supply, making brewing a very common cottage industry. Women who brewed for their families would often brew excess for sale, allowing them to bring in a bit of money. Because brewing was a craft that could be learned at home, women could be employed as brewers in larger commercial breweries.

We find women in the brewing trade consistently: records show them paying taxes on their gains from brewing, and registering with the authorities who oversaw standards. When someone performed below these standards, they were frequently written up, so we can find the women who were not meeting them. The Durham Court Rolls from 1365 record that Agnes Postell and Alice de Belasis were fined twelve denarii for selling bad ale, about the equivalent of two days' work for a skilled craftsman. Similarly Alice de Belasis was separately fined two shillings, or the equivalent of five days wages, for poor-quality ale, which a court proved had no strength at all.[18] Punishments for brewing bad ale could range from fines to ritualized humiliation. In England, the Domesday Book first recorded the use of the cucking stool (which would become the ducking stool in the early modern period) in Chester to punish those who sold bad ale or ale in incorrect measures. They would be forced to sit in a chair outside their home and be jeered at by locals. Fourteenth-century Scottish laws noted that any alewife who made "evil ale" was either fined "eight shillings" or placed in the cucking stool, a nod to women as the primary brewers in the region who could face the largely gendered humiliation as a result.[19]

We also learn of women in the brewing profession through records of accidents. For example, one coroner's roll indicates that at around noon on October 2, 1270, Amice Belamy was carrying a tub full of gruit, an agent for flavoring ale, with Sibyl Bonchevaler at her work in Lady Juliana de Beauchamp's brewhouse in Staploe, Eaton Socon. As they went to dump the gruit into the boiling vat of beer, Amice slipped and fell into it and was trapped by the tub that fell on top of her. "Sibyl immediately jumped towards her, dragged her from the vat and shouted; the household came and found her scalded almost to death." She was given the last rites of the church and died on the day following.[20] This harrowing story reminds us what a physically tasking and dangerous job brewing, especially in large quantities, could be.

This episode is also interesting because the two women were working for another woman, and a lady at that, Juliana de Beauchamp. Brewing was commonly associated with women across class lines, since the brewhouse is listed as belonging to the Lady Juliana.

All in all, during these years a woman was just as likely to be brewing ale as a man, if not more likely in some instances.

Women were also employed in any number of part-time occupations in the countryside. They were day laborers, doing a range of jobs from breaking rocks for roads to thatching roofs and mowing hay. They were also specialist goods sellers. A woman might be an egg monger who brought her wares into town for market, although she likely had the same numerous duties back in her cottage as the other peasant women. They would be expected to roll up their sleeves and take on all the never-ending tasks in a household. There would always be wool to spin, bread to bake, ale to brew, wood to collect, and animals to feed, alongside any special seasonal work.

Although a working rural woman had any number of roles, she can often be harder to find in records than men due to coverture, her status as under the protection or authority of her husband or father. These women are therefore listed by a male relative's name rather than their own. William Shepherd in Staffordshire, England, was fined repeatedly for making bad ale, although the records show that it was his wife, not he, who was doing the brewing.[21] We should expect that many more women were being paid for their labor than what we can read in the historical record.

City Workers

Plenty of women living and working in towns also worked at jobs (some in trades not traditional for women), but unlike their rustic counterparts, they—like anyone who lived in a city for a year and a day—were considered free. Before that time elapsed, though, those who were fleeing serfdom and had been lured to the city by the promise of work could be taken back home by their lord.

In the earlier medieval period, escape to the city was much less possible, simply because there were fewer cities. In 800, a young woman in the Alps could not likely seek work thee hundred miles away in the city of Metz. For one thing, she would have to get there on foot while evading her lord the entire way.

The possibility of urban life expanded greatly in the high medieval period, partially as a result of new and innovative farming and land cultivation methods. The three-field system meant that crops were coming in more reliably. More food led to an expanding population and a greater demand for land for them to live on. The European population expanded into previously uninhabitable areas, such as the lowlands. Present-day Belgium and the Netherlands were settled in this period because of the new ability to drain and reclaim land. As people put in a series of dikes there, they turned an unoccupiable swamp into usable land.

Reclaimed land wasn't always easy to grow crops on, but it was ideal for raising sheep. The animals could happily graze on grasses that grew in soil that was once under water. They also quite happily produced wool, one of the most important medieval commodities. In a world without central heating, where a huge amount of labor was done outdoors in any and all conditions, the miracle fiber that stays warm even while wet was in high demand, especially in northern Europe. Denizens of the lowlands quickly set up an enviable economic engine. Shepherds sold on their wool to traders, who quickly transported it through the series of canals that diverted the water that had previously covered the area. Next, cities emerged, powerhouses like Ghent and Bruges that soon bustled with people who serviced the wool trade. While the low countries are a pronounced medieval urbanization story, they were by no means the only one. Medieval Cologne, Prague, and Marseille became cities when once they were merely towns. Meanwhile established cities like Milan, Venice, Paris, and London expanded, flush with new migrants.

The population growth aided the expansion of cities for several reasons. First, once farming was efficient enough to feed an entire population, people could live in cities and be assured that they would be able to trade cash or goods for the necessary food. Second, an expanding population made it less necessary for a landlord to track down every errant serf that left his lands, provided they had enough hands farming the land and paying taxes.

But women migrating to cities from the country often faced hardships that men did not. The assumed sexual profligacy of women meant that an unaccompanied woman was often read as a theoretical threat. There was no telling what a woman alone, without a man's supervision, might do. As a result, some cities required that women had to join households rather than live on their own or had to live together with other unsupervised women. Especially in late medieval England, women on their own were given deadlines either to amalgamate into a household or to leave the city.

Being a part of a household meant contributing to its economic output. As such, the most common way for a woman to find a place in a household was to take up work in service. Overall, by the fourteenth century, servants accounted for about a third of all city dwellers in England, and just under half were women.[22] Service was considered an especially appropriate option for young single women.

Urban women could find work as scullery maids, helping in the kitchens of larger households. This entry-level job could lead to promotions for those who worked diligently. From scullery maid, one could be promoted to kitchen maid, then possibly to cook. The work was difficult. Scullions were often required to be the first person awake in the house to ensure that fires were lit and usable when higher-ups needed them. They washed floors, swept ashes from fireplaces, cleaned pots and pans, and did all the grimiest work. Kitchen maids aided with meal preparation, chopping vegetables, kneading dough, and washing dishes. Cooks ruled the kitchen and weren't determined by sex. They would be responsible for feeding both the family and the servants of a household. Similarly, chambermaids from the countryside could find gainful employment in the city's wealthy houses, especially if they had sewing prowess, which was in great demand in larger households.

Not all women who reached the city came as runaways from the countryside. Girls from more well-to-do backgrounds could join a few industries as apprentices. Since cloth production was a trade dominated by women, young women were allowed to train in it. Silk production in particular was a feminine enterprise, with large communities of silk weavers in cities including Catanzaro in Calabria and, later, Lyon and London. In Paris, women dominated the trade, and the rules between apprentices and the higher levels of professionals were set out in the 1270 *Book of Crafts* (*Livre des métiers*).[23]

These regulations give a great overview of how the apprenticeship system worked and its objectives. In general, parents would pay a fee and hand over their children, from about the age of twelve, to apprentice in the house of their mistress. There they would start out doing the more menial jobs required for the trade and eventually learn how to make silk. A longer term of apprenticeship would mean a cheaper fee in return for the training, as the mistress would presumably get more work out of her charge. In theory, if a child was pledged for a decade, no fee would be required for the apprenticeship, allowing poorer girls into the trade. In reality, the poor would have had difficulty making connections with the well-to-do women who ran the silk craft in Paris, though it was not unheard of.

Once a woman completed an apprenticeship, usually after three to ten years, she became a journeywoman, allowed to work in the craft in the city where she had trained. After that she could become a mistress herself and set up her own business. Only those who came through this system were allowed to participate in the craft within the city. Trades formed guilds, similar to unions, that ensured that the work would be of the highest order and in return guaranteed that buyers would pay the craftspeople adequate compensation. It was also protectionist. No one from outside the guild was allowed to practice the craft. A board comprised of three masters and three mistresses of the silk guild ensured that those engaged in silk weaving met the requirements "to safeguard the craft" from those who were not properly trained. Clearly then, women in the silk-weaving profession enjoyed a certain amount of parity with their male counterparts.

While the time-intensive nature of cloth making meant that there was always demand for carders, spinners, and weavers, men often controlled cloth production outside the Parisian silk guild. As a fairly lucrative industry, those who made their living in it were eager to restrict the number of competitors. This was usually done through the guild structure.

The fullers were one group in Paris that found a way to limit the number of people in their field. Their job was to cleanse the wool cloth, removing oil and other impurities, and then to thicken it. The process was difficult and required training. The Parisian fullers had a system of apprenticeship not unlike the silk workers, but it was open only to boys. However, women could become fullers through family connections. Daughters, stepdaughters, and wives of fullers could learn the craft, and "if a Master dies, his wife may practice the craft and keep the apprentices." There was a limitation to this sanction, however. If a widow remarried to a man who was not a fuller or a fulling apprentice, she had to give up her position.[24]

Regulations in towns and cities like those of the Parisian fullers hint that in most professions, guilded or not, women were usually working alongside their husbands, doing the same work. Further, fullers' widows had an advantage on the marriage market with single male fullers. A wife who knew what she was doing in the business world was a boon, and it was extraordinarily common for people to marry within occupations. The daughter of a fuller, for example, likely would marry a fuller, since she knew the trade.

Unskilled women in their midtwenties and up who lived in cities and had no prior work experience were considered to have aged out of service or apprenticeship. If a woman was free to remain in the city, however, a number of trades were still open to her. At the lower end of the social spectrum, many women worked in market stalls.

They might sell foodstuffs that they had made, such as bread or pretzels. Or they might sell fruits and vegetables, eggs, and other goods that could easily be grown in gardens or on small plots of land near the city. The plus side of such work was that it usually held no legal barriers to entry and didn't require a large outlay of cash to start.

Similarly, the work that women did in the countryside was still needed in the city. Many who could pay to have their laundry done would hire out, and washerwomen were a familiar sight in every urban center. Itinerant washerwomen took in laundry from smaller houses that had no laundry facility of their own and set to work, often at public waterways. These same women often did mending, like dry cleaners and laundry services today. Larger households that had their own laundry facility and enough laundry would have live-in washerwomen as part of the general household. The work wasn't particularly well paid, but it wasn't expensive to get into the trade, and the only rule governing it was usually where the wash could be done.

In cities, washing was often the preserve of working women. Any medieval person who wanted to adhere to the beauty standard had to bathe (see Chapter 2). In the later medieval period, a city's bathhouses were generally considered integral to the health of the city itself. A clean populace was a healthy populace, and the practice of ensuring that a city was adequately served by bathhouses was a part of what the historian Guy Geltner has called "healthscaping," along with seeing to sewage and waste disposal.[25] In Hungary, which still retains a vibrant public bathing culture, the first recorded public bathhouse was established by Anna of Antioch (d. 1184), who married Béla III of Hungary (ca. 1148–96). This royal woman saw it as a public service to introduce bathhouses, though her own upbringing in the Middle East and at court in Constantinople probably also meant that she simply enjoyed public bathing and wanted it to catch on.[26] Anna's interest in introducing public baths to medieval Buda

also is indicative of the fact that medieval people considered bathing really fun. City dwellers could frequent bathhouses and enjoy a
nice soak without having to carry and heat water themselves.

Bathhouses needed workers at various levels, and bathhouse
attendants were often women. They fetched and discarded water,
looked after the fires that heated the water, and sometimes collected
bathers' admission fees.[27] A woman who had more money might run
a bathhouse. Many enterprising bathhouse keepers were women,
though men were also in the trade. Parisian codes for bathhouse
keepers stated that their rules applied to either men or women who
had sworn to uphold the standards of the trade.[28]

But such regulations did not prove some sort of parity of the genders in the Parisian bathhouse trade. While women were free to
enter the trade, they could not join the regulatory body of bathhouse
keepers that ensured that their fellow tradespeople were adhering
to the rules. Instead, three male bathhouse keepers were elected to
oversee the trade.[29] Parisian women who kept bathhouses thus faced
not so much a glass ceiling as a regular ceiling. They could make a
good living as bathhouse keepers, but they could never rise to super-
visory roles.

Women who had the funds might also work in a bakery. They
could bake and sell bread and other sundries, or they could charge
people to use the baker's oven to bake their own bread. Both men
and women were bakers. In fact, women bakers were so common
that they didn't arouse comment, and so one of the major ways we
know about these women is when they got into legal trouble.

Much as women brewers could be punished if they sold "bad"
ale, bakers could be fined if they were caught selling loaves that did
not meet the standardized weight. In fourteenth-century London,
Rogeer le Paumer, the sheriff, weighed bread that was being sold by
Sarra Foting, Christina Terrice, Godiyeva Foting, Matilda de Boling-
tone, Christina Prichet, and Isabella Pouveste, all of whom were bak-

ers from Stratford. The sheriff found that the women were selling halfpenny loaves that were lighter than they should have been, for about eight shillings each.[30]

These women were living in Stratford—now firmly a part of Greater London, but then a village within reasonable walking distance. Living outside the city, they were able to take advantage of the relatively low cost of living in a village yet have access to the many potential customers in the city. In other words, they were commuters. Likely their entry into the city was part of why they came to the attention of the sheriff, as goods brought into London were regularly inspected to ensure not only that they were up to code but that they were taxed at the correct level.

Despite their infraction, these women got off relatively lightly. Ordinarily, bread found to be underweight would be forfeited, sometimes used to feed prisoners or given to alms or lazar houses. Because it was cold by the time it reached London, the sheriff simply ordered the women to sell their bread at a price closer to its actual weight. It was not a terrible outcome, but the women likely thought twice before attempting the same scam in the future.

Women who rented out their ovens for baking were once involved in a scheme to steal bits of dough from loaves left in their care. In 1327 Alice de Brightenoch and Lucy de Pykeringe took dough from the loaves their customers brought in to bake. This complex ruse involved a hole in the table and someone in their household hiding under it, opening the hole, stealing the dough from the unbaked loaves bit by bit, and combining it to make new loaves for sale. Apparently, this scheme worked well, but when they were caught, they were condemned for taking dough "falsely, wickedly, and maliciously; to the great loss of all [their] neighbours and other persons living near." It was quite the scandal, in that they were literally taking the food from the mouths of their customers and neighbors to enrich themselves.

Alice and Lucy were sentenced to serve time in Newgate Prison, along with their male counterparts who had been working the same scam. But the men were put in the pillory, with stolen dough hung around their necks to shame them further. The women, meanwhile, pleaded that they were both married and that "said deed was not their deed"—rather, their husbands were responsible for the dough-stealing hole. Rather than be set up for public scorn, they were given time in Newgate to think about what they had done while all the tables with holes were destroyed.[31]

What we can glean from this incident is that some of the bakers of London chose to augment their income with a bit of light crime, and that women bakers could be treated with a bit more leniency. The fact that the women involved in this case were married shows us that women did not cease to work upon marriage. Yes, women had to drop out of service if they started a family, but they could use those skills in professions elsewhere. However, they should be careful of marrying men who were open to criminal activity.

Women in cities, like these wayward bakers, were often employed in the same work as women in the countryside. Women who could come up with the money for a business premise could be found brewing, or making and selling food. Many women worked at inns, doing domestic tasks for money, as they cooked meals, served patrons, and kept rooms. Shopkeepers sold items beyond basic needs. Both professions could be taken on only by women who had some wealth, as renting or buying a physical premises was expensive. So could filling shops with the sort of goods that an upscale clientele would want.

With high entry fees, however, came the possibility of high rewards, and we can often see just how well women did for themselves by looking at their wills. The 1359 will of the general shopkeeper Mechthild von Bremen, who lived in Lübeck, in present northern Germany, noted a fortune of 51 marks, or about four years' worth of wages for a skilled craftsman, that she disbursed to various individuals. Little wonder then that a fair number of women pursued shop- and inn-keeping businesses. In 1429 Basel, in present Switzerland, boasted some thirty tax-paying shopkeeping women. More dramatically, that same year in the Alsatian town of Beinheim, a baggage train of pack horses and two-wheeled carts carrying wholesale items bound for shops across Switzerland was robbed, with the result that sixty-one shopkeepers lost out on goods, thirty-seven of them women. Clearly, women commonly kept shops and inns in the city, but also in communities in the countryside if there was a large enough population to sustain them.[32]

Husbands and wives worked together in virtually every rung of working society. Bathhouse attendants often worked alongside their husbands who were the listed bathhouse keepers. At a higher level, Rose of Burford was a fifteenth-century wholesale wool merchant based in London. Her husband, also a wealthy merchant, lent a considerable sum of money to the crown. After he died, Rose petitioned the crown repeatedly for the repayment of her husband's loan, while still apparently running a very successful wool export business. Eventually, perhaps despairing at the slow repayments, she proposed that the crown simply subtract the amount owed from her taxes on her wool business.[33] This accomplished woman not only ran a prosperous business but was also adept enough with legalities that she felt comfortable approaching the crown with an alternative credit arrangement.

Rose was remarkable because of her connections at court, but women being intimately involved in a family's successful business was the standard. The wife of Regensburg wholesale merchant Matthias Runtinger (1385–1407) appears to have witnessed sales deeds, purchased items for the business, and like many businesswomen, kept the books. Eventually she oversaw the family's registration of currency exchanges, no small task in a place where merchants might be dealing with currency from Italian city-states, Hungary, the Czech lands, and German-speaking lands. Runtinger was lucky to have a wife who paid considerable attention to detail and who had skill with numbers. Although she was clearly an adept member of her extended family's business, we do not know her name.[34]

Artists

Medieval Europeans regarded embroidery as an art, much as we today consider painting. It was considered a female task, and even chambermaids were expected to be competent in it. Yet it was a coveted line of work, as one early Irish law tract stated that "the woman who embroiders earns more profit even than queens."[35] Embroiderers could find employment with professional clothing makers or in tapestry workshops.

By the thirteenth century, given that embroidery was held in high esteem and could bring in money, the field contained plenty of men as well. In England, over time women come up less frequently on the lists of embroiderers than men and more often in conjunction with a husband, even when their work was exceptional. In May 1317 "Rose, the wife of John de Bureford, citizen and merchant of London," sold "an embroidered cope for the choir" to the French queen Isabella (ca. 1295–1358), who gave it as a gift "to the Lord High Pontiff." Rose was clearly a very skilled artist, since she was commissioned by the queen, but was not skilled enough to be named as an artist in her own right.[36] We don't know how many other working embroiderers were subsumed into their husbands' workshops with even their first names lost to us. Once a field became truly profitable, men nudged women out of it. It was all well and good to let ladies have fun with a needle and thread. But if there was cash to be made, men suddenly showed up front and center and excluded women from the role.

Beyond textiles, women were also commonly associated with the production and decoration of books. Christine de Pizan in *City of Women* credited Anastaise as being a specialist in making borders and backgrounds in manuscripts.[37] While Anastaise was fictional, we know that women were producing manuscripts since at least the sixth century.

Manuscript production was often linked to monasteries and nunneries. Nuns were particularly well suited for such holy work, as they were expected to be literate. Much of the work was purely scribal—an important job in and of itself. But many women worked on the art as well, some of whom were widely celebrated. In 730, Boniface (ca. 675–754) gave a silver stylus to Eadburg, "so that her words might shine in gold to the glory of the Father in heaven." Around the same time, a ninth-century hagiography noted that the Flemish sisters Harlinde and Renilde "wrote and painted so much that it would seem laborious even to robust men of our day."[38]

Lay women also worked as illustrators, sometimes in professional circumstances. Some may have worked during daytime in scriptoria in nunneries. The thirteenth-century German artist Claricia was behind what we now call the Claricia Psalter. Some historians believe that she drew herself into it, swinging happily from a Q as its tail, her name written above her head. But others argue that the woman may not be Claricia but an allegory of vanity, the subject of the passage.[39] With her long blond hair, high forehead, and stylish long-sleeved dress, she would have qualified as attractive by the medieval standard. Either way, the provenance of the manuscript indicates that it was made by a woman, although we cannot conclusively say whether she was a nun.

We do know, however, that women worked as illustrators outside nunneries. Using Parisian tax records, historian Françoise Baron uncovered several women painters and illuminators working in the city during the thirteenth and fifteenth centuries. Sadly, we know that Agnes *la paintresse* and Henriete *l'ymagiere* existed only due to the charitable donations they made or received. We can't connect them to any of their artistic output, in contrast to the men whose family workshops these women seem to have been laboring in. For them, the tax records give their specific commissions.[40] Again, there is an entire class of employed women whose work we are estranged from. Nevertheless, we know they were there, and some celebrated names shine through.

Baron uncovered women painters and sculptors in Paris, but medieval women worked as artists all over Europe. They made altar

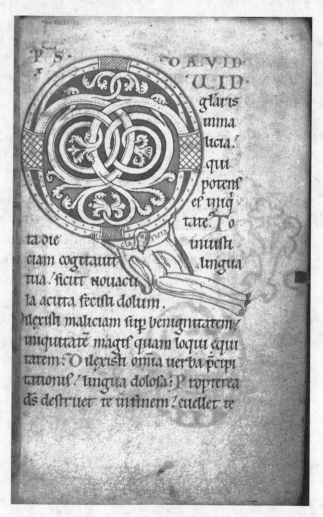

Claricia, Claricia Psalter, late twelfth century, Augsburg (?).
THE WALTERS ART MUSEUM, BALTIMORE.

clothes and stained glass. They illustrated books and painted. They practiced in their families' artistic workshops. But their names are unknown, not just because of coverture but also because our society is less interested in the artisans who crafted textile works, illustrated beautiful manuscripts, and made religious stained glass than in individual painters or sculptors, who happened to get recorded more often when they were men. While our records for practicing women artisans are fairly detailed, we tend to overlook them because we don't value the arts that they were engaged in. We are every bit as responsible for the erasure of women artists as our medieval counterparts were.

Medical Professionals

Women also made a comfortable living by participating in the field that never ceases to be in demand: medicine. Medieval professional medicine was very different from our own. It did not, by and large, require formal training. The great school at Salerno trained physicians, but if you lived in a far-flung rural place in, say, what is now Scotland, whoever treated you didn't train there. Instead, various levels of professionalism and training existed in the medieval medical marketplace, and one could encounter medical professionals with various amounts of training at various price points: physicians who had university training, surgeons and barbers who were trained through guilds, and midwives who were trained by seniors in the profession. Women could be found throughout these groups, though they faced restrictions.

One of the most common ways for a medieval woman to become a medical professional was to become a nun, because hospitals then were almost exclusively branches of monasteries or nunneries. Essentially, ill people could go to the nearest habitation of monks or nuns, and they would be cared for and prayed for, given "cloister medicine." Nuns and monks copied medical texts as well as religious

Nuns working in a ward, wood engraving of a miniature, sixteenth century, Hôtel-Dieu, Paris. PICTORIAL PRESS LTD / ALAMY STOCK PHOTO.

and philosophical ones. The nuns who worked in Paris's Hôtel-Dieu, for example, would have been reasonably current with medical learning coming out of the University of Paris (now known as the Sorbonne) as well as from their own libraries.

However, more monks than nuns worked in hospitals, as it was considered a gamble to allow religious women to work with the general public, lest they be tempted into sexual sin (of course). As a result, monks were more likely to be running hospitals than were nuns. Indeed, libraries in nunneries had distinctly fewer medical texts than those in monasteries. Even nuns who were directly connected to hospitals often had fewer medical texts to work from, indicating that hierarchies kept women from practicing medicine and relegated them to more caregiving work.[41] Still, women did work in hospitals, and many medieval people would have interacted with them when in need.

While nuns were involved with academic medicine, which

depended on the same classical texts that were used at universities, and were copied and shared among various religious institutions, most women were locked out of becoming educated physicians. Medieval university students were counted as clergy members, specifically clerics. As I mentioned in Chapter 1, the primary reason was to make sure that rowdy, usually wealthy students who ran out on bar tabs were judged in ecclesiastical courts rather than lay ones. This clever device not only kept young men from experiencing consequences but also excluded women from university attendance, since they were not allowed to be clerics. What was initially, early in the medieval period, a frustrating barrier to attaining legal or theological qualifications would become exclusionary when university training became a legal requirement for those practicing as physicians.

Women often had more luck approaching medical guilds, such as those of barbers or surgeons, medical professionals who performed procedures that involved cutting. Surgeons were held in more esteem, and in the fourteenth century in Paris, Philip IV (1268–1314) pronounced that to gain entry to the guild, surgeons, referencing women in this trade, must be examined by other master surgeons.[42] In general, surgeons would perform more complex procedures such as cataract surgery. Barbers, in contrast, would lance boils or do bloodletting. Women could join these guilds if they were the wives or daughters of medical practitioners or had apprenticed with women in the field to learn the craft. These professions had lower status than that of physicians, but they were still lucrative and important enough that guilds built up around them to limit access and to direct customers to those who were trained by guild members.

Regardless of their place in the medical professions, women could become medical authorities in their own right. Hildegard of Bingen wrote two extensive volumes on medicine, *Physica* and

Causa et Curae, which stressed herbal remedies as well as diet. She covered the usual diagnostic processes such as urine analysis, gave recipes for common aliments including toothaches and hiccoughs, and tackled more severe illnesses such as leprosy and epilepsy. She gave guidance on bleeding patients and on alternative treatments such as cupping. Another impactful medieval medical thinker was Trota of Salerno, who may not have existed. Her *Trotula* was a compendium of works, not all of which she composed. But one she apparently did; the earliest references to the gynecological text *On Treatments for Women*, inside the *Trotula*, say it was written by Trota.[43] Both Trota and Hildegard were outliers in terms of the reverence their work was held in—their medical works were some of the most widespread in the medieval period. Clearly then, women could be considered medical authorities even if their opportunities to practice were limited.

There was one professional medical field that almost all women had recourse to in their lifetime and that was dominated by women: midwifery. The danger of childbirth was acknowledged widely in the medieval period. Most women wanted medical guidance when they struggled through labor. If a woman was looking for a medical career and found herself locked out of the university, midwifery was a solid and reliable option. In the countryside, the local midwife might be engaged in any number of other types of work in addition to her vocation, given the way the rural economy worked.

Trota's *Sickness of Women* marks out sixteen "unnatural" issues that women might face while giving birth. For most of them, the prescribed remedy was for a midwife to oil her hands with a mixture of linseed and fenugreek so as to "replace the child in its place and . . . in its correct position" for a more expedient birth.[44] Should a midwife's intervention fail, and the mother died, midwives were also tasked with performing cesarean sections. This task was considered to be primarily a religious intervention: in the late fourteenth and early fifteenth centuries, the Augustinian canon regular John Mirk wrote in *Instructions for Parish Priests* that in such sad cases, "teach the midwife that she hurry / For to undo her with a knife / In order to save the child's life / And hurry that it christened be / For that is a deed of charity."[45] The exhortation for emergency baptism indicates the low expectation of success from the procedure. Whereas midwives did not enjoy the same social status as physicians, they were responsible for complex medical procedures and were expected to do them well. Midwives not only attended births, they also treated pregnant women's ailments and helped them through postpartum issues. They looked after gynecological concerns more generally and at times the common health concerns of their community. In most smaller towns, a midwife was likely to be consulted for coughs and colds, fevers, aches, and pains. Because they were considered lower than other medical professionals, and generally had more affordable services, midwives likely did the medical care for most people.

Midwives also provided abortions, which would later lead to accusations in the *Malleus Mallificarum* that "witches who are midwives in various ways kill the child conceived in the womb, and procure an abortion; or if they do not do this offer new-born children to devils."[46] The whole "offering new-born children to devils" thing here is a bit over the top. But in general, the *Malleus* considered that a woman's willingness to assist with an abortion was indicative of her willingness to serve the devil in any number of ways. But this association was limited to women who offered abortion services—it was not applied to midwifery generally. After all, midwives hardly ceased to work, even at the height of the seventeenth-century witch panic. They simply had to be careful about what medical services they offered if they wished to remain on the right side of the law. Those who kept their abortion services quiet, or did not offer them, could look forward to an important and necessary career untroubled by witch-hunters.

Sex Workers

Sex work also required walking a tight legal rope. Sex work in the medieval period was considered a necessity, especially in cities, because of concern that unmarried men might not be having enough sex. Both Augustine and Aquinas warned of the dangers of pent-up lust in urban environments. They cautioned that if unmarried men were unable to have sex, they would exercise violence, as there was no other way to expel the heat that their hot, dry constitutions built up. As a result, both saints advised that brothels were necessary to avoid riots.[47]

Almost every major metropolitan area in the medieval period was home to thriving centers of sex work, but with a number of provisos. Especially in the Holy Roman Empire, sex workers had to work in brothels, as opposed to their own homes, and the brothels had to have a municipal charter. Further, there were often rules about where those brothels could be located. Sex workers commonly had to ply their trade either outside the walls of the city, or close to its edge. Cities commonly forbade brothels to operate out of bathhouses; some legislated that sex workers had to wear dress that marked them as such. In London they had to wear a "hood of ray," a headdress made of black-and-white-striped cloth.

These laws meant that sex workers had an assured place in medieval Europe. Those who stuck by the rules could count on municipal support. In Prague, a zealous local priest tried to run sex workers in the municipal brothel Obora out of their building; a band of sex workers called on the city magistrates to intervene.[48] Their persecutor, the tenacious Master Ulrich, complained bitterly about the sinfulness of commercial sex, but it didn't matter: the women had a right to ply their trade, and the legal system backed them up.

While the law protected the sex workers of Obora, it also necessarily restricted them. In the north of Prague, off Wenceslas Square, several complaints were registered about "suspect women" presumed

Valerius showing emperor Tiberius the decadence of a bathhouse brothel, by the Master of Anthony of Burgundy, ca. 1470. BERLIN STAATSBIBLIOTHEK.

to be working in unlicensed brothels in Krakow Street. In response, the archdeacon announced that the women in question could be "extirpated" from their homes on pain of excommunication.[49] Similarly, London restricted where sex workers could live, even when they were not working. In 1393 the city announced that it forbade any sex worker to "go about or lodge in the . . . city, or in the suburbs thereof, by night or by day; but they are to keep themselves to the places thereunto assigned, this is to say, the Stews [bathhouse brothels] on the other side of [the river] Thames, and Cokkeslane; on pain of losing and forfeiting the upper garment she shall be wearing, together with her hood" if she did not comply.[50] In other words, if a sex worker was found outside the approved area, she would be stripped to her waist and marched back to where she "belonged," a powerful form of public shaming.

Despite this treatment, sex workers could be found in most cities. The trade was open to just about any woman who would put up with the restrictions around it. If you didn't want to live as someone else's servant, weren't allowed to join a trade like fulling, and didn't have a husband who could bring you into a craft, sex work was a way for you to make a living, fast. This was especially relevant for women recently arriving from the countryside who needed a place to stay and a ready income without flagging their whereabouts to the authorities and possibly the landlords they had left behind.

However, not all sex workers came to the trade freely. Some women were fooled into it through outright lies. In London, Elizabeth, the wife of Henry Moring, was accused of posing as an embroiderer, taking in young women for apprenticeships, but instead "after so retaining them, she incited [them] . . . to live a lewd life, and to consort with friars, chaplains, and all other such men as desired to have their company, as well as in her own house."[51] Meanwhile in Prague women sometimes took to the trade as a result of incurring debt. Newly arrived women might take out a loan as they attempted to settle in the city, and lenders commonly insisted that unpaid debts be compensated through labor. A woman who fell into arrears learned that the labor in question was sex work. Because sex work was legal, so were such arrangements, and duped women had little recourse. In one case, the unfortunate Dorothy of Strygl found herself indebted to the madam Ann Harbatová in a contract that required her to work until her debt was repaid, on pain of death.[52]

Again, the ramifications of such behavior depended on the individual's ability to follow the law. The procuress Elizabeth got in legal trouble because her ensnared women were working in places that they shouldn't be (the city of London, as opposed to Southwark), and were serving clientele that they oughtn't (members of the clergy as opposed to unmarried laymen). Ann Harbatová, meanwhile, was able to extort the unwilling Dorothy because she had obeyed the rules of the city. The experiences of unwilling sex workers might differ greatly from city to city, neighborhood to neighborhood, or even person to person, depending on how canny exploiters were about legalities.

Though it was legal to be a sex worker, and even sometimes to force others into the trade, it was never considered a laudable path. The existence of sex workers may have been theologically necessary, but by having sex outside marriage, they were still committing fornication, and it was still deemed a sin, even if a lesser one. Sex workers, then, were considered to be in a state of sin when they plied their trade. Those who died while still in the profession were considered to have died outside the protection of the Church. Much like those who took their own lives, still-practicing sex workers were excluded from burial in consecrated ground.

In London, women of the stews were buried in Southwark in a plot now known as Crossbones Graveyard. Many of these sex workers had worked and lived in houses owned and rented out by the archbishop of Winchester, whose summer palace sat on the south bank of the Thames alongside bathhouses and brothels. For a bishop of the Church to make money from the proceeds of the sex trade was acceptable, but when the women from whom he took money died earning it for him, they were considered outside his care. These sex workers were buried without ceremony or sacrament, a stone's throw from the bishop's palace, in unhallowed ground, as an enduring symbol of their place outside the community they served. Sex workers might be necessary, but they were also expendable.

Death while out of communion with the Church was not the only danger that sex workers faced. As I mentioned in Chapter 3, theo-

logians generally agreed that sex workers could not become pregnant. William of Conches said that because they were having sex for
work, not for pleasure, they were not releasing the sperm necessary
to conceive. While this is not true, some sex workers likely became
sterile as a result of sexually transmitted infections (STIs) picked
up in the line of work. The "leprosy" that women could apparently
pass to their sex partners without harm to themselves might have
been gonorrhea. Symptoms of gonorrhea are often more evident
in men than in women, but when left untreated, it can cause steril-
ity in women. There was concern about STIs at the time, especially
among sex workers: an 1161 decree by Henry II of England (1133–
89) stated that the brothel owners in the London Stewes were not
"to keep any woman that hath the perilous infirmity of burning"
in their employ.[53] In 1256 the French king and later saint Louis IX
(1214–70) decreed that those found to be suffering from the disease
would be banished from the kingdom. Women who became ill faced
very real consequences, both legally and physically.

In 1495, syphilis was introduced into Europe.[54] It triggered a
health and moral panic and made life even more dangerous for
sex workers, though in a world before condoms, there were always
health risks to the trade, and social stigma followed becoming ill.
These medieval infections undermined the health of women who
were already in a socially precarious position and could hasten the
prospect of a death out of communion with the Church.

Many sex workers did not expect to die while in the trade. Women
who were forced into sex work through deceit or debt might find it
hard to exit the trade for legal or extralegal reasons, but those who
had picked it up from convenience or ease were not faced with the
same issues. A necessary part of urban life, sex work could conceiv-
ably be done and then left behind. Those who wished to exit the
trade had only to go to their parish priest, confess their sins, and
request penance, which as advocated by Pope Innocent III (1160/61–
1216), was to marry and, if possible, start a family.[55] Men who mar-

ried former sex workers were promised a remission of their own sins to sweeten the deal. The penance of marriage hints at what the societal issue with sex workers was. Obviously, sex workers were needed to control unruly lust, but they were also a concern not just because of their sexual availability but because they were outside the control of men. If they adhered to their city's laws, they could exist entirely outside familial patriarchal authority, living on their own, spending money as they pleased, and engaging in the work that they had chosen. Asking sex workers to marry was about more than commanding them to leave a dubious trade behind. It was about seeing that they came back under the control of an individual man.

Plenty of women had taken up sex work because they wanted to leave traditional family life behind them in the countryside. They might be less enamored of the work but still not entirely ready to step into the role of wife and mother. Some former sex workers, it turned out, decided that when they wanted to "repent" of sex work, they really meant repent, particularly those who had been forced into sex work because of debt. Those who had never intended to get into sex work were probably more likely to see what they had been doing as sinful and distasteful and wanted to respond by going as far as they could in the other direction. Luckily, plenty of religious people were more than happy to help former sex workers down this road, the bishop of Winchester notwithstanding.

One such individual was the fourteenth-century Czech preacher Jan Milíč of Kroměříž (d. 1374). Milíč established a community called Jerusalem in the house of a former brothel that had been donated to him by a repentant madam. There he would pay off the debts of a reformed woman. If she did not wish to rejoin society, she could stay in the house and dedicate herself to religious contemplation.[56] Eventually, Jerusalem came under scrutiny for, among other things, housing both repentant sex workers *and* male preachers, but it enjoyed widespread support from the Prague community. In general, medieval people seemed to understand that those leaving sex work needed support to do so, and Milíč and the Jerusalem community could offer it.

Jerusalem is an example of direct intervention, part of a long European tradition. In France, such houses had existed in Paris, Toulouse, and Marseille in the thirteenth century; one called Les Filles-Dieu received financial support from the aforementioned Louis IX. Others were in the German and Italian lands.[57] In 1375 Pope Gregory IX (ca. 1145–1241) established a formal group of nuns, the Repentant Sisters of Saint Mary Magdalene, to offer such women a stable life as nuns. The rules were: devotees had to renounce their old lives before age twenty-five; pay for minor infractions by taking up a diet of bread and water; and face imprisonment for more serious offenses.[58] These requirements may have been enough to put off some potential converts, and for this reason less formal communities like Jerusalem continued to thrive, often in the same cities as the Magdalene order. Eventually, the Magdalenes ceased their outreach to sex workers and became an order of nuns like any other. Former sex workers had numerous religious groups eager to take them in, but they weren't necessarily going to become religious women. However, if they did decide to take up the cloth, they could join any number of orders, many doing interesting work.

Religious Women

Nuns have cropped up repeatedly in this discussion because so many were involved in scholastic and community-oriented work. Nuns came into being as part of the monastic movement. Soon after Benedict of Nursia founded the first monastery—Monte Cassino—and formalized his Benedictine rule in 516, Caesarius (ca. 478–542), the bishop of Arles, wrote the first rule for convents in 534. For monasteries and nunneries alike, rules sought to create a parallel world outside the secular one where members could dedicate themselves to a life of prayer and work, *ora et labora,* "in order to evade, with

God's help, the jaws of spiritual wolves." The nuns agreed to wear a distinctive habit, which marked them out as separate from the secular world, and they subordinated their own will to that of the abbess who ruled the nunnery without question. They vowed to "never [leave] the monastery until death."[59] There throughout the day they performed multitudinous mundane tasks. Different groups of nuns gardened, scrubbed floors, cooked, washed dishes, did laundry, and worked wool, everything needed for the convent to function.[60]

But the working lives of nuns differed from those of monks in one important respect: enclosure. In the thirteenth century, new monastic orders came into being. These mendicants, who included the Franciscans, were dedicated to lives of poverty and to administering to the religious needs of their communities. They preached and provided additional religious instruction to individuals who wanted more than their traditional parishes offered. In return, they received alms, which helped them to pay for the running of their monasteries. Their sisters, the Poor Clares, in contrast, remained confined to their convents. Their orders may have been based on the same principles, but women, especially religious ones, were not to mix in public.

A woman who left the secular world behind could look forward to a life of the mind and an opportunity to devote herself to her faith. Some nuns came in as child oblates, as Hildegard did. Others joined later in life. Some young single women could, in theory, listen to sermons about the horrors of married life and choose to forgo marriage in favor of a life of contemplation and communion with God. However, a woman didn't have to be single to serve God. A married woman could join an order with the agreement of her husband. Similarly, widows seeking the solace of the convent could take holy vows. In theory then, except for the very young, a medieval woman could choose to put aside her life among the laity, serve a trial period of six months during which her devotion was evaluated, and take up a new life as a nun serving God.

In reality, the life of the nunnery was largely reserved for the wealthy—Hildegard, for example, came from a lower noble family. A family willing to give up a young daughter to a life of prayer had to be sufficiently well off that they didn't need the extra pair of hands around the house. The average peasant needed the help that a daughter could bring with milking, animal husbandry, and eventually spinning or brewing. Moreover, when a family gave a child as an oblate to a nunnery, it also provided a gift of land or money to assure her upkeep until she became a full working member. There were exceptions to this rule: orphans could be surrendered to nunneries if they lacked other family to care for them. But as a general rule, oblates came from money.

Women who wished to join later in life faced similar difficulties. The literacy requirement prevented the uneducated from being admitted at older ages, even if they had the means. If you could not contribute to the daily life of the order immediately, you were not of much use to those who saw themselves as tasked with working for God constantly. Moreover, it seemed useless to educate a seventy-something widow who might at any point become infirm. The Magdalenes forwent such requirements, needing their members simply to be young, contrite, and willing to be beaten for infractions. Most commonly, if a woman who had no money wanted to become a nun, she could, but she had to put up with a very restrictive rule and order. Women of means, on the other hand, could join orders where rules were more relaxed and beatings less frequent.

Those from lower stations did not necessarily give up hope of a religious vocation. Rather, many sought out lives of religion in various other guises. Like the former sex workers of Jerusalem who lived alongside Milíč, some groups of women lived a religious life but remained members of the laity.

Beguine is a catchall term for a woman who lived a religious life outside the nunnery, in the late twelfth and early thirteenth centuries. Beguine communities were set up in towns that were large enough to absorb and support them, particularly Amsterdam, Ghent, Liège, and Bruges. Beguines often had the same mission as the mendicant Franciscans: They sought to live an apostolic life dedicated to active service, and as a result, they needed to be in towns with large enough populations to serve.

How Beguines took up the religious life varies widely. Some continued to live with their families but devoted themselves to prayer, preaching, and reflection in their spare time. Others lived together in communities called *béguinages*, where they supported themselves through manual labor and committed themselves to religious activity. All had to be unmarried or to have set their husbands aside with their consent. Beguines mostly lived lives of austerity, not unlike the apostolic poverty that the Poor Clares cultivated. The major differences between Beguines and nuns were that the Beguines lacked a rule and a religious vow, often drew members from a lower economic class, and were not enclosed. One could hardly serve a community from behind a closed *béguinage* wall.

Because being a Beguine could mean disparate things, there were various responses to them. Some people actively sought to promote the religious women as paragons of virtue. Jacques de Vitry (ca. 1160–1240), a theologian and canon, wrote a life of the Beguine saint Marie d'Oignies (1177–1213) that aided in her eventual canonization as a saint. Marie, who urged Jacques to take up preaching, was dedicated to "work with her hands . . . in order to afflict her body through penance, and also furnish life's necessities for those in need."[61] Marie had grown up wealthy and chose to marry a man whom her parents opposed. She became deeply devout and practiced physical acts of penance. She slept on wooden planks with a rope tied around her midsection to deprive herself of sleep. She fasted constantly, refused to eat meat, and ate bread so stale it cut her mouth. Eventually, she devoted herself to chastity, a decision that her equally devout husband accepted. She and her husband dedicated themselves to nursing people with leprosy. Marie experienced divine visions and was said to have had healing powers, including curing a sick man by giving him a lock of her hair. In short, she was grade A saint material, and Jacques was able to make his case directly to the papacy.

While Marie had all the desired hallmarks of a Beguine, others did acts that were considered unseemly. Marie never preached, but some Beguines had no compunctions about preaching to their communities just as their models the Franciscans did. The mystic Marguerite Porete (d. 1310) even wrote her own religious work, *The Mirror of Simple Souls,* an extended meditation on the concept of *agape* or universal love. Written in the vernacular French instead of Latin, it described how the individual soul passes through seven stages of "annihilation," eventually being subsumed into Oneness with God. She associated the concept of love with God: "I am God, says Love, for Love is God and God is Love, and this Soul is God by the condition of Love. I am God by divine nature and this Soul is God by righteousness of Love."[62] This train of thought did not go down well. The bishop of Cambrai ordered Marguerite to burn all copies of her work. She refused, was tried for heresy, and in 1310 the inquisitor of France, the Dominican friar William of Paris (d. 1314), had her burned at the stake.

Marguerite exemplified the worst-case scenario, a woman who lived a religious life without oversight. Because women were thought to be intellectually inferior, they were seen as easy targets for heretics who could infect their minds with unacceptable thoughts. If they then took up preaching, they could spread their erroneous ideas to the communities they served. Women simply weren't able to understand when they had transgressed the teachings of the Church. Those like Marguerite who were corrected but refused to change were another story, but there were plenty who just didn't know the difference between religious idealism and heresy.

So reviews of Beguines were mixed. Regardless of the feelings of their contemporaries, however, Beguines offered a life of religious

vocation and community-oriented work for women who would otherwise have no recourse to a spiritual life. These women, heretical
or not, were often valued by their communities and worked hard
within them. Theirs was not always a societally "legitimate" form
of female work. But the existence of Beguines shows that women
across class desired to carry out work that they considered meaningful. They created their own communities that gave them opportunities that otherwise would have been available only to the better off.
Moreover, the life of a Beguine was one of the very few options for a
woman who wanted a religious life but also the opportunity to better her community. A life of piety and contemplation behind closed
doors was laudable. But if a woman wanted to change her society
while cleaving to a life of prayer, joining the Beguines was the way to
do it, detractors be damned.

Those Who Ruled

It is no coincidence that the medieval women that we tend to hear
the most about also had the highest status. Noble and royal women,
bearing heavy burdens of power and prestige, have received outsize
emphasis, even though they were only, in truth, a handful of exceptional individuals. The emphasis on them has, at times, distracted
writers from the much richer lives of ordinary medieval women.

Still, these women, no matter how small their number, had lives
that were almost wholly subsumed by their work. In many ways,
their concerns about their futures fueled more widespread ideas
about beauty standards and fears about sexuality. As soon as she
was born, such a woman was seen as a potential bride. Her looks,
deportment, and spirituality were not simply features, but adver-
tisements for her as a future wife and mother. But on the way to
this future noblewomen also held other jobs. They could work as
ladies-in-waiting and be moved between noble and royal courts.
Once married, they were hardly "just" mothers, not that that role is

easy. They were often directly involved in political negotiations and religious ceremonies. Some traveled alongside their husbands to and from wars and conferred on military tactics. Those who stayed home when their husbands were away often did so because it was their job to run household estates numbering in the hundreds of people and to oversee complex bookkeeping, which required constant attention. Overall, noble and royal women enjoyed luxuries, but they were not idle.

Women from the ruling class were often educated at home. Young ladies might be taught some reading and writing to better be prepared for their future duties. Often, their first teachers were their mothers, setting the tone for the sort of work that would be expected of them once they became mothers. Rich young girls could learn at their mothers' knees, especially, from the thirteenth century onward, from their mothers' books of hours. But much of the education they received from their mothers, even among the wealthy, was oral.

Once a young woman had learned as much as she could from her mother, many wealthy households employed women as private teachers. Indeed, the most prominent royal and noble households employed women to educate both boys and girls up until the age of seven or so. For older girls, the women, generally drawn from the upper classes, would impart more domestic forms of learning. Eleanor of Castile (1246–90), a queen of England, employed Edeline Popiot, from Ponthieu, in Picardy, to serve as the teacher for her daughter, Princess Joan (1220–79).[63] Such teachers could help with deportment, embroidery, and other feminine tasks, but they would not necessarily take one's daughter through complex questions of philosophy. Nor were they meant to do so.

Daughters raised in these powerful households, after receiving their education, often went on to become damsels at puberty. Damsels, like women throughout society, were expected to make themselves useful in multiple ways. Principally, they were to act as company for other elevated women. They acted as maidservants who went with and served these women as they visited their homes, and they provided companionship during trips to other women of their class. At marriage, foreign princesses were commonly accompanied to their new homes by a collection of their compatriots to ease their transition into a new court. When Anne of Bohemia (1366–94) left her father's imperial court in Prague to marry Richard II of England, she was accompanied by several other young Czech girls, who once in London seem to have introduced a taste for the horned headdress and a proclivity for riding sidesaddle.[64]

Damsels were expected to take on all the tasks that busy women in any household might put their hands to, including spinning, weaving, sewing, and embroidering. They might help with gardening, or with making medicines or makeup. Often high-status maidens would launder their mistress's bedding and make their beds. Young maidens were also employed more explicitly as a symbol for well-to-do households, especially in the later medieval period. A woman who arrived at a household or court with a bevy of young women wearing expensive, beautiful clothing told anyone watching how important she was.

Well-born women sometimes enacted specific and intimate acts of service at public occasions such as feasts. In 1487, Dame Katherine Grey and Mistress Ditton served at Elizabeth of York's coronation in a peculiar way: they "went under the table where they sat on either side of the Queen's feet all the dinner time." Similarly, the countesses of Oxford and Rivers "kneeled on either side of the Queen, and at certain times held a kerchief before her Grace."[65] While it surely is handy to have someone pass a napkin, such an action is not needed except to make a ceremonial point. The new queen's body was seen as needing to be carefully attended by high-ranking women from across the realm, showing her place at the top of a vanishingly small pecking order.

The payoff to a life of hiding under the queen's table was often

meant to be a good marriage, but not all those in service necessarily retired to run their own homes once they made such a connection. Ladies-in-waiting, especially in the later medieval period,
could be married and gain important titles. Countesses knelt at
the side of Queen Elizabeth of York, for example. These older
women were often tasked with complicated business dealings for
their royal mistresses. In 1312 Isabella of France (ca. 1295–1358)
sent two of her *damicellae* to London to represent her business, and
another married damsel, Alice de la Lagrave, to Lady Christine de
Marisco, "to have a talk with her concerning certain affairs touch-
ing the queen herself."[66] Plenty of women kept working at royal
courts during their marriages because there was plenty of work to
be done at court, especially as women aged. A queen like Isabella—"the She Wolf" who would later be famous for openly keeping a
lover and who was rumored to have deposed her husband, Edward
II (1284–1327), in favor of her son, Edward III (1312–77)—was not
likely to entrust her business to a fifteen-year-old girl, no matter
how pretty and well dressed.

While some women chose to stay at court and see what errands
they might be sent on, others opted instead to become mistresses of
their own domains, which was no small feat. Women were expected
to oversee their households, and in a great house that could mean
the planting of crops, managing a team of workers, and handling
the budget that paid and fed them, often in the absence of their husbands. As Christine de Pizan noted, ladies who lived on their own
land spent a lot of time running their houses while their husbands
were absent, either at court or abroad. To manage their property
and all its revenue, the ladies had to know what legal rights they
had, what they were supposed to take in as taxes from the harvest,
and how to manage the accounts as well as the staff and tenants
and farm laborers. Meanwhile they also needed to oversee their own
daughters and the work they were doing, as well "many more such
tasks as these which would take too long to describe here."[67]

Principal among the "other tasks" noted by Christine was over-seeing the kitchen, cellar, and larder. Feeding a large household appropriately was a huge undertaking, and mistresses often had the help of a steward to assist them in keeping accounts of what was being consumed and what it cost. One fifteenth-century lady, Dame Alice de Beryene, had her steward John report what was eaten and by how many, so we know exactly how much was con-sumed in her house between 1412 and 1413. On October 2, Dame Alice was informed that six people had breakfast, eighteen dinner, and twelve supper. She was told that the house's holdings now com-prised forty-four white and six black loaves of bread (a type of dark rye bread made with whole wheat), wine from an extant purchase, ale from their own stock, half a salt fish, and one stockfish for the kitchen. And she was told that the house had purchased a hundred oysters for two denarii, a hundred smoked herrings for eighteen denarii, and thirty-three merlings and nine plaice (types of fish) for fourteen denarii. For some reason, bread was purchased for a merchant's horse at half a denari, while the stable fed the six horses of the lady and her company with hay as well as a bushel of oats. In total, the purchases came to two shillings and ten denarii. In the fifteenth century, this was the equivalent of about a week's wages for a skilled tradesman.

The next day the kitchens used a quart of wheat to make 236 white loaves and thirty-six black loaves. Meanwhile out in the brew-ery, two quarters of malt were used to make 112 gallons of ale. Great feasts, such as a New Year's banquet, required an outlay of some fifteen shillings (about thirty-seven days of wages for a craftsman), in order to take care of an influx of people including "Thomas Mal-cher with 300 tenants and other strangers" who showed up expect-ing to be fed. While John the steward recorded these amounts for the running of the household, it was ultimately Alice who had to oversee and understand what was being spent.[68]

While all this routine domesticity was certainly work enough, women from the noble orders also planned for occurrences of a military nature. Not for nothing were the nobility often referred to as "those who fight," and great houses could be targets for violence. Over the thousand-plus years of the medieval period, the wealthy might be targets of, among other groups, Vikings, each other, invading royal armies, and disgruntled peasants. Among the wealthy Pastons (who were of the English gentry, or very-well-to-do people who fell just outside the category of nobility through lack of a title), the wives were involved in planning for violent eventualities, as their letters show. Margery Paston asked her husband to "get some crossbows, and windeases to bend them with, and quarrels [crossbow bolts]; for your houses here are so low that no one can shoot out with a long bow, though we have never so much need. . . . And also I would ye should get two or three short poleaxes to keep indoors, and as many jacks."[69] Her concern here is instructive as it shows that outside houses of those tasked with licit violence, women helped plan for violent defense.

Noblewomen were also supposed to engage in patronage and artistic display. The sponsorship of poets and artists highlighted what it meant to be noble and set these women apart by their education and refinement. As a result, commissioning, reading, and displaying books constituted a necessary role. It was as much a part of the job as overseeing a household, albeit an extraordinarily pleasant part.

Noblewomen had a heavy workload even before any political work that they might do to assist their husbands. The political marriages that noblewomen entered into, and that they had to be prepped for with careful education by their mothers, brought ongoing responsibilities. Noblewomen might confer with and advise their husbands on political matters. They could intercede with family members on behalf of their in-laws and could cultivate relationships with other powerful women to do the same. The connections they made while in service could and did come in handy when they were back on their estates. Even a quiet life in the country was busy and had the potential to be as political as any man's.

Any discussion of medieval women's work will eventually focus on the women about whom we hear more than anyone else: queens. All the work of noblewomen was also expected of royal women, with an extra emphasis on affairs of state and on public ritual. As the busy ladies-in-waiting to Queen Isabella show, queens often had their own goals and motivations that kept them busy. They often mediated between their families of origin and their new kingdoms, acting as high-level diplomats who could balance the concerns of both. In a particularly important role, queens interceded with their husbands or sons. If a king took a certain course of action, then had to walk back from it, making him appear weak or foolish, queens could intercede directly, asking for leniency. This allowed kings to save face while also avoiding mistakes of rash decision making.

When Anne of Bohemia wasn't busy introducing English women to new fashions in pointed hats, she managed to work in favor of her subjects. Her husband Richard II was, from the point of view of the common people, a difficult man. He had overseen the violent suppression of his peasant subjects when they rebelled in 1381 seeking better wages and more rights. By 1392, the king seems to have learned very little from that episode and found himself embroiled in a conflict with the people of London. That June the king had requested a loan of ten thousand pounds, but the city, struggling with a new outbreak of plague and food shortages, refused. Richard did not take it well. In retaliation, he suspended the liberties of the city, deposed the mayor and aldermen, moved the royal law courts to York, and put his captain in charge of the city. He also demanded a fine of one hundred thousand pounds (or about £9 million in today's currency) from the struggling Londoners, presumably for hurting his feelings.

He was deliberately attempting to strip London of its prominence. It was not a great move, considering the city's outsize importance as a place of trade. Anne was able to talk her husband out of destroying the most important city in his kingdom, pleading with him directly in Windsor and in Nottingham to reinstate the mayor and forgive the fine. The Londoners, for their part, agreed to capitulate to the king if their liberties were reinstated. They offered to pay a fine of ten thousand pounds (the amount of the initially rejected loan). The king and queen then held a lavish ceremony at Westminster Hall, where Anne got on her knees in front of her husband, once again pleading for forgiveness for London. He then raised her from her knees and placed her back at his side, a sign that he would forgive London. He did not fully restore the liberties of London until 1397, and even then, it was contingent on agreement to another loan.

Queens could also intercede between kings and the Church. In 1141, when Pope Innocent II (d. 1143) appointed Pierre de la Chatre (d. 1171) as archbishop of Bourges, Louis VII of France (1120–80) tried to veto his choice. In return, the pope placed Louis under interdict. The protracted disagreement resulted in war between Pierre's supporters and the crown and culminated in the death of a thousand people in Vitry when the king besieged the city. In 1144 Louis's wife, Eleanor of Aquitaine, visited with Bernard of Clairvaux (1090–1153), a friend of the pope who was soon to be made a saint. She demanded that the pope undo the excommunication of those on the king's side in return for the confirmation of his first choice of bishop. Her request was granted.

Queens could also wield military power, and Eleanor, once again, is the archetype. Louis, wracked with guilt over the deaths that his assault at Vitry had caused, decided to go on Crusade to atone. Eleanor took part in the Second Crusade not just as the king's wife but as the leader of Aquitaine, recruiting her ladies-in-waiting as well as her Aquitanian subjects. She also corresponded with her uncle Raymond of Poitiers (ca. 1099–1149), then prince of Antioch, to ascertain how much military support would be needed to prop up the failing Crusader states. The Second Crusade ended in defeat, mainly due to Louis's poor military knowledge. The marriage of Louis and Eleanor did not survive this trip, and the pair were granted an annulment on grounds of consanguinity. In general, it is agreed that the capable queen Eleanor was humiliated by her husband's military ineptitude. A queen who could and did marshal her own forces could not, and didn't have to, abide by such a husband.

Eleanor of Aquitaine is an outlier among outliers. Her military interventions, though not unheard of, were still rare among her women peers. There is a reason that hers is one of the few medieval women's names that people know. Still, she was able to achieve what she did because she was working within the framework of queenship. It might have been an unusual way to wield royal power, but it was not an impossible one.

Queens who did not go into the battlefield still had any number of important jobs. Like noblewomen, they acted as important patrons of both the Church and the arts. One such notable patroness was Margaret of Anjou (1430–82), who stands out as one of the hardest-working queens in several areas. French, she married Henry VI of England (1445–71) and was often in charge of the kingdom's affairs while her husband struggled with mental illness. Like Eleanor of Aquitaine in her role as a military leader, Margaret was called upon to lead the Lancastrian faction during the Wars of the Roses. Still, with all these responsibilities, she found time to be a prolific patron. Queens College in Cambridge was founded in 1448 at her request. She was also instrumental in raising the profile of women-dominated textile industries in England and imported skilled wool workers from Flanders to bolster the trade. Even more notably, she was responsible for the introduction of silk weaving into the country. Queen Margaret brought in silk workers from Lyon to teach the craft and founded the Sisterhood of Silk Women in London. Though Margaret would eventually be captured in battle at Tewkesbury and returned to France, to live out her days in exile, Spitalfields silk, which was created as a direct result of her patronage, remained a sought-after commodity well into the nineteenth century.

Medieval queens, while living impressive, rarefied lives, nonetheless had to perform complex and difficult tasks. They had to balance power with kings, bear and raise children, manage the details of castles and palaces, support a host of artists and artisans, and ease relationships between the king and the Church leadership, all while maintaining strong connections with her and the king's friends and relatives, and at times command an army. But we must not pay attention to queens to the exclusion of the other women in the period. For every queen living a life of riches and diplomatic employment, there were thousands of hardworking peasant women who kept households, worked fields, and got involved in village politics. We must acknowledge the work of queens, but it was ordinary women's work that kept medieval Europe alive and thriving.

Women have always been workers. In addition to domestic chores, they worked in farming, brewing, and the like, laboring for rather a lot more hours than most men did. For this reason, medieval women might attempt to warn others off of married life and point them toward the somewhat less stressful confines of the nunnery instead. The idea that women didn't work until recently is, ironically, a modern construction. Medieval people may not have lauded women for their professions, but working women were common enough that they didn't necessarily bear mentioning.

Where then, did we get this idea? Partially it has to do with the way that medieval people approached both women and work. Women were understood less as individuals than as commodities. They were traded through marriage to be productive laborers, working alongside their husbands and carrying out reproductive labor as well. Even if they managed to leave their family while unwed, they were expected to labor within a household, or to join an order of religious women, performing religious labor and praying for their families. While an argument could be made that the combination of domestic, reproductive, and religious labor was an overlooked sink of energy for women, we don't need to get that theoretical. Women were working at every level of society alongside or in partnership with men—and received almost no credit for doing so.

The idea that a woman would need to be credited for being a worker in her own right was alien to medieval people because women didn't necessarily exist in their own right. Much as male family members needed to watch women to ensure that they were behaving appropriately, women's work took place under the auspices of an appropriate and respectable collective that could control them. Women then worked not for themselves but in service of their family, their household, or, failing that, the Church, reflecting an institution and not themselves as individuals. It's become our job to find these women and to name what they did for what it was: worthwhile and necessary work.

5

WHY IT MATTERS

MEDIEVAL PEOPLE HAD A DIFFERENT FRAMEWORK FOR judging women's status from our own, a different set of beauty standards, a different way of relating to women's sexuality, and different expectations about women's lives and work. But we tend to ignore that fact. This could be chalked up to chance. After all, misunderstanding a complex period of history that ended half a millennium ago isn't necessarily a problem in and of itself. However, it obscures the fact that the stories we *do* tell about the medieval age allow us to claim that modern thinking about and treatment of women are superior to those of the earlier age.

It is easy to buy into the idea of the distant past as more oppressive than our own time, even if both share the supposition that women are inferior to men. We tend to look at our individual life experience and then make assumptions about history based on that. If we perceive that our personal attitudes toward women have become more equitable over the course of our lives, we presume that previously conditions must have been worse. To be sure, during the course of our lifetimes, women have made major strides toward equality because of the feminist movement's concentrated attempts to counteract negative constructs about women. Feminism—which the writer Marie Sheer famously defined in 1986 as "the radical notion that women are people"—has been one of the hallmarks of later modernity.[1] From the eighteenth through the early twentieth centuries, the movement called for legal recognition of equality between the sexes and for the right of suffrage (although often specifically for white women, it should be noted). In the so-called second wave, from the 1960s to the '90s, it advocated for reproductive rights and examined the limited concept of sexuality. From the late 1990s until now, feminism has been in its third wave, which has been informed by postcolonial and postmodern thinking and calls for a greater emphasis on intersectionality and subjectivity for women.

Because of its cultural prominence, feminism is sometimes presented to us as a fait accompli. Indeed, the themes explored in this book have been directly discussed in the feminist canon for decades. In 1929 Virginia Woolf wrote of the social pressure to maintain appearances by asking "what your beauty means to you, or your plainness, and what is your relation to the ever changing and turning world of gloves and shoes."[2] In 1963 Betty Friedan's *The Feminine Mystique* questioned the role of women as mothers and carers. Women's sexuality was front and center of the feminist debate during the so-called sexual revolution of the 1960s.

These women made real impacts in terms of turning the tide of social consciousness, and as a result, the treatment of women in many places in the world has improved. This advance allows us to construct an idea of our own society as a time of postfeminist egalitarianism, sharply delineated from a regressive and backward past. We are told that women have achieved equality as their numbers in the workforce rise, or when cosmetics companies run "diverse" beauty campaigns, or when advertising campaigns for sex toys label them as a necessity for "wellness." If anything seems still to be unfair, well, that is likely the result of certain immutable and biological facts that no amount of philosophical arguing or political agitation can change.

The trouble with that argument is that just a cursory glance at the Middle Ages shows that there has never been one stable reason why women continue to struggle with these issues.

Women's Nature, or How Are Women Inferior? Let Me Count the Ways

As we have seen, medieval Europeans created their gender beliefs using a mixture of classical Greek and Roman philosophy and meticulous Christian theology. From Aristotle to Aquinas, their verdict was unanimous: women were *created* as secondary to men. The default human in both classical and Christian cosmology was a man. Men were rational, pious, equanimous, strong, and brave. They had downsides like quick tempers due to their hot and dry humoral complexions, but that was a natural outcropping from their virtues and could not be helped.

In contrast, the cold and wet women were irrational, garrulous, oversexed, and cowardly. Their positive attributes were limited to the domestic world, where they could be nurturing. So intrinsic was women's unpleasant and sinful nature that the medieval feminine ideal, the Virgin Mary, had to go through a theological loophole to be born without the original sin that corrupted the rest of her sex.

Enlightenment thinkers created a neat fissure between outdated medieval superstitions and religious ideas and the more rational and scientific concepts. The Enlightenment philosopher Voltaire (1694–1778) popularized our view of the medieval period as a "Dark Ages" whose ideas had to be banished and superseded. The names given to the Renaissance and the Enlightenment show how thoroughly the earlier age had to be buried.

However, even as late as the Enlightenment, certain medieval philosophical frameworks were retained, even if dressed up as rational. John Locke (1632–1704), philosopher and physician, put forward the idea that the superiority of men over women was natural, based on an interpretation of the Fall of Man. He stated that "God, in [the creation myth] . . . foretells what should be the woman's lot, how by this providence he would order it so that she should be subject to her husband, as we see that generally the laws of mankind and customs of nations have ordered it so." Because of Eve's fall into temptation, society ordered itself to control for the various weaknesses of women. As a result, men "naturally" came out on top. For example, in domestic disputes it "being necessary that . . . the rule should be placed somewhere, it naturally falls to the man's share, as the abler and stronger."[3] It may surprise you to learn that this take was considered almost radically pro-woman for the time. Saying that men were in the controlling and decision-making role because of their strength was an advance over saying men ruled the world because God said so.

Others concurred about the place of women but gave different reasoning. Philosopher Jean-Jacques Rousseau (1712–1778), for one, insisted that women didn't "naturally" devote themselves to domestic acts like childrearing. Domesticity, he argued, was a habit that women picked up as they lived alongside their offspring. In a natural state, women nursed and cared for their children "almost without effort" and in theory got on with their lives like any other animal. But because European society underwent great advances, women became wholly domestic, putting the relations between the sexes on a par with "civil society, the arts, commerce, and all that is claimed to be useful to men."[4] In other words, segregating women into a specifically domestic role, which happened to be considered inferior to men, was not "natural" but was a major achievement of his civilization.

The "Female" Brain

Bolstered by the allegedly progressive spirt of the Enlightenment, we are reevaluating our concepts of sex-related behavior through scientific understanding. Now the fact that women and men have certain *biological* differences is used to explain why women *are* inferior to men in all the ways that our society privileges. Who would have thought?

In his 2003 book *The Essential Difference: Men, Women, and the Extreme Male Brain*, the renowned Cambridge psychology professor Simon Baron-Cohen waded into the discussion of differentiation between the sexes with a new theory. He claimed that there are three kinds of human brain: "empathizing" (type E), "systemizing" (type S), and between the two of them, "balanced" (type B). He argued that most men have a type S brain, which means that they are more interested in things than in people, and that their interest in mastery over items allows them to gain expertise in a range of subjects and hardwires them as leaders. Women, in contrast, are more likely to have a type E brain, which sets them up to gossip, make friends, and be mothers.

Baron-Cohen came to this conclusion by way of an experiment with day-and-a-half-old babies who were not yet burdened with social expectations and therefore, in theory, were more likely to display intrinsically biological reactions. The experiment was simple: show the babies a person's face for about a minute and an object (a mobile) for about a minute, record their eye movements, and see which the baby elected to look at for a longer time. Baron-Cohen reported that overall, boy babies looked at the mobile for about 51 percent of the time, and at the face for 41 percent of the time, while the remaining 8 percent showing no marked difference in attention. The girls, in contrast, looked at the face 49 percent of the time and the mobile 41 percent. The remaining 10 percent of girls showed no difference in attention between face and object.

We as a society absolutely love this sort of experiment, as it gives us authoritative data for a phenomenon that we have been noticing at least since Plato. The trouble is that its conclusion doesn't seem to be correct. When other researchers attempted to recreate the study, they did not come to the same conclusion—even Baron-Cohen himself did not, in later instances.[5] This should probably not be surprising, given that newborn babies aren't even able to hold their heads up on their own. All those in the study were held by a parent and probably ended up looking at whatever was most comfortable for them given the way that they were held.

Moreover, as University of Melbourne professor Cordelia Fine has pointed out, newborn babies are also in want of a well-developed attention span. Most studies that ask which stimulus a baby prefers present two options side by side and see where the baby elects to focus. "If you don't, and instead present them one after the other," Fine observes, "then you don't really know whether the baby looked at stimulus A more because she genuinely found it interesting, or whether she was irritated by some inner rumblings, about to fall asleep, or simply a little tired when stimulus B was on show."[6] But the fact that Baron-Cohen's study results were not repeatable and therefore scientifically moot has done little to keep them from cropping up when useful.

Baron-Cohen's study is just one that contributes to flawed ideas about a neurological sex differentiation that the psychologist Diane F. Halpern terms "neuromythologies." She highlights the case of a medical doctor who cheerfully informed viewers of a CBS-TV news program that "men have six and a half times more gray matter than women do" while women have "ten times more white matter," making men better at information processing and women better at multitasking. Almost everything in this statement is incorrect, including the assumption that a differentiation in cell bodies in gray matter and myelinated axioms in white have any bearing on these processes. Even worse, it ignores the fact that "our brains change in response to experience, so any purported brain differences between males and females could have been caused by (and not the cause of) different life experiences."[7]

Elsewhere, Halpern records a teacher in a sex-segregated public-school class explaining that she separated boys and girls because "brain researchers have proven that boys learn differently to girls."[8] But it has been shown that when groups of children are segregated along the lines of characteristics, they infer that the groups do differ in important ways, and develop biases as a result. Separating boys and girls at an early age thus reinforces to them that there are specific gender differentiations in learning, which they will take with them into adulthood.[9] The same conceit is found in the infamous 2017 "Google Memo" case, where an employee of the data giant was fired after posting a pseudo-scientific treatise claiming that women's biology prevented them from working to the same level as men at technology companies. The memo, incidentally, alluded to Baron-Cohen's work.[10]

When women's brains are not being cited as theoretical proof of their inevitable status as mothers, their hormones are blamed as likely culprits. Teams of hormonal researchers have identified that women who have higher levels of estrogen have "higher maternal tendencies." They apparently reached this conclusion by asking a group of women how many children they wanted and when, then measuring the levels of estrogen in their urine.[11] Such studies back up received psychological wisdom about the ticking "biological clock" that urges women into motherhood and that some researchers have linked to the pituitary gland or simply to the "essential" natures of women.[12]

Although scientists and the general public alike assure themselves that women's hormones mean that they are destined to be mothers, many more studies have found that no such link exists. As the sociologist Nancy J. Chodorow noted as far back as 1987, there is as yet "no evidence to show that female hormones or chromosomes make a difference in human maternalness, and there is substantial evidence that nonbiological mothers, children, and men can parent just as adequately as biological mothers and can feel just as nurturant."[13] This remains the case.

Overall, there is no real problem with the idea that women's hormones are a help if they become mothers. Motherhood, after all, should be a neutral state that women do or do not enter. However, the fact of motherhood is often enough to make people consider women as less competent than their male or childless-female peers. The sociologists Shelley Correll, Stephan Benard, and In Paik recently found that working mothers were seen as 10 percent less competent than their childless peers. They were also perceived as 12 percent less committed to their jobs than women with no children. Maddeningly, fathers, in contrast, were seen as being 5 percent more committed to their jobs than men with no children. These same working mothers were also paid less and were more heavily scrutinized by their peers, especially for perceived problems with punctuality.[14] In all, the average working mother in America loses about $16,000 in wages due to "the motherhood penalty."[15] Women's theoretical hormonal destiny as mothers is thus an active impediment to their participation and advancement in the workforce.

You will note that regardless of whether the modern concept of sexual differences rests on a social or a scientific explanation, neither disputes the unassailable fact that women are in their current societal place due to an irresistible force. If we keep women from public life for social reasons, it is because we are compelled to do so. Who will raise the children if not women?

The Changing Beauty Standard

One thing that modern and medieval society agree on is that the most important thing about women is the way they look. Moreover, each society has decided that women, to be beautiful, require specific traits. Our modern emphasis on women's looks is common enough that we are almost inured to it. We are constantly barraged with commercials in which beautiful young women try to sell us, well, anything really, and media in all formats are populated by women who stand out for their attractiveness. This observation is not groundbreaking, and most women are hyperaware that they will almost always be judged by how they present themselves and are perceived. Sociological researchers have proved repeatedly that whether in Germany, China, or the United States, women who are perceived as attractive by the national standard are paid more for the same jobs as their counterparts who are considered less attractive.[16]

This predilection, everyone from psychologists to fitness magazines assures us, is scientific and has nothing to do with objectifying women. In numerous research articles, men show their preference for an hourglass figure—small waist and wide hips—as measured in the "waist-to-hip ratio" (WHR). In an article in *Frontiers of Psychology*, the author acknowledges that "the effect of WHR on attractiveness is widespread." A low WHR is hypothesized as a way of men recognizing a woman *as* a woman; a cue of reproductive age in women; a way of telling whether a woman is currently pregnant and what her fecundity is more generally; or even an indicator of parasitic load.[17] Overall, however, the most commonplace reasoning for the emphasis on the hourglass figure is that men are attracted to it because they "know without knowing" that women who boast it are fertile and have likely never been pregnant before.[18]

The "natural" and "evolutionary" preference for hourglass shapes would be news to medieval male Europeans, who as we have seen were much more interested in pear shapes. How do we explain medieval men's desire for pot bellies if men analyze women's bodies for signs that they may be pregnant and eschew them if they are? And what about today's high fashion models who are tall, have small to medium-sized breasts, and slim hips yet are considered the epitome of the ideal body? All these designations of attractiveness leave out most women, even if they turn to a surgical option.

Further, our society does not praise most of the other medieval beauty preferences. We may still regard blond hair as a beauty ideal, but we are fickle on much else. In the last fifty years, we have lauded tanned skin and fair complexions—note that Black and brown women's skin tones don't even enter into Western beauty standards. Eyebrows go from pencil thin to bushy. And we don't share the medieval penchant for "high free" foreheads. If standards are based on evolutionary processes, why do our current preferences differ from older ones, and why have ours changed even during different decades?

There is no single and consistent beauty ideal that has existed over time, even within Europe. Beauty is a social construct and has different characteristics in different ages. Justifying social beauty norms through scientific means is as much a social construction as Matthew of Vendôme's effort was, and we can pay them exactly as much heed. Maybe less, because at least Matthew was giving us some poetry to read as well.

So while women must meet mostly impossible requirements of beauty, medieval and modern societies also prefer that the women should simply *be* beautiful and unaware of the fact, fitting in with a modesty that helps to keep them in inferior positions. We no longer threaten women with ghastly tortures in hell if they take an interest in makeup, but we still want them to be effortlessly beautiful, and creating that effect requires a lot of money and sometimes surgery. At the same time, the fashion industry aggressively markets to women, with omnipresent reminders that one must have this season's newest look or be labeled a drudge. The beauty expectations that women live under have created a juggernaut of closely linked global industries, selling everything from frocks to facelifts, and even then, those products are treated as fripperies—fundamentally unserious endeavors to achieve an ideal that women should nevertheless embody effortlessly. And once a woman knows she is beautiful and fashionable, she can safely be dismissed as vain.

The other thing our society has carried over from the medieval period is that it is easier for rich women to be considered beautiful. Certainly, among white women, a preference for blondes is still very much in play, and blondeness is now easily achievable through artificial means. Women with expendable cash can have their hair dyed professionally and achieve a "natural" look, while the less affluent can dye their hair at home, although that too requires some spare cash, which isn't always available. A preference for white skin among white people has given way to a preference for tanned skin, but since more women now work indoors, a sun-kissed glow is a nod to an abundance of leisure time outside and away from computers and housework. It is tied in our minds to vacations to beaches in exotic locales, which are certainly not open to everyone. Meanwhile, the pressure to live up to European standards of beauty sees many Black and brown women avoiding the sun or purchasing skin-whitening products.

An interest in small breasts has given way to a preference for larger ones, which those with a budget for plastic surgery can readily purchase. Less invasive options are also on the table, such as push-up bras, but they too require money, even if less than going under the knife. Similarly, while we have shed the preference for a pot belly in favor of a flat stomach, the ripped abs that women now aspire to require serious exercise, which requires free time that is not always available to those who work long hours for little pay and go home to childcare responsibilities. Moreover, Pilates classes aren't necessarily going to sculpt poor women in the ways that rich women can achieve by hiring a surgeon.

Women's fashion today, like medieval fashion, favors the rich and often nods to idleness as the most fashionable possible state. Women who are on their feet all day working, or who need to take public transportation or walk to work, simply cannot wear extremely high heels. Those who wear such fashionable items can sit during transport and need only to cover short distances, reclining in comfort when they arrive. They are, as a friend of mine once stated, "the sort of shoes you wear from the taxi into the restaurant." Similarly, pristine, fashionable clothing is hardly achievable to women who work in agriculture, or who wear uniforms to blue-collar jobs, or who run after children upon their return home.

Fashion thus reinforces ideas about luxury and beauty. Now that fashion is its own industry, those messages are perhaps even more heightened than they were in the medieval period, when society actively fought to stop others from emulating the styles of the ruling class. Everyone is now encouraged to buy luxury brands, though the vast majority of people will never be able to.

Our society also still holds questionable concepts of attractiveness and maidenhood. Young women in the public eye are trotted out year over year, sexualized, yet asked to perform purity at the same time. Then they are castigated for not meeting that impossible standard. In 2019 the teen pop star Billie Eilish stated that she wore baggy clothes to avoid the hyperfixation and sexualization that the music industry and culture imposes on women. She was still the subject of hypersexualization and a media frenzy when, wearing a tank top, she took a picture with a fan. As one interviewer put it, "She's a minor, and even CNN wrote a story about Eilish's boobs."[19] Two years later, and a legal adult, Eilish graced the cover of *British Vogue* wearing a corset and faced immediate backlash, ultimately losing "100,000 followers [on Instagram], just because of the boobs."[20] This was a specific backlash to Eilish's agency. It was fine to sexualize her against her will, but the moment she presented herself willingly in a revealing top, there was a problem.

Clearly, our society is still preoccupied with the theoretical sexual innocence of women. At times this can be dressed up as yet another evolutionary trait, where those interested in ogling sexually inexperienced young women can tell themselves that they do so because surely any children they would have with such women would be "theirs." But that argument is basically interchangeable with the medieval emphasis on virginity, even if it replaces God and parents with a theoretical biological "drive." We also continue to place young sexually inexperienced women in positions where they are expressly meant to be viewed in a sexualized manner. Whether it is damsels at court, or pop stars on fashion covers, we, like our medieval counterparts, are more than willing to leer at young women, then get upset when they confront that gaze head on.

"Purity" as a form of attraction continues to spill over even after a woman has had sex for the first time. We fret about the number of sex partners women have, explicitly stating that a woman can have sex with only a finite number and still be considered attractive. Even in a world that is more accepting of queer relationships, our societal preoccupation with women's sex partners seems to focus almost exclusively on heterosexual encounters. Men worry about women having sex with other men, while same-sex contact between women is not considered to "count." Conversely, a woman's attraction to or experience with other women is often held up as a specific attraction point in itself. We may think we have moved beyond religious concepts of appropriate behavior, but we clearly still uphold a concept of purity based on just that. We get to the same outcome through new and ever more contrived means.

The ideal medieval beauty looked nothing like the modern model, but our social relationship to beauty is similar. While this is incredibly frustrating, it also means that there is a possibility for positive change. We can refuse to participate in a game rigged against women and open the world up to diverse ideas of beauty and undercut its importance in women's lives.

Shifts in Sexuality

Since the medieval period, our idea of sexuality and of women more broadly has changed, but you wouldn't necessarily know that because, in general, we have yet to treat the contemplation of sex with the same seriousness as medieval intellectuals. We have only recently begun to regard the study of sex as legitimate, and even then, we still treat it as a distraction from more serious scholarly topics. Despite our familiarity with Alfred Kinsey, Dr. Ruth, and Dr. Debby Herbenick, discussing sexuality outside a clinical environment is often treated as fundamentally unserious. As a result, we still face barriers to sexual research, or even to sexual health services because of government opposition to funding them.[21]

One reason for our society's reluctance to come to grips with sexuality as a field of study is that we are convinced that we know what sex is. Sex, we are taught (if we are lucky enough to have received any sex education), is something that a man and a woman do when they love each other very, very much and decide they want to have a baby. As we age, we learn the process for such encounters: kissing, groping, mutual masturbation, oral sex, and finally "real" sex, which we are to understand as penis-in-vagina sex, as it was for medieval people.

We are also fairly convinced of how sexuality and relationships break down according to gender. Men put up with relationships in order to have sex. Women put up with sex to have relationships. However, European society has a far longer tradition of women as sexually rapacious than our newly agreed upon idea of them as frigid.

Interestingly, Christian philosophers in the ancient and medieval periods spent a lot of time attempting to nudge people into forsaking all sex other than procreative sex. However, we too tend to believe that the only type of sex that counts is the penis-in-vagina kind. Everything else, including the types of sex that those with a clitoris consider more enjoyable, is transformed into foreplay. Think of the baseball metaphor for sex that counts kissing as first base, over-the-clothes or upper-body fondling as second, manual or oral sex as third base, and penile penetration as a home run. Sexologists spend a great deal of their time attempting to debunk this "sexual script."[22]

Our views of sex, then, resemble those of medieval people in that we agree on discounting the types that women may have more interest in. Pietro d'Abano's description of orgasms produced through clitoral stimulation as "indiscreet" is very much like Freud's description of clitoral orgasm as "infantile" or "immature."[23] Both regard orgasm achieved through any means other than penile insertion as somehow silly or childish and speaking to an improper understanding of the real purpose of sex. What changed between d'Abano and Freud is the reason *why*.

The medieval world put clitoral orgasm achieved through sex that couldn't lead to procreation off-limits. Augustine and Aquinas thought having too much fun during sex was an affront to God and therefore had to be stopped. In contrast, we often characterize these same actions as distractions. That we as a society may have taken to heart the millennia of hectoring to knock off all that sodomy and stick to procreative sex doesn't occur to us.

We assure ourselves that our sexual ideas, especially when it comes to women, are based purely on biological urges, unsullied by anything that the Church ever told us. This is ridiculous. Even medieval people would find laughable the idea that we engage in sex only because biological urges to have children compel us to. As they point out, why then do women want to engage in sex when they are menstruating, when conception isn't possible? If our focus on penis-in-vagina sex now is simply reflecting a physical biological reality about what is pleasurable, then why are clitorises external? If all this was just the way sex was, why did philosophers and theologians spend scores of centuries begging people to stop having the sorts of sex that didn't count? Our attitudes toward sex certainly are driven by some biological underpinnings, but our hegemonic ideas about sex are a product of society.

Modern thinkers, like medieval ones, continue to define women largely by their procreative potential. The concept of women engaging in sex in order to trap a man hinges on the idea that they are baby-makers first and foremost. When it comes to sex, "respectable" women are never considered as sexual agents in and of themselves. They are involved because they wish to be mothers. In contrast, women who are interested in sex, or sex with more than one person, are often expressly presented as damaged, untrustworthy, and expressly unfeminine. The fact that we have accepted this framing would absolutely delight medieval theologians. After all, women were created to serve men and help them multiply. When we accept the framing of sex as something that women engage in to have children, we are doing the work of the medieval Church for them. They would probably be amazed to hear that women were "naturally" chaste and monogamous, but they would likely take it, provided we accepted that sex was only a means to a procreative end.

Because of their idea that women's sexuality is depraved, medieval thinkers spent their time marveling at women's sexual capacity and the pleasure that they experienced during sex, even if they thought it of lesser quality than men's. Our modern recasting of women as mere receptacles for men's sexual pleasure, on the other hand, has seen new ways of thinking about female orgasm. Indeed, evolutionary psychologists wonder why women orgasm at all, given that it is not necessary for reproduction. Some have tackled this quandary by arguing that women might experience pleasure during sex in order to "seal the pair bond" between themselves and men, or to encourage "sperm upsuck." Most gallingly, some dismiss it as an "incidental by-product of male orgasm, much like male nipples [which] apparently have no function and are incidental by-products of the fact that females have nipples."[24]

Amusingly, as our contemporary focus has shifted to accept the Church's preferred attitude toward sex, so has our idea of who enjoys sex. Now that sex is considered a "good" as a means to a procreative end first and foremost, our society has decided that it is men who like it, and they like it ideally with a lot of different partners. In contrast, women are now faithful creatures hoping to grit their teeth through sex with one man in order to get a baby and a committed husband out of it. Yet no matter how many articles are written about how women are "naturally selective" about their mates, the fact remains that for most of recorded European history, women were considered to be wishing for hot sex with whoever would give it to them.

In contrast, some holdovers from the medieval period remain, including our attitudes toward women who have experienced sexual assault. We have decided, like our medieval counterparts, that women who have had sex against their will were likely "asking for it." Our definition of rape is of a brutal act perpetrated against the woman and not, as for medieval people, against the men responsible for her. However, we often blame women for these assaults, despite the decades-long advancement of feminist ideas and a few legal wins.

When a woman is assaulted, we ask what she was wearing, how much she had drunk, why she was alone, why she had been on a date with the man if she wasn't interested in sex—anything to explain away her experience of unwanted sexual attention. It is simply easier to file away women who complain about their sexual assaults as the wrong sort of woman than to accept that a man has done something awful. Thus, when the idea that women are frigid no longer serves the patriarchy, it can be discarded. Instead, the medieval idea of women returns: overtly sexual and hoping to damage the men around them through the use of their sexuality.

Thankfully, we no longer accuse women of witchcraft, and the idea that women might be practicing occult rites to have sex with men has gone by the wayside. What we still retain, however, is the idea that women have a powerful, perhaps bewitching, sexual hold over men. What else could drive men, who would otherwise have been minding their own business, into assault?

Clearly then, while many of our attitudes toward women's sexuality have changed since the medieval period, one thing has remained the same: women are not sexual in the correct way. Our society is still determined to declare women's relationship to sex disordered. Many millions of people are having sex outside a heteronormative context, and from them we may learn some lessons that will help to break down our assumptions about sex. One lesson is to reject the theological and falsely "scientific" idea that sex exists purely to beget children. Then we can to begin to sort it into a range of activities that we may or may not be interested in. Those accused of a lack of interest in sex may turn out to be a lot more engaged when the things they enjoy are on the table and treated as viable options. Unlinking our ideas about sex from ideas about procreation also allows us to move away from defining women by their procreative capacity.

With the benefit of historical insight, we can reject the idea that our culture's particular framing of sexuality is inevitable. We need to make a conscious decision to stop treating women as the "other" in opposition to men, who know how to have sex correctly. We just might find that everyone is happier that way.

New Justifications, Old Expectations

Expectations for women are another area where our society struggles to come to terms with the past. Medieval women were expected to become wives and mothers, and we can hardly claim to hold a much different view today. Our society's attitudes toward women's marital status have shifted very little. From childhood, girls are fed a steady diet of fairytales that end in a happily-ever-after of marriage to the right man, they play at wedding with dolls in bridal dresses. This expectation does not die with age. Women are still presented with the "ladies sports pages" in the *New York Times* "Vows" column; an endless parade of reality television focuses on finding a husband; and the expanding wedding industry has grown to the point of being dubbed the "wedding industrial complex." For the "most important day in a woman's life," we sink ever-increasing amounts of money into the display—the average American wedding costs about $29,000. That would confuse a medieval European audience, whose focus was much more on marriage than on weddings, but the result is the same.[25] Women are primed to believe that *the thing* about their lives will be the fact that they marry.

After marriage, women are to fulfill their biological destiny to become mothers. The same "scientific" studies that inform us that there has always been one standard of beauty and that women aren't sexual also tell us that women, first and foremost, are child bearers. Just as every relationship women have is supposedly predicated on selecting successful partners who will provide for them and their children, the organizing principal of women's lives is supposed to be reproductive.

At times, these ideas about women spill over into real-world policy. During the George W. Bush administration in the United States, for example, the Centers for Disease Control and Prevention made the socially conservative case that women of childbearing age should consider themselves as "pre-pregnant." The thing about all younger women, you see, is that they might be mothers someday, not that they are people whose health and happiness matters in and of itself. Lest you convince yourself that this is a relic of a far-off decade and an especially retrograde American government, as recently as June 2021 the World Health Organization announced that "appropriate attention should be given to prevention of . . . drinking among . . . women of childbearing age."[26] That would include fourteen-year olds and women who have decided to never have children as well as women who have had as many children as they want. When it comes to women's health, nothing, but nothing is more important than the possibility that they might make more people. After all, they might manage to have a son whose enjoyment of life would matter.

Medieval women were also expected to marry and become mothers, and with them the wealth of farms and fortunes and political influence were anticipated. What is interesting, however, is that back then the expectation of marriage and motherhood was more of a probability and less of a goal than in our experience. Women maintained their chastity or enhanced their beauty to be considered good marriage prospects, absolutely, but that was their lot in life. The point was the continuation of families, not the dreams of little girls.

Our society continues to see marriage and children as a woman's role, but it has trussed it up in fantasy. You will be a princess for a day. You will live through the success of your children. You might get to see your own little princess grow up and be "given away" by her father to another man at a wedding. That will be the narrative of your life.

Interestingly, if our attitudes to marriage and motherhood have largely remained the same, our expectations about women and work have changed dramatically. As we have seen, medieval women worked hard, but we are often told that women's presence in the workplace is a product of the postwar twentieth century, when women emerged from the domestic sphere to take up a place in the work world. If the average person thinks this is true, they can be forgiven. Even academics have fallen victim to this argument. In 1963 the sociologist William Goode remarked on "the statistically unusual status of western women today . . . [and] their high participation in work outside of the home," which, he argued, was "due to the gradual logical philosophical extension to women of originally Protestant notions about the rights and responsibilities of the individual undermined the traditional idea of 'women's proper place.' "[27] Yet medieval women worked and indeed expected to work. Why then do we treat the working woman as a modern invention?

Modern ways of thinking about both gender and work color the way we look at the past. Medieval women and their work were considered unimportant for the theological and philosophical reasons I've spoken of before. Women were inferior to men, and their work was viewed similarly.

In Enlightenment thought, for women to participate in challenging careers or the public sphere was to go against nature. Rousseau argued that women were better at domestic tasks that required "details," while men were more intellectual, which created a mutual dependence that benefited "social relationships." The best way for these "social relationships" to thrive was for women to retreat entirely from the public sphere and into a domestic life that limited their own intellectual pursuits to whatever made life easiest for men.

These arguments weren't revolutionary, but their effect was. As they took hold, women in the middle and upper classes retreated from the workshop, the storefront, and the political realm into the back of the home with their children. The philosopher Mary Wollstonecraft (1759–1797) argued for the place of women in society, but overall it was increasingly common to associate women with the private sphere. As the modern period wore on, and a nebulous concept of science was increasingly used to validate the way the world was organized, more arguments like these followed. This is how a psychologist like Baron-Cohen is able to tell us that women are inherently nurturers, so human society assigned them to the responsibility to make the home the way it assigned men to make money.[28]

But the house-bound domestic mother was never, even in the modern period, common. Domesticity was a privilege accorded to those who could get by on a husband's wage or who inherited wealth. Working-class women have always worked—the hint is in the name. Women were part of the agricultural labor force throughout the modern period, although they, like their medieval counterparts, might not have been counted separately from their husbands. Industrial-age textile mills were almost exclusively the realm of working-class women. In families with money, women worked as maids and cooks, laundresses and gardeners. Women have worked at part-time or full-time jobs before they married, while they were married, and after their children grew up.

We are complicit in this erasure of pre-twentieth-century working women for a number of complex reasons. Chief among these is our desire to think about history as one constant march toward progress. Women must have entered the workplace only recently because now must be the best time ever to be a woman. We celebrate that women can now enter professions and have careers, but we slight the fact that women have worked over the centuries at jobs that they were supposed—and not supposed—to do. We don't like to admit that even if women are not working outside the home, doing the tasks of a home—cleaning and repairing the interior, making and mending clothing, raising a family, tending to children's education—is work. Medieval people had no doubt that being a mother was difficult and took time in a way that we simply do not.

To be fair, we have begun to acknowledge this domestic labor. In 1989, Arlie Hochschild coined the term the *second shift* for all the work that women do when they get home from their paying jobs.[29] And much like medieval people, if we have money and the option, we almost immediately attempt to hand household chores off to other people, and by people, I mean poorer women. The armies of caregivers, nannies, and house cleaners are testimony to the fact that domestic labor is work. But because a negative assessment is attached to this "home work," the mostly women workers are paid low wages.[30] Still, we push women toward these roles by insisting that it is natural for them to do these tasks, and we start teaching domestic responsibilities to girls at very young ages.

Yet it goes beyond these domestic tasks to whatever work women do. When women take over a field previously dominated by men, the pay for that profession drops.[31] Conversely, in fields where women were the majority, but men eventually outplaced them, such as computing, the pay increases. Meanwhile women in any profession are routinely paid less than their male counterparts in the same job, a phenomenon referred to as the gender pay gap, and women are regularly underrepresented at the higher levels of these same professions. The same proclivities were on display in the medieval period. However, medieval people were honest about why they did it—they just didn't like women.

To tell ourselves that we are the newly liberated, women-respecting heroes is to ignore millennia of women who got up, did their jobs, took care of their kids, and were every bit as engaged in and integral to society as men were.

We obfuscate these women and their history if we tell a story about ourselves rather than the past. The stories that we tell about the history of women and work, like those about beauty standards and sex, show us in the best possible light but often have very little to do with history. If we are to confront these false narratives, we first have to make room in our minds for the factual story of women and work. Only then can we begin to understand why our narrative differs so much from the reality, and what we are avoiding when we write it.

Studying medieval women and their society is interesting in and of itself. Learning more about the world that made ours can be endlessly fun, if challenging, and it is a net good. However, by looking more deeply into the medieval understanding of women, we also can divine our own world and its expectations of women. Turns out that the way we think about and treat women is socially malleable, and while some of our constructs have changed, we continue to treat women as inferior to men.

On its surface the constancy of women's place in society is depressing, but the thing about social constructs is that they are just that—

constructs. Fundamentally if we have created these strictures, then we can deconstruct them and make new ones. Seeing the past and rejecting it allows us to imagine new futures and make the changes that are necessary to create a more equitable world. It's time to start constructing that different future.

ACKNOWLEDGMENTS

This book, like any project, was made possible by the people around me. I would first like to thank Amy Cherry, my indefatigable editor, for her insight, wit, and support through the process. The effort and patience of editorial assistant Huneeya Siddiqui was also invaluable, as I navigated the differences between academic and trade publishing. My agent, William Callahan, must also be thanked for helping me to shape the project from the outset.

I would also like to thank the Walters Art Museum, the Staatsbibliothek zu Berlin, and the Koninklijke Bibliotheek for their help with image permissions, and their commitment to supporting authors.

My profound thanks to my dear friend Sara Öberg Strådal for her help with reading drafts of the book and help killing my darlings. Thanks too, to Simon Thomas Parsons for help attempting to navigate the French library system and looking over my Latin translations for me. He is a better friend than I can say. Thanks also are due to the wonderful Estelle Paranque for her insight and help thinking about queens and patronage.

The theoretical elements in this book would not have been possible without innumerable conversations with Justin Hancock, and easy access to his bookshelf. Nor can I ever thank him enough for the endless cups of coffee and perfect meals which appeared in front of me while I wrote.

As always, Blair McLennan was infinitely patient as I grumbled, wrote, and was generally totally absorbed into the book for over a year. He somehow remains an enthusiastic cheerleader.

I would also like to thank my PhD supervisor, the peerless Martyn Rady, who told me repeatedly I should be writing for the general public. I remain in his debt.

Lastly, I would also like to thank the vast army of my fellow historians, podcasters, and writers from all genres who agreed to help let other people know that this book exists. They are too many to name, and for that I am incredibly blessed. Having such a supportive and wonderful group of friends and colleagues remains my greatest accomplishment. I am nothing without them.

NOTES

INTRODUCTION

1. Ivan Hlaváček and Zdeňka Hledíková, eds., *Protocollum visitationis archidiaconatus Pragensis annis 1379–1382 per Paulum de Janowicz archidiaconum Pragensem factae* (Prague: Academia, 1973), 71.

CHAPTER 1: BACK TO BASICS

1. Geoffrey de La Tour Landry, *The Book of the Knight of the Tower, Landry: Which he Made for the Instruction of his Daughters,* ed. and trans. Alexander Vance (Dublin: Moffat & Co., 1868), 17–19.

2. See Jeffrey A. Norton et al., *Surgery: Basic Science and Clinical Evidence* (New York: Springer-Verlag, 2008), 4. For Hippocrates's writings, see Hippocrates, *Places in Man,* ed. Elizabeth M. Craik (Oxford: Clarendon Press, 1998). For more on the man and his life, see Herbert S. Goldberg, *Hippocrates: Father of Medicine* (Lincoln, Neb.: Universe Press, 1963, 2006).

3. I use the term "Western Roman Empire" here because at the time there were *two* Roman Empires—the Western Empire, headquartered in Rome, and the Eastern Empire, which we now call Byzantium, with its capital in Constantinople (where Istanbul now is). The Eastern Roman Empire would continue on

into the fifteenth century, and Byzantine citizens absolutely thought of themselves as and called themselves the Roman Empire. I have a lot of respect for this level of self-promotion and defer to it.

4. Hippocrates, *Aphorisms*, trans. Francis Adams, http://classics.mit.edu/Hippocrates/aphorisms.1.i.html.

5. Perhaps the best introduction is *Airs, Waters, Places*. You can find it in Hippocrates, *Ancient Medicine. Airs, Waters, Places. Epidemics 1 and 3. The Oath. Precepts. Nutriment*, ed. and trans. Paul Potter, Loeb Classical Library 147 (Cambridge, Mass.: Harvard University Press, 1923), 65–138.

6. Sherry Sayed Gadelrab, "Discourses on Sex Differences in Medieval Scholarly Islamic Thought," *Journal of History of Medicine and Allied Sciences* 66, no. 1 (2011): 48.

7. Hippocrates, *On Generation*, in Iain M. Lonie, *The Hippocratic Treatises: "On Generation," "On the Nature of the Child," "Diseases IV": A Commentary* (Berlin: Walter de Gruyter, 1981), 4.

8. See M. H. von Standen and H. von Staden, "The Discovery of the Body: Human Dissection and Its Cultural Contexts in Ancient Greece," *Yale Journal of Biology and Medicine* 65, no. 3 (1992): 223–41.

9. For more about Plato, try Danielle S. Allen, *Why Plato Wrote: Blackwell-Bristol Lectures on Greece, Rome, and the Classical Tradition* (Hoboken, N.J.: Wiley-Blackwell, 2012).

10. Plato, *Timaeus*, in *Oeuvres complètes*, ed. and trans. Léon Robin (Paris: Société d'édition Les Belles Lettres, 1962), 4:60–62. See also Plato, *Timaeus*, trans. and ed. Andrew Gregory and Robin Waterfield (Oxford: Oxford University Press, 2009).

11. Plato's ideas on penises and uteruses are summarized well in Joan Cadden, *Meanings of Sex Difference in the Middle Ages: Medicine, Science, and Culture* (Cambridge, U.K.: Cambridge University Press, 1993), 14.

12. A nice introduction to Aristotle is Carlo Natali, *Aristotle: His Life and School* (Princeton, N.J.: Princeton University Press, 2013).

13. Aristotle, *Politics*, trans. H. Rackham (Cambridge, Mass.: Harvard University Press, 1944), 1254b 13–14.

14. Aristotle, *History of Animals*, 608 b 1–14.

15. For more on the transmission of Galen, see Petros Bouras-Vallianatos and Barbara Zipser, eds., *Brill's Companion to the Reception of Galen*, Brill's Companion to Classical Reception 17 (Leiden: Brill, 2019).

16. Editions of this work abound, but an excellent one can be found in Galen, *Three Treatises: "On My Own Books," "On the Order of My Own Books," and "That the*

Best Physician Is Also a Philosopher": An Intermediate Greek Reader: Greek Text with Running Vocabulary and Commentary, trans. and ed. Evan Hayes and Stephen A. Nimis (Oxford, Ohio: Faenum, 2014). A nice introduction to his life is Susan P. Matten, *The Prince of Medicine: Galen in the Roman Empire* (Oxford: Oxford University Press, 2013).

17. Moreover, in Hellenistic and Roman society, voting rights and citizenship were hardly universal even for men. Both societies were propped up by a huge population of slaves who were not considered, either in Aristotelian thought or in law, as full humans. Slaves, as not-quite-people, were forbidden to vote even if they were men, which rather contradicts the idea of Hellenistic society as a beacon of democracy.

18. There is so little on Themistoclea that you have to read about her in tandem with other women philosophers as a part of a grab bag. Try Mary Ellen Waithe, "Early Pythagoreans: Themistoclea, Theano, Arignote, Myia, and Damo," in *A History of Women Philosophers,* vol. 1, *600 BC–500 AD,* ed. Mary Ellen Waite (Dordrecht: Martinus Nijhoff, 1987), 11–18.

19. I wish I could refer you to a book about Hipparchia, but I can't! Even more depressing, if you want more on her, she is always inextricably bound up with her husband, Crates. This is the problem right here, but anyway more of her work and work on her can be found in Robert Dobbin, trans. and ed., *The Cynic Philosophers: From Diogenes to Julian* (New York: Penguin, 2012), 79–98.

20. Socrates of Constantinople, *Historia Ecclesiastica,* 7.15, https://www.early churchtexts.com/public/socrates_the_murder_of_hypatia.htm.

21. David Coward, *A History of French Literature* (Hoboken, N.J.: Blackwell-Wiley, 2002), 13.

22. The entire "history" is very much worth your time. An excellent edition is Geoffrey of Monmouth, *The History of the Kings of Britain: An Edition and Translation of "De gestis Britonum (Historia regum Britanniae),"* ed. Michael D. Reeve, trans. Neil Wright (Woodbridge, Suffolk: Boydell Press, 2007).

23. Medieval historians are enamored of the Carolingian Renaissance, so it is difficult to narrow down where to start with it, but as good a place as any is Jean Hubert, Jean Porcher, and Wolfgang Fritz Volbach, *The Carolingian Renaissance* (New York: G. Braziller, 1970).

24. Again, literature on the subject is thick on the ground, but a seminal text is Charles Homer Haskins, *The Renaissance of the Twelfth Century* (Cambridge, Mass.: Harvard University Press, 1927).

25. Ernesto Bonaiuti, "The Genesis of St. Augustine's Idea of Original Sin," trans. Giorgio La Piana, *Harvard Theological Review* 10, no. 2 (1917): 162–63.

26. Augustine, *De trinitate* 12.7.10; *Patrologia Cursus Completus, Series Latina*, ed. Jean-Paul Migne (Paris: Garnier Fratres, 1865), 42:1003. To his credit, Augustine did also say here that women—in conjunction with men—can be considered the image of God. Just not on their own. Unlike men, who can. So I guess that's better?

27. Tertullian, *Tertulliani de cultu feminarum*, bk. I, at http://thelatinlibrary.com/tertullian/tertullian.cultu1.shtml. For more on him, see Eric Osborn, *Tertullian: First Theologian of the West* (Cambridge, U.K.: Cambridge University Press, 2008).

28. You may have noted a lack of a reference to Lilith here. Lilith appears as a demon in various Hebraic sources, including the Babylonian Talmud. In the eleventh century, the Talmudist Isaac ben Jacob Alfasi ha-Cohen (1013–1101), who worked in what is now Algeria and Spain, wrote that Lilith had been intended as Adam's first wife, but she refused to be subservient with him, instead having sex with the archangel Samael and leaving the Garden of Eden. See Kristen E. Kvam et al., *Eve and Adam: Jewish, Christian, and Muslim Readings on Genesis and Gender* (Bloomington: Indiana University Press, 1999), 220–21. She does not, however, appear in medieval Christian biblical sources, though they are based on the original Jewish works. Instead, the references to her in the book of Isaiah are translated so that her name is figured as "Lamia," a type of child-eating monster from Greek mythology. The conception of Lilith as Adam's first wife would gradually make its way into Christian thinking in the early modern period and was seized upon in particular by romantic writers such as Goethe.

29. This is a very simplified version of a very complex issue. A better summation can be found in Christiaan Kappes, "Gregory of Nazianzen's Prepurified Virgin in Ecumenical and Patristic Tradition: A Reappraisal of Original Sin, Guilt, and Immaculate Conception," in *The Spirit and the Church*, ed. J. Isaac Goff (Eugene, Ore.: Wipf and Stock, 2018).

30. Augustine, *De natura et gratia*, 36.42; *Patrologia Cursus Completus, Series Latina*, ed. Jean-Paul Migne (Paris: Garnier Fratres, 1865), 44:267.

31. There are hundreds upon hundreds of medieval monasteries around Europe, so many that it would be impossible to list them all. The large number of monasteries, and their importance to the educational process in Europe, cannot be stressed enough. For a good introduction, see J. Patrick Greene, *Medieval Monasteries* (New York: Continuum, 1992).

32. C. Warren Hollister, *Henry I* (New Haven, Conn.: Yale University Press, 2001), 23.

33. For more on changes in medieval education, see Nicholas Orme, *Medieval Schools: From Roman Britain to Renaissance England* (New Haven, Conn.: Yale University Press, 2006), which looks at England in particular.

34. Hildegard of Bingen, *Causae et curae: Liber compositae medicinae*, ed. Paul Kaiser (Leipzig: B. G. Teubner, 1903), 2:46–47. For more on Hildegard's life, check out Sabina Flanagan, *Hildegard of Bingen: A Visionary Life* (New York: Routledge, 1989).

35. Christine de Pizan, *The Book of the City of Ladies* (1405), trans. Rosalind Brown-Grant (London: Penguin, 1999). For more on Christine, see Charity Cannon Willard, *Christine de Pizan: Her Life and Works* (New York: Persea Books, 1984).

36. Lest you are tempted to think of this as backward, I beg you to consider that schools today have summer vacation not because everyone wants a nice little break but because all hands were once needed on farms over the summer. We are all, at most, only a few generations removed from bringing in the harvest.

37. For more on the *Glossa Ordinaria*, "the ubiquitous text of the central Middle Ages," see Lesley Smith, *The "Glossa Ordinaria": The Making of a Medieval Bible Commentary* (Leiden: Brill, 2009), 1.

38. David d'Avray, "Method in the Study of Medieval Sermons," in *Modern Questions About Medieval Sermons: Essays on Marriage, Death, History and Sanctity*, ed. Nicole Bériou and David d'Avray (Spoleto: Centro italiano di studi sull'Alto medioevo, 1994), 3–29.

39. Mervyn James, "Ritual, Drama and Social Body in the Late Medieval English Town," *Past and Present* 98, no. 1 (1983): 6–7.

40. Jarmila F. Veltrusky, *Mastičkář: A Sacred Farce from Medieval Bohemia* (Ann Arbor: Michigan University Press, 1985).

CHAPTER 2: MEN LOOKING AT WOMEN

1. Robert Grosseteste, *De unica forma omnium*, in L. Bauer, ed., *Die philosophischen Werke des Roberts Grosseteste*, Beiträge 9 (Münster, 1912), 107–8, following Edgar de Bruyne, *The Esthetics of the Middle Ages*, trans. Eileen B. Hennessy (New York: Ungar, 1969), 71.

2. Paulus Diaconus, *Historia Langobardorum*, in *Monumenta Germaniae historica inde ab anno Christi quingentesimo usque ad annum millesimum et quingentesimum. Scriptores rerum Langobardicarum et Italicarum saec. VI–IX*, III, ed. G. Waitz (Hanover: Impensis Bibliopolii Hahniani, 1878), 134–35; *Chronicae que dicuntur Fredegarii*, in *Monumenta Germaniae historica . . . Scriptores rerum Merovingicarum*, II, IV, c. 51, ed. Bruno Krusch (Hanover: Impensis Bibliopolii Hahniani, 1888), 145–46; *Vita Balthildis*, in *Monumenta Germaniae historica . . . Scriptores rerum Merovin-*

gicarum, II, c. 2, ed. Krusch, 438; Theganani Gesta, *Vita Hludowici Imperatoris*, in *Monumenta Germaniae Historica . . . Scriptores* cit., c. 26, ed. Georg Heinrich Pertz (Hanover: Impensis Bibliopolii Hahniani , 1829), 214.

3. *Vita Balthildis* A (MGH, Script. rer. Mer., II), c. 2, p. 438.

4. Mayke de Jong, "Queens and Beauty in the Early Medieval West: Balthild, Theodelinda, Judith," in *Acting as a Woman: Models and Practices of Representation (6th–10th Centuries)*, ed. M. C. La Rocca, proceedings of conference in Padua, February 18–19, 2005 (Turnhout, Belgium: Brepols, 2007), 235–48.

5. See Ferdinand Otto Meister, ed., *Daretis Phrygii De excidio Troiae historia*, Bibliotheca Scriptorum Graecorum et Romanorum Teubneriana (Leipzig: Teubner, 1873), 16, 17.

6. Ibid., 14.

7. Sappho, fragment 23.

8. Current scholars don't necessarily accept the individual personhood of Maximianus, thinking that his poems may have been composed by several authors. See Richard Webster, *The Elegies of Maximianus* (Princeton, N.J.: Princeton University Press, 1900), 7–11.

9. Maximianus, *Elegies*, 1.93, in Edmond Faral, *Les arts poétiques du XIIe et du XIIIe siècle: Recherches et documents sur la technique littéraire du Moyen Âge* (Paris: Champion, 1924), 80, translated by author.

10. While he may have been ubiquitous, Maximianus was not always loved. At one point the twelfth-century teacher, author, and poet Alexander of Villedieu (ca. 1175–ca. 1240) described his poetry as "trifles." Alexander of Villedieu, *Das "Doctrinale" des Alexander de Villedieu*, ed. Dietrich Reichling, Monumenta Germanic Pedagogica 12 (Berlin: A. Hofmann, 1893), 2:24–25.

11. Matthew of Vendôme, *Ars Versificatoria*, in Mathei Vindocinensis, *Opera*, ed. Franco Munari (Rome: Edizioni di storia e letteratura, 1977), 83.

12. Ibid., 85–86.

13. To study or teach at a medieval university one had to be a member of the clergy. This is why Geoffrey had to apologize to the archbishop and was well connected enough to give gifts to the pope. Incidentally, it also meant that women were precluded from studying at university level because they could not be clergy members. For more on Geoffrey, see James J. Murphy's excellent *Three Medieval Rhetorical Arts* (Berkeley: University of California Press, 1971), 29–31.

14. Caroline Spurgeon, *Five Hundred Years of Chaucer Criticism and Allusion: 1357–1900* (London, 1925), 1:17, 49; James J. Murphy, "A New Look at Chaucer and

the Rhetoricians," *Review of English Studies* 15 (1964): 1–20; Karl Young, "Chaucer and Geffrey of Vinsauf," *Modern Philology* 41 (1943): 172–82.

15. Geoffrey of Vinsauf, *Poetica Nova,* in Faral, *Les ars poétiques,* 214–15.

16. Guillaume de Lorris, *Le roman de la rose par Guillaume de Lorris et Jean de Meung,* ed. Ernest Langlois (Paris: Firmin-Didot, 1914–24), 2:51–52. See also *The Romance of the Rose,* trans. Frances Horgan (Oxford: Oxford University Press, 2009).

17. Ibid., 2:28, 44.

18. F. J. E. Raby, *A History of Secular Latin Poetry in the Middle Ages* (Oxford: Clarendon Press, 1934), 2:239. According to Raby, the Judith in question might have been an abbess at the Remiremont abbey in what is now France, but there's no way of proving the case, sadly. We may never know who, in fact, was this attractive.

19. Ibid., 2:244–45.

20. Geoffrey Chaucer, "The Miller's Tale," *The Canterbury Tales,* 1, lines 3245–62.

21. John Tzetzes, *Antehomerica,* trans. Ana Untila (n.p., 2014), 356–58, https://archive.org/details/TzetzesANTEHOMERICA/mode/2up.

22. Ibid., 115–22.

23. Walter Mettmann, "'Ancheta de caderas.' Libro de buen amor, C. 432 ss," *Romanische Forschungen* 73, nos. 1–2 (1961): 141–47; and Michael Ray Solomon, trans., *The Mirror of Coitus: A Translation and Edition of the Fifteenth-Century "Speculum al foderi"* (Madison: Hispanic Seminary of Medieval Studies, 1990), 8.12

24. Luce López-Baralt, "La bella de Juan Ruiz tenía los ojos de hurí," *Nueva Revista de Filología Hispánica* 40 (1992): 73–83.

25. Faral, *Les ars poétiques,* 80.

26. "Colla nivi . . . ," ibid., 84.

27. "Succuba sit capitis pretiosa colore columna / Lactea, quae speculum vultus supportet in altum." Geoffrey of Vinsauf, *Poetica Nova,* ibid., 215.

28. See, for example, Peter Dronke, *Medieval Latin and the Rise of European Love-Lyric* (Oxford: Oxford University Press, 1965), 1:193; Matthew of Vendôme, *Ars Versificatoria,* trans. Aubrey E. Galyon (Ames: University of Iowa Press, 1980), 39.

29. D. S. Brewer, "The Ideal of Feminine Beauty in Medieval Literature, Especially 'Harley Lyrics,' Chaucer, and Some Elizabethans," *Modern Language Review* 50, no. 3 (1955): 260; Anonymous, "Alysoun," https://rpo.library.utoronto.ca/poems/alysoun.

30. Francisco A. Marcos-Marín, "Masculine Beauty vs. Feminine Beauty in Medi-

eval Iberia," in *Multicultural Iberia: Language, Literature, and Music,* ed. Dru
Dougherty and Milton M. Azevedo (Berkeley: University of California Press,
1999), 31.

31. Guillaume de Machaut, "Le Jugement dou Roy de Behaingne," in *Guillaume
de Machaut: The Complete Poetry and Music,* vol. 1, *The Debate Series,* ed. R. Barton Palmer, Domenic Leo, and Uri Smilansky, trans. R. Barton Palmer and
Yolanda Plumley (Kalamazoo: Medieval Institute Publications, 2016), https://d
.lib.rochester.edu/teams/text/palmer-machaut-thedebateseries-bohemia,
lines 365–66; Chaucer, *Troilus,* 2.1247, and *The Book of the Duchess,* lines 953–54.

32. Geoffrey of Vinsauf, *Poetica nova,* 215.

33. Matthew of Vendôme, *Ars Versificatoria,* in Mathei Vindocinensis, *Opera,* 85.

34. Ibid., 84.

35. Geoffrey of Vinsauf, *Poetica nova,* 215.

36. Machaut, "Le Jugement dou Roy," lines 369–70.

37. Monica H. Green, ed. and trans., *The Trotula: An English Translation of the Medieval Compendium of Women's Medicine* (Philadelphia: University of Pennsylvania
Press, 2001), 85.

38. Matthew of Vendôme, *Ars Versificatoria,* 85.

39. Machaut, "Le Jugement dou Roy," lines 373–75.

40. Matthew of Vendôme, *Ars Versificatoria,* 85.

41. See, for example, Machaut, "Le Jugement dou Roy," lines 376–77.

42. Matthew of Vendôme, *Ars Versificatoria,* 85.

43. Geoffrey of Vinsauf, *Poetica nova,* 215.

44. Ibid.

45. Machaut, "Le Jugement dou Roy," lines 377–79.

46. There are notable exceptions to this rule, especially among royalty and nobility. However, those exceptions are indeed notable. For more on marriage and
maidens, see Kim M. Phillips, *Medieval Maidens: Young Women and Gender in
England, 1270–1540* (Manchester: Manchester University Press, 2003), 36–42.

47. M. C. Seymour et al., eds., *De puella,* in *On the Properties of Things: John Trevi-
sa's Translation of Bartholomaeus Anglicus "De proprietatibus rerum": A Critical Text*
(Oxford: Oxford University Press, 1975), col. 1, lib. 6, cap. 6, quoted in Phillips, *Medieval Maidens,* 6–7.

48. Phillips, *Medieval Maidens,* 7.

49. The coldness of women, noted throughout the medieval period, was debated
by many of the great physicians and natural philosophers. See, for example,
Pseudo Albertus Magnus, *Women's Secrets: A Translation of Pseudo-Albertus Mag-*

nus' "De secretis mulierum," with Commentaries, ed. and trans. Helen Rodnite Lemay (Albany: SUNY Press, 1992), 60–70; Mazhar H. Shah, *The General Principles of Avicenna's "Canon of Medicine"* (Karachi: Naveed Clinic, 1966), 33–34.

50. Caroline Walker Bynum, *The Resurrection of the Body in Western Christianity, 200–1336* (New York: Columbia University Press, 1995), 122; Mary Dove, *The Perfect Age of Man's Life* (Cambridge, U.K.: Cambridge University Press, 1986), 21–25.

51. Malcolm Andrew and Ronald Waldron, eds., *The Poems of the Pearl Manuscript* (Exeter, U.K., 1987), lines 197–204.

52. Neu-Karsthans, "Gesprech biechlin neüw Karsthns," quoted in Michael Baxandall, *The Limewood Sculptors of Renaissance Germany* (New Haven, Conn.: Yale University Press, 1980), 88.

53. Anne-Laure Lalouette, "Bains et soins du corps dans les textes médicaux (XIIe–XIVe siècles)," in *Laver, monder, blanchir: Discours et usages de la toilette dans l'Occident medieval*, ed. Sophie Albert (Paris: Presses de l'Université Paris-Sorbonne, 2006), 33–49.

54. Etienne de Boileau, *Le Livre des métiers*, in *Women's Lives in Medieval Europe: A Sourcebook*, ed. Emilie Amt (New York: Routledge, 1993), 162. The denier, from which we get the modern term *penny*, was the smallest and most common coin. Laborers and servants in the thirteenth century were generally paid somewhere between one and a half and two and a half deniers per day, whereas tradesmen could earn between three and nine deniers per day depending on their skill set. See Jeffrey L. Singman, *Daily Life in Medieval Europe* (Westport Conn.: Greenwood Press, 1999), 61.

55. Georges Vigarello, *Concepts of Cleanliness: Changing Attitudes in France Since the Middle Ages*, trans. Jean Birrell (Cambridge, U.K.: Cambridge University Press, 1988), 21–22.

56. Olivia Remie Constable, "Cleanliness and Convivencia: Jewish Bathing Culture in Medieval Spain," in *Jews, Christians and Muslims in Medieval and Early Modern Times*, ed. Arnold E. Franklin et al. (Leiden: Brill, 2014), 257–58.

57. On the survival of *hammams*, see, for example, Catherine B. Asher, "The Public Baths of Medieval Spain: An Architectural Study: Cross-Cultural Contacts," in *The Medieval Mediterranean: Cross-Cultural Contacts*, ed. Marilyn J. Chait and Kathryn L. Reyerson (St. Cloud, Minn.: Northstar Press, 1988); On suspicion about women's bathing habits, see, Alexandra Cuffel, "Polemicizing Women's Bathing Among Medieval and Early Modern Muslims and Christians," in *The Nature and Function of Water, Baths, Bathing and Hygiene from Antiquity through the Renaissance*, ed. Cynthia Kosso and Anne Scott (Leiden: Brill, 2009).

58. Kevin M. Dunn, *Caveman Chemistry: 28 Projects from the Creation of Fire to the Production of Plastics* (Irvine, Calif.: Universal, 2003), 233.

59. Hildegard of Bingen, *Hildegard von Bingen's Physica: The Complete English Translation of Her Classic Work on Health and Healing*, trans. Priscilla Throop (Rochester, Vt.: Healing Arts Press, 1998), ch. 4.

60. Monica H. Green, ed. and trans., *The Trotula: An English Translation of the Medieval Compendium of Women's Medicine* (Philadelphia: University of Pennsylvania Press, 2001), 115.

61. Ibid.

62. Geoffrey de La Tour Landry, *Le Livre du Chevalier de La Tour Landry pour l'enseignement de ses filles*, ed. Anatole de Montaiglon (Paris: P. Jannet, 1854). For English, see Geoffroy de La Tour Landry, *The Booke of Thenseygnementes and Techynge that the Knyght of the Towre Made to his Doughters*, trans. Gertrude Burford Rawlings and William Caxton (London: G. Newnes, 1902).

63. Jan Milíč of Kromčříž, "Sermon on the Last Day of the Lord," in *The Message for the Last Days: Three Essays from the Year 1367*, ed. Milan Opočenský and Jana Opočenská (Geneva: World Alliance of Reformed Churches, 1998), 49.

64. Bernard P. Prusak, "Woman: Seductive Siren and Source of Sin? Pseudepigraphal Myth and Christian Origins," in *Religion and Sexism: Images of Women in the Jewish and Christian Traditions*, ed. Rosemary Radford Ruether (Eugene, Ore.: Wipf and Stock, 1998), 89–116.

65. La Tour Landry, *Le Livre du Chevalier*, 112, following Susan Udry, "Robert de Blois and Geoffroy de la Tour Landry on Feminine Beauty: Two Late Medieval French Conduct Books for Women," *Essays in Medieval Studies* 19 (2002): 100.

66. Montserrat Cabré, "Beautiful Bodies," in *A Cultural History of the Human Body in the Medieval Age*, ed. Linda Kalof (New York: Bloomsbury, 2014), 135.

67. Joanne B. Eicher, ed., *Dress and Ethnicity: Change Across Space and Time* (New York: Bloomsbury, 1999), 1–16.

68. Green, *Trotula*, 115–16.

69. Ibid., 118.

70. Ibid., 121.

71. La Tour Landry, *Le Livre du Chevalier*, 109–10, cited in Udry, "Robert de Blois and Geoffroy de La Tour Landry on Feminine Beauty," 99.

72. Chaucer, "The Miller's Tale," *The Canterbury Tales*, lines 137–138.

73. Antoninus of Florence, *Confessionale: Defecerunt scrutantes scrutinio* (Delft: Jacob van der Meer, 1482), chap. 21, "De immodestia mulierum," fol. 1.11, https://archive.org/details/ned-kbn-all-00001853-001. See John Block Friedman,

"Eyebrows, Hairlines, and 'Hairs Less in Sight': Depilation in Late Medieval Europe," in *Medieval Clothing and Textiles,* ed. Robin Netherton and Gale R. Owen-Crocker (Woodbridge, U.K.: Boydell & Brewer, 2018), 14:102.

74. Friedman, "Eyebrows, Hairlines," 14:95.

75. Ibid., 14:113.

76. Montserrat Cabré i Pairet, "La cura del cos femení i la medicina medieval de tradició llatina. Els tractats 'De ornatu' i 'De decorationibus mulierum' atribuïts a Arnau de Vilanova, 'Tròtula' de mestre Joan, i 'Flors del tresor de beutat' atribuït a Manuel Díeç de Calatayud" (Ph.D. diss., University of Barcelona, 1996), 202, cited ibid., 14:87.

77. Margaret Scott, *Fashion in the Middle Ages* (Los Angeles: J. Paul Getty Trust, 2018), 21-24.

78. W. Nelson Francis, ed., *The Book of Vices and Virtues* (Oxford: Oxford University Press, 1942), 43-44.

79. James Tait, ed., *Chronica Johannis de Reading et Anonymi Cantuariensis 1346-1367* (Manchester: Manchester University Press, 1914), 88-89, in *The Black Death,* ed. and trans. Rosemary Horrox (Manchester: Manchester University Press, 1994), 131.

80. Scott, *Fashion in Middle Ages,* 20.

81. Quoted in Phillips, *Medieval Maidens,* 180.

82. Peter Von Moos, " 'Public' et 'privé' à la fin du Moyen Age: Le 'bien commun' et la 'loi de la conscience,'" *Studi medievali* 41, no. 2 (2000): 505-48; Etienne Dravasa, " 'Vivre noblement.' Recherches sur la dérogeance de noblesse du XIVe au XVe siècles," *Revue juridique et économique du Sud-Ouest* 16 (1965): 135-93.

83. L. Gilliodts-Van Severen, ed., *Cartulaire de l'ancien grand tonlieu de Bruges, faisant suite au Cartulaire de l'ancienne estaple: Recueil de documents concernant le commerce inférieur et maritime, les relations internationales et l'histoire économique de cette ville* (Bruges: Plancke, 1901), 2:312.

84. Catherine Kovesi Killerby, " 'Heralds of a Well-instructed Mind': Nicolosa Sanuti's Defence of Women and Their Clothes," *Renaissance Studies* 13, no. 3 (1999): 255-82.

85. G. Bistort, "Il magistrato alle pompe nella Repubblica di Venezia. Studio storico," *Miscellanea di storia veneta,* ser. 3, 5 (1912): 74-75.

86. Ibid., 71-73.

CHAPTER 3: HOW TO LOVE

1. Augustine, *City of God*, bk. 14, p. 26. *Generation in paradise would have occurred without the shame of lust.*

2. P. J. Payer, *The Bridling of Desire: Views of Sex in the Later Middle Ages* (Toronto: University of Toronto Press, 1993), 185.

3. Augustine, *On Genesis*, bk. 11, p. 41.

4. Augustine, *City of God*, bk. 14, p. 20, *The ridiculous indecency of the cynics.*

5. Ibid., 7, *The scriptural terms for love.*

6. Ambrose, *On Virginity*, trans. Daniel Callam, Peregrina Translation Series 7 (Toronto: Peregrinqa, 1989), 13, 81.

7. Hermann Theodor Bruns, *Canones apostolorum et conciliorum saeculorum IV, V, VI, VII: Recognovit atque insignioris lectionum varietatis, Notationes subiunxit* (Berlin: G. Reimeri, 1839), 2, 6.

8. Canons 3 and 21, in *Medieval Sourcebook: Ninth Ecumenical Council: Lateran I 1123*, https://sourcebooks.fordham.edu/basis/lateran1.asp.

9. Johannes Gerson, *De pollutione* (Cologne: Ludwig von Renchen, n.d.). See also Cadden, *Meanings of Sex Difference*, 141–42; James A. Brundage, *Law, Sex, and Christian Society in Medieval Europe* (Chicago: University of Chicago Press, 1987), 400–1.

10. Aquinas, *Summa Theologica*, pt. 2, ques. 154, art. 5.

11. Quoted in Jeffrey Richards, *Sex, Dissidence and Damnation: Minority Groups in the Middle Ages* (New York: Routledge, 1994), 23–24.

12. Brundage, *Law, Sex, and Christian Society*, 430.

13. Quoted in Pierre J. Payer, *The Bridling of Desire: Views of Sex in the Later Middle Ages* (Toronto: University of Toronto Press, 1993), 118.

14. Augustine, *City of God*, bk. 14, p. 16. *The evil of lust, in the specifically sexual meaning.*

15. Aquinas, *Summa Theologica*, pt. 2, ques. 154, art. 4.

16. Jerome, *Against Jovinianus*, trans. W. H. Fremantle, G. Lewis, and W. G. Martley, in *A Select Library of Nicene and Post Nicene Fathers of the Christian Church*, ed. Philip Schaff (Buffalo, N.Y.: Christian Literature, 1893), 6:367.

17. Ibid., 6:386.

18. Aquinas, *Summa Theologica*, pt. 1, ques. 98, art. 2.

19. Burchard of Worms, *Corrector*, in *Die Bußordnungen in der abendländischen Kirche* (Halle: F.W.H. Wasserschleben, 1851), 642.

20. Aquinas, *Summa Theologica*, pt. 2, ques. 154, art. 11.

21. For more on Alexander of Hales see James A. Brundage, "Let Me Count the

Ways: Canonists and Theologians Contemplate Coitus Positions," *Journal of Medieval History* 10 (1984): 81, 86. On William of Pagula, see ibid., 87.

22. *Fragmentum Cantabrigiense*, MS. Add. 3321 (I), fol. 23v, Cambridge University Library. See Brundage, "Let Me Count," 85.

23. James A. Brundage, "Sex and Canon Law," in *Handbook of Medieval Sexuality*, ed. Vern L. Bullough and James A. Brundage (New York: Garland, 1996), 157.

24. Ibid., 36.

25. Quoted in Brundage, "Let Me Count," 84.

26. Ibid., 86.

27. Isiodore, *Etomologias*, xi.24.43.

28. Brundage, *Law, Sex, and Christian Society*, 451–52.

29. Jerome, *Against Jovinianus*, 367.

30. This absolutely massive subject has been discussed at length in Cadden, *Meanings of Sex Difference*, 117–29.

31. Ibid., 65.

32. Avicenna, *Liber Canonis*, bk. 3 fen. 21 tr. 1, ch. 2, quoted in Ruth Mazo Karras, *Sexuality in Medieval Europe: Doing Unto Others*, 3rd ed. (2005; reprint New York: Routledge, 2017), 106.

33. Brian Lawn, ed., *The Prose Salernitan Questions: Edited from a Bodleian Manuscript* (London: Open University Press, 1979), 4.

34. For the wet wood analogy, see William of Conches, *A Dialogue on Natural Philosophy (Dragmaticon Philosophiae)*, trans. Italo Ronca and Matthew Curr (Notre Dame: University of Notre Dame Press, 1997), 2:135. For the iron, see Danielle Jacquart and Claude Thomasset, *Sexuality and Medicine in the Middle Ages*, trans. Matthew Adamson (Princeton, N.J.: Princeton University Press, 1988), 28.

35. Jacquart and Thomasset, *Sexuality and Medicine*, 81.

36. Pseudo Albertus Magnus, *Women's Secrets: A Translation of Pseudo-Albertus Magnus' "De secretis mulierum" with Commentaries*, ed. and trans. Helen Rodnite Lemay (Albany: SUNY Press, 1992), 51.

37. Albert the Great, *Alberti Magni. Opera omnia*, vol. 12, *Quaestiones super de animalibus*, ed. Ephrem Filthaut (Münster: Aschendorff, 1955), 5.Q4.Q6.

38. Vincent of Beauvais, *Speculum naturale*, bk. 31, chap. 5.

39. Quoted in Joan Cadden, "It Takes All Kinds; Sexuality and Gender Differences in Hildegard of Bingen's *Book of Compound Medicine*," *Traditio* 40 (1984): 159.

40. Quoted in Joyce E. Salisbury, "Gendered Sexuality," in *Handbook of Medieval Sexuality*, ed. Vern L. Bullough and James A. Brundage (New York: Garland, 1996), 93.

41. Mazo Karras, *Sexuality in Medieval Europe*, 16–17.

42. *Wife of Bath's Prologue,* lines 44–46, translation the author's own, from Larry D. Benson and F. N. Robinson, eds., *The Riverside Chaucer,* 3rd ed. (Oxford: Oxford University Press, 2008), 105.

43. Georg Heinrich Pertz, ed., *Monumenta Germaniae Historica* (Hanover: Hahn, 1835), 1:345.

44. Aquinas, *Summa Theologica,* pt. XP, ques. 58, art. 1.

45. Jacquart and Thomasset, *Sexuality in Middle Ages,* 171.

46. R. H. Hemholz, *Marriage Litigation in Medieval England* (Cambridge, U.K.: Cambridge University Press, 1974|), 89; Mazo Karras, *Sexuality in Medieval Europe,* 94.

47. Quoted in Jacquart and Thomasset, *Sexuality in Middle Ages,* 173.

48. Thomas of Chobham, *Summa Confessorum,* ed. F. Broomfeld (Louvain: Editions Nauwelaerts, 1968), 184. See also Catherine Ryder, "Magic and Impotence in the Middle Ages," *Societas Magicas Newsletter* 13 (Fall 2004): 1.

49. Giovanni Boccaccio, *The Decameron,* trans. G. H. McWilliam (New York: Penguin, 1972), 240.

50. Jean de Meun, *The Romance of the Rose,* trans. Harry W. Robbins (New York: E.P. Dutton, 1962), 172, 182.

51. John C. Jacobs, trans., *The Fables of Odo of Cheriton* (Syracuse, N.Y.: Syracuse University Press, 1985), 143. See also Mazo Karras, *Sexuality in Medieval Europe,* 115.

52. Michael Goodich, ed., *Other Middle Ages: Witnesses at the Margins of Medieval Society* (Philadelphia: University of Pennsylvania Press, 1998), 111.

53. Geoffrey de La Tour Landry, *Le Livre du Chevalier de La Tour Landry pour l'enseignement de ses filles,* ed. Anatole de Montaiglon (Paris: P. Jannet, 1854), 24, 96.

54. Andreas Capellanus, *The Art of Courtly Love,* trans. John Jay Parry (New York: Columbia University Press, 1960), 27.

55. Ibid., 28, 30.

56. Ibid., 32, 145.

57. Ibid., 150.

58. Ibid., 23.

59. Ibid., 175.

60. Ibid., 171.

61. Ibid., 194–97.

62. Ibid., 208.

63. Avicenna, *Canon,* bk. 3, fen 21, tr. 1, ch. 9, quoted in Jacquart and Thomasset, *Sexuality and Medicine,* 130.

64. Justin Hancock, conversation with author, February 17, 2021.

65. Pietro d'Abano, *Conciliator* (Venice: O. Scoti, 1521), in Jacquart and Claude Thomasset, *Sexuality and Medicine*, 46.

66. Avicenna, *Canon*, bk. 3, fen 21, tr. 1, ch. 9, quoted in Jacquart and Thomasset, *Sexuality and Medicine*, 130–31. Interestingly, Avicenna also identifies the "seat of pleasure" in women as "between the anus and the vulva," showing us that his own observations about pleasure may have been personal.

67. William of Conches, *Dialogue on Natural Philosophy*, 136.

68. Aquinas, *Summa Theologica*, pt. SS, ques. 154, art. 7.

69. Ibid.

70. William of Conches, *Dialogue on Natural Philosophy*, 137.

71. Humber of the Romans, *To the Leprous*, in Goodich, *Other Middle Ages*, 147.

72. Odette Pontal, trans., *Les statuts de Paris et le synodal de l'Ouest (XIIIme siècle)* (Paris: Bibliothèque nationale, 1971), 205–7.

73. P. de Koning, trans., *Trois traités d'anatomie arabe* (Leiden: Brill, 1903), 403–5, cited in Jacquart and Thomasset, *Sexuality and Medicine*, 72. Interestingly, the other parts of the body, which are classified as "white" in nature were created from sperm from both the father and mother.

74. William of Conches, *Dialogue on Natural Philosophy*, 137–38.

75. Quoted in Benjamin Lee Gordon, *Medieval and Renaissance Medicine* (London: Peter Owen, 1960), 534.

76. Green, *Trotula*, 97, 98, 127–28, 133–34.

77. Ibid., 71.

78. Quoted in Jacquart and Thomasset, *Sexuality and Medicine*, 174.

79. Green, *Trotula*, 72.

80. John of Gaddesden, *Rosa Anglica practica medicine a capite ad pedes*, ed. N. Scyllacius (Augsburg: Augustae Vindelicorum, 1595), 596–96. See also Jacquart and Thomasset, *Sexuality and Medicine*, 176.

81. Jacquart and Thomasset, *Sexuality and Medicine*, 176.

82. *De Animalibus*, bk. IX, tr. I, ch. 1, p. 7, cited in Joan Cadden, "Western Medicine and Natural Philosophy," in *Handbook of Medieval Sexuality*, ed. Vern L. Bullough and James A. Brundage (New York: Garland, 1996), 59.

83. Quoted in Jacqueline Murray, "Twice Marginal and Twice Invisible: Lesbians in the Middle Ages," in Bullough and Brundage, *Handbook of Medieval Sexuality*, 197.

84. Burchard of Worms, *Decretorum Liber*, in *Patrologiae Cursus Completus. Series Latina*, ed. Jacques-Paul Migne (Paris: Migne, 1856), 140:971.

85. Hincmar of Reims, *De divortio Lotharii et Theutbergae reginae*, in *Patrologia Cursus Completus, Series Latina*, ed. Jean-Paul Migne (Paris: Migne, 1852), 125: 692–

93, cited in Boswell, *Christianity, Social Tolerence,and Homosexuality: Gay People in Western Europe from the Beginning of the Christian Era to the Fourteenth Century* (Chicago: University of Chicago Press, 2015), 204.

86. Burchard of Worms, *Corrector and Doctor,* in *Medieval Popular Religion, 1000–1500: A Reader,* ed. John R. Shinners, 2nd ed. (Toronto: University of Toronto Press, 2006), 469.

87. "Gerard Cagnoli (d. 1342) and the Exorcism of Lust," in *Other Middle Ages: Witnesses at the Margins of Medieval Society,* ed. Michael Goodich (Philadelphia: University of Pennsylvania Press, 1998), 143–44.

88. "Bridget of Sweden (d. 1371)," ibid., 144–45.

89. Whether the *Malleus*'s second attributed author, the Dominican Inquisitor Jacob Sprenger (c. 1436–95), was actually involved in the production of this influential work is currently up for debate. See, for example, Hans-Christian Klose, "Die angebliche Mitarbeit des Dominikaners Jakob Sprenger am Hexenhammer, nach einem alten Abdinghofer Brief," in *Paderbornensis Ecclesia. Beiträge zur Geschichte des Erzbistums Paderborn. Festschrift für Lorenz Kardinal Jäger zum 80. Geburtstag,* ed. Paul-Werner Scheele (Paderborn: Verlag Ferdinand Schöningh, 1972), 197–205.

90. Heinrich Kramer and James Sprenger, *Malleus Malificarum* (1487), trans. Montague Summers (New York: Dover, 1971), 41–48.

91. Ibid., 43–47.

92. Ibid., 121.

93. Ibid., 117.

94. Ibid., 48.

95. Ibid., 1.

96. Ibid., 104.

97. Ibid., 119.

CHAPTER 4: HOW TO BE

1. Max L. W. Laistner, *Christianity and Pagan Culture in the Later Roman Empire: Together with an English Translation of John Chrysostom's "Address on Vainglory and the Right Way for Parents to Bring up their Children"* (Ithaca, N.Y.: Cornell University Press, 1951), 8.

2. Bella Millett and Jocelyn Wogan-Browne, eds., *Medieval English Prose for Women: Selections from the Katherine Group and Ancrene Wisse* (Oxford: Clarendon Press, 1990), 31.

3. "St. Jerome: Virginity and Marriage (4th c. A.D.)," in *Women's Lives in Medieval Europe: A Sourcebook*, ed. Emilie Amt (New York: Routledge, 1993), 26.

4. Millett and Wogan-Browne, *Medieval English Prose for Women*, 23, 25, 21.

5. Judith Bennett, *Women in the Medieval English Countryside: Gender and Household in Brigstock Before the Plague* (New York: Oxford University Press, 1987), 56.

6. Henrietta Leyser, *Medieval Women: A Social History of Women in England, 450–1500* (London: Weidenfeld & Nicolson, 1995), 143–44.

7. "Survey of Alwalton: Obligations of Peasants (1279)," in Amt, *Women's Lives in Medieval Europe*, 182–84.

8. Zvi Razi, "Family, Land, and the Village Community in Later Medieval England," *Past and Present* 93, no. 1 (1981): 5.

9. Emilie Amt, ed., *Women's Lives in Medieval Europe: A Sourcebook* (New York: Routledge, 1993), 181.

10. Ibid., 182.

11. Millett and Wogan-Browne, *Medieval English Prose for Women*, 35.

12. Heath Dillard, *Daughters of the Reconquest: Women in Castilian Town Society, 1100–1300* (Cambridge, U.K.: Cambridge University Press, 1984), 150; Leyser, *Medieval Women*, 152.

13. Martine Segalen, *Love and Power in the Peasant Family: Rural France in the Nineteenth Century*, trans. Sarah Matthews (Chicago: University of Chicago Press, 1983), 138–39.

14. Peter Ward, *The Clean Body: A Modern History* (Montreal: McGill-Queen's University Press, 2019), 89.

15. Burchard of Worms, *Corrector and Doctor*, in *Medieval Popular Religion, 1000–1500: A Reader*, ed. John R. Shinners, 2nd ed. (Toronto: University of Toronto Press, 2006), 461.

16. "Descriptions of Maidservants' Work (12th–13th c.)," in Amt, *Women's Lives in Medieval Europe*, 181.

17. Aelfric, *Ælfric's Colloquy: Translated from the Latin*, trans. Ann E. Watkins, http://www.kentarchaeology.ac/authors/016.pdf, 13.

18. "Manorial Court rolls (14th c.)," in Amt, *Women's Lives in Medieval Europe*, 185.

19. Llewellyn Jewitt, "A Few Notes on Ducking Stools," *Green Bag* 10 (1898): 522. The cucking stool is an early iteration of the ducking stool and was just a chair that people would be strapped into while their neighbors walked past and made fun of them.

20. "Coroners' Rolls: Violent Incidents (13th–14th c.)," in Amt, *Women's Lives in Medieval Europe*, 189.

21. Helena Graham, "'A Woman's Work . . .': Labour and Gender in the Late Medieval Countryside," in *Woman Is a Worthy Wight: Women in English Society, c. 1200–1500* ed. P. J. P. Goldberg (Wolfeboro Falls, N.H.: Alan Sutton, 1992), 141; Leyser, *Medieval Women*, 147.

22. Leyser, *Medieval Women*, 156.

23. "Parisian Guild Regulations (13th c.)," in Amt, *Women's Lives in Medieval Europe*, 194.

24. Ibid., 196.

25. Guy Geltner, "Healthscaping a Medieval City: Lucca's *Curia Viarum* and the Future of Public Health History," *Urban History* 40, no. 3 (2013): 396–400.

26. Christopher Mielke, "Rub-a-dub-dub, Three Maids in a Tub: Women in Bathhouse and Secondary Sites of Sex Work in Medieval Hungarian Towns," in *Same Bodies, Different Women: "Other" Women in the Middle Ages,* ed. Christopher Mielke and Andrea-Bianka Znorovszky (Budapest: Trivent, 2019), 118–20.

27. Ibid., 121.

28. Ibid., 197.

29. Ibid.

30. "Infractions of Commercial Regulations (13th–14th c.)," in Amt, *Women's Lives in Medieval Europe*, 202.

31. Ibid., 202–3.

32. Erika Uitz, *Women in the Medieval Town* (London: Barrie & Jenkins, 1990), 44.

33. Ibid., 40.

34. Ibid., 41.

35. Quoted in Jenifer Ní Ghrádaigh, "Mere Embroiderers? Women and Art in Early Medieval Ireland," in *Reassessing the Roles of Women as "Makers" of Medieval Art and Architecture,* ed. Therese Martin (Leiden: Brill, 2012), 93.

36. Charles Henry Hartshorne, "English Medieval Embroidery," *Archaeological Journal* 1, no. 1 (1844): 322.

37. Dorothy Miner, *Anastaise and Her Sisters: Women Artists of the Middle Ages* (Baltimore: Walters Art Gallery, 1974), 20–21.

38. Annemarie Weyl Carr, "Women as Artists in the Middle Ages," *Feminist Arts Journal* (Spring 1976), 6.

39. Pierre Alain Mariaux, "Women in the Making: Early Medieval Signatories and Artists' Portraits (9th–12th c.)," in Martin, *Reassessing the Roles,* 399–409.

40. Françoise Baron, "Enlumineurs, peintres et sculpteurs parisiens des XIIIe et XIVe siècles, d'après les rôles de la taille," *Bulletin archéologique du Comité des travaux historiques et scientifiques* 4 (1968): 37–121; and Baron, "Enlumineurs, peintres et sculpteurs parisiens des XIVe et XVe siècles, d'après les archives de

l'hôpital Saint-Jaques-aux-Pèlerins," *Bulletin archéologique du Comité des travaux historiques et scientifiques* 6 (1971): 77–115.

41. Katrinette Bodarwé, "Pflege und Medizin in mittelalterlichen Frauenkonventen / Cure and Medicine in Medieval Nunneries," *Medizinhistorisches Journal* 37, no. 3–4 (2002): 231–63.

42. Vern L. Bullough, "Training of the Non-University-Educated Medical Practitioners in the Later Middle Ages," *Journal of the History of Medicine and Allied Sciences* 14, no. 4 (1959): 448.

43. Monica H. Green, ed. and trans., *The Trotula: An English Translation of the Medieval Compendium of Women's Medicine* (Philadelphia: University of Pennsylvania Press, 2001), xii–xiv.

44. Green, *Trotula*, 80.

45. Leyser, *Medieval Women*, 127.

46. Sprenger and Kramer, *Malleus Malleficarum*, 66.

47. Augustine, *De ordine*, in *Corpus scriptorum ecclesiasticorum Latinorum*, ed. P. Knöll, 63 (Leipzig, 1922), 155; Aquinas, *Summa Theologica*, pt. Iia–IIae, ques. 10, art.11.

48. Ivan Hlaváček and Zdeňka Hledíková, eds., *Protocollum visitationis archidiaconatus Pragensis annis 1379–1382 per Paulum de Janowicz archidiaconum Pragensem factae* (Prague: Academia, 1973), 118.

49. Ibid., 62.

50. "Carpenter's Specifications: A Town House (1308)," in Amt, *Women's Lives in Medieval Europe*, 213.

51. Ibid., 211.

52. John Martin Klassen, *The Nobility and the Making of the Hussite Revolution* (New York: Columbia University Press, 1978), 20.

53. John Noorthouck, *A New History of London Including Westminster and Southwark* (London: R. Bladwin, 1773), bk. 3, ch. 1 "Southwark," note 11, https://www.british-history.ac.uk/no-series/new-history-london/pp678-690.

54. John E. Lobdell and Douglas Owsley, "The Origin of Syphilis," *Journal of Sex Research* 10, no. 1 (1974): 76–79.

55. Emile Friedberg, ed., *Corpus iuris canonici: Editio lipsiensis secunda post Aemilii Ludouici Richteri curas ad librorum manu scriptorum et editionis romanae fidem recognouit et adnotatione critica instruxit Aemilius Friedberg* (Graz: Akademische Druck, 1879–81), 2:668.

56. *Vita venerabilis presbyteri Milicii, praelati ecclesiae Pragensis*, in Josef Emler, ed., *Fontes Rerum Bohemicarum* (Prague: Musea Království českého, 1871–73), 1:418.

57. Leah Lydia Otis, *Prostitution in Medieval Society: The History of an Urban Institution in Languedoc* (Chicago: University of Chicago Press, 1985), 72–73.

58. Ibid., 73–76.

59. "Caesarius of Arles: Rule for Nuns (ca. 512–534)," in Amt, *Women's Lives in Medieval Europe*, 221–22.

60. Ibid., 223.

61. James of Vitry, "The Life of Mary of Oignies," in *The Essential Writings of Christian Mysticism*, ed. Bernard McGinn (New York: Modern Library, 2006), 65.

62. Marguerite Porete, *The Mirror of Simple Souls*, trans. Ellen L. Babinsky (New York: Paulist Press, 1993), 104.

63. Phillips, *Medieval Maidens*, 74.

64. Agnes Strickland, *Lives of the Queens of England from the Norman Conquest* (Philadelphia: Lea & Blanchard, 1841), 308.

65. Phillips, *Medieval Maidens*, 118.

66. Ibid., 114.

67. "Christine de Pisan: Advice to Noblewmoen (1405)," in Amt, *Women's Lives in Medieval Europe*, 164–65.

68. "Household Accounts of Dame Alice de Bryene (1412–13)," ibid., 166–68.

69. "The Paston Family: Letters (15th c.)," ibid., 173.

CHAPTER 5: WHY IT MATTERS

1. Marie Shear, "Media Watch: Celebrating Women's Words," *New Directions for Women* 15, no. 3 (May–June 1986): 6.

2. Virginia Woolf, *A Room of One's Own* (1929; reprint London: Renard Press, 2020), 105.

3. John Locke, *Two Treatises of Government* (Cambridge, U.K.: Cambridge University Press, 1969), 37, 16.

4. Jean-Jacques Rousseau, *Second Discourse*, trans. Roger and Judith Masters (New York: St. Martin's Press, 1964), 108, 112, 216.

5. Gina Rippon, *The Gendered Brain: The New Neuroscience that Shatters the Myth of the Female Brain* (London: Vintage, 2020), 176.

6. Cordelia Fine, *Delusions of Gender: The Real Science Behind Sex Differences* (London: Icon, 2010), 113.

7. Diane F. Halpern, "How Neuromythologies Support Sex Role Stereotypes," *Science* 330, no. 6009 (2010): 1320–21.

8. A. Memrick, *Gaston Gazette*, January 15, 2011, quoted in Diane F. Halpern et al., "The Pseudoscience of Single-Sex Schooling," *Science* 333, no. 6050 (2011), 1706–7.

9. Lacey J. Hilliard and Lynn S. Liben, "Differing Levels of Gender Salience in

Preschool Classrooms: Effects on Children's Gender Attitudes and Intergroup Bias," *Child Development* 81 no. 6 (2010): 1787–98.

10. James Damore, "Google's Ideological Echo Chamber: How Bias Clouds Our Thinking About Diversity and Inclusion," July 2017, https://s3.documentcloud .org/documents/3914586/Googles-Ideological-Echo-Chamber.pdf.

11. M. J. Law Smith et al., "Maternal Tendencies in Women Are Associated with Estrogen Levels and Facial Femininity" *Hormones and Behavior* 61, no. 1 (2012): 12–16.

12. E. James Anthony and Therese Benedek, eds., *Parenthood: Its Psychology and Psychopathology* (New York: Little, Brown, 1997); Mardy S. Ireland, *Reconceiving Women: Separating Motherhood from Female Identity* (New York: Guilford, 1993), 48.

13. Nancy J. Chodorow, *The Reproduction of Mothering: Psychoanalysis and the Sociology of Gender* (Berkeley: University of California Press, 1987), 29.

14. Shelley J. Correll, Stephen Benard, and In Paik, "Getting a Job: Is There a Motherhood Penalty? 1." *American Journal of Sociology* 112, no. 5 (2007): 1297–338.

15. Michelle Fox, "The 'Motherhood Penalty' Is Real, and It Costs Women $16,000 a Year in Lost Wages," CNBC, March 25, 2019, https://www.cnbc .com/2019/03/25/the-motherhood-penalty-costs-women-16000-a-year-in-lost -wages.html.

16. Eva Sierminska, "Does It Pay to Be Beautiful?" *IZA World of Labor* (2015): 161; Eva M. Sierminska and Xing (Michelle) Liu, "Beauty and the Labor Market," in *International Encyclopedia of the Social & Behavioral Sciences,* ed. James D. Wright, 2nd ed. (Amsterdam: Elsevier, 2015), 383–91; Daniel S. Hamermesh, *Beauty Pays: Why Attractive People Are More Successful* (Princeton, N.J.: Princeton University Press, 2011); Jason M. Fletcher, "Beauty vs. Brains: Early Labor Market Outcomes of High School Graduates," *Economics Letters* 105 (2009): 321–25; D. S. Hamermesh and J. E. Biddle, "Beauty and the Labor Market," *American Economic Review* 84 (1994): 1174–94; M. T. French, "Physical Appearance and Earnings: Further Evidence," *Applied Economics* 34 (2002): 569–72; D. S. Hamermesh, X. Meng, and J. Zhang, "Dress for Success—Does Primping Pay?" *Labour Economics* 9 (2002): 361–73.

17. William D. Lassek and Steven J. C. Gaulin, "Evidence Supporting Nubility and Reproductive Value as the Key to Human Female Physical Attractiveness," *Evolution and Human Behavior* 40, no. 5 (2019): 408–19; Jeanne Bovet, "Evolutionary Theories and Men's Preferences for Women's Waist-to-Hip-Ratio: Which Hypotheses Remain? A Systematic Review," *Frontiers in Psychology,* June 4, 2019, https://doi.org/10.3389/fpsyg.2019.01221.

18. Will Lassek, Steve Gaulin, and Hara Estroff Marano, "Eternal Curves," *Psychology Today*, July 2012; Devendra Singh, "Universal Allure of the Hourglass Figure: An Evolutionary Theory of Female Physical Attractiveness," *Clinical Plastic Surgery* 33, no. 3 (2006): 359–70; Daniel Davies, "Why Science Says Men Go for Women with Hourglass Figures: It's in Our Nature Apparently," *Men's Health*, June 18, 2019; Gad Saad, "Men's Preference for the Female Hourglass Figure: The Appeal of Women with Curves, Latest Data," *Psychology Today*, February 2010.

19. De Elizabeth, "Billie Eilish Reveals the Reason for Her Baggy Clothes in New Calvin Klein Ad," *Teen Vogue*, May 11, 2019; Eve Barlow, "Billie Eilish Has Already Lived a Hundred Lives—And She's Only 17," *Elle*, September 5, 2019.

20. Leyla Mohammed, "Billie Eilish Said Her Experimental Vogue Cover Was Meant to Be 'A Specific Aesthetic for a Photo Shoot' and 'Not a New Style' After Critics Called Her Out for Wearing Lingerie and Form-Fitting Clothes," *BuzzFeed News*, December 2, 2021, https://www.buzzfeednews.com/article/leylamohammed/billie-eilish-responds-to-backlash-over-vogue-cover.

21. "House Republicans Balk at Sex-Research Funding," *Washington Times*, July 9, 2003, https://www.washingtontimes.com/news/2003/jul/9/20030709-110059-9087r/; Liam Beattie, "Tory Cuts Are Causing a Sexual Health Crisis," *Tribune*, December 12, 2020 https://tribunemag.co.uk/2020/12/tory-cuts-are-causing-a-sexual-health-crisis.

22. Meg-John Barker and Justin Hancock, *Enjoy Sex How, When, and If You Want To: A Practical and Inclusive Guide* (London: Icon, 2017), 1–7.

23. Pietro d'Abano, *Conciliator controversarium, quae inter philosophos et medicos versantur* (1472), in Danielle Jacquart and Claude Thomasset, *Sexuality and Medicine in the Middle Ages*, trans. Matthew Adamson (Princeton, N.J.: Princeton University Press, 1988), 46; Sigmund Freud, *Three Essays on the Theory of Sexuality* (1905), in *The Standard Edition of the Complete Psychological Works of Sigmund Freud*, vol. 7 *(1901–1905): A Case of Hysteria, Three Essays on Sexuality and Other Works* (London: Hogarth Press, 1975), 123–246.

24. David M. Buss, "Evolutionary Psychology: A New Paradigm for Psychological Science," *Psychological Inquiry* 6, no. 1 (1995): 5.

25. Jamie Cuccinelli, "Marriage in the 'New' America: A Pandemic, Equality, and an Industry Ready for Change," *Brides*, December 13, 2021.

26. World Health Organization, *Global Alcohol Action Plan 2022–2030 to Strengthen Implementation of the Global Strategy to Reduce the Harmful Use of Alcohol*, June 2021, https://cdn.who.int/media/docs/default-source/alcohol/action-plan-on-alcohol_first-draft-final_formatted.pdf?sfvrsn=b690edb0_1&download=true.

27. William Goode, *World Revolution and Family Patterns* (New York: Free Press of Glencoe, 1963), 56.

28. Simon Baron-Cohen, *The Essential Difference: Men, Women, and the Extreme Male Brain* (London: Allen Lane, 2003), 185.

29. Arlie Russell Hochschild, *The Second Shift: Working Parents and the Revolution at Home* (New York: Viking Penguin, 1989).

30. Peter Kay Chai Tay, Yi Yuan Ting, and Kok Yang Tan, "Sex and Care: The Evolutionary Psychological Explanations for Sex Differences in Formal Care Occupations," *Frontiers in Psychology*, April 17, 2019, https://doi.org/10.3389/fpsyg.2019.00867.

31. Asaf Levanon, Paula England, and Paul Allison, "Occupational Feminization and Pay: Assessing Causal Dynamics Using 1950–2000 U.S. Census Data," *Social Forces* 88, no. 2 (December 2009): 865–91.

INDEX

Note: Page numbers in *italics* indicate figures.